Dedicated to fulfilling the dream

of every new teacher —

that of making a difference.

Annette L. Breaux

Harry K. Wong

NEW TEACHER INDUCTION:

How to

Train,

Support,

and

Retain

New Teachers

ANNETTE L. BREAUX   AND   HARRY K. WONG

HARRY K. WONG PUBLICATIONS, INC.

Copyright © 2003 by Harry K. Wong Publications, Inc.

To request permission to reprint or quote or to order copies of this book please contact the publisher:

Harry K. Wong Publications, Inc.
943 North Shoreline Boulevard
Mountain View, California 94043
TEL 650-965-7896
FAX 650 965-7890
www.effectiveteaching.com

ISBN: 0-9629360-4-9
Library of Congress Control Number: 2001095120

Executive producer: Rosemary T. Wong
Production Assistant: Tim Chen
Book Production: H. Heath Design
Illustrations: Heidi Heath Garwood
Editor: Mark Colucci

Printing: CS Graphics, Singapore
10 9 8 7 6 5 4 3 2 1

Cover Photo: New teacher Nicole Benoit gets a warm welcome to the teaching profession from Annette Breaux, director of the Lafourche Parish new teacher induction program.

What We Believe

- Every child—and every new teacher—should be treated with dignity and respect.

- Every child—and every new teacher—can learn and succeed.

- Every new teacher is a valued human resource, a person who has invested years in preparing for a life dedicated to helping young people; we have a responsibility to ensure that these new teachers will learn and succeed—just as we have a responsibility to ensure that every child will learn and succeed.

- New teachers must be trained if we want them to succeed; it is much better to train new teachers and risk losing them than not to train them and risk keeping them.

- An induction process is the best way to send a message to your teachers that you value them and want them to succeed and stay.

I Teach

I light a spark in a darkened soul

I warm the heart of one grown cold

I look beyond and see within

Behind the face, beneath the skin

I quench a thirst, I soothe a pain

I provide the food that will sustain

I touch, I love, I laugh, I cry

Whatever is needed, I supply

Yet more than I give, I gain from each

I am most richly blessed—I teach.

— Annette L. Breaux

Why We Wrote This Book

For just as a work of art long outlives the artist, a teacher's influence outlives the teacher.

We have found many successful schools and school districts that are providing induction programs that train, support, and retain highly qualified teachers. First and foremost, we have written this book to share the stories of these successful programs with you and provide you with a basic how-to approach—a blueprint for structuring a successful new teacher induction program.

> Effective induction programs not only retain highly qualified new teachers; they also ensure that these teachers are teaching effectively from the very first day of school.

Our motivation for writing this book stems from four sources:

1. Our love of children
2. Our belief in the value of a quality education
3. Our reverence for the teaching profession
4. Our concern over the fact that school districts are plagued with the problem of attracting and retaining highly qualified teachers for their classrooms

We believe that the inability to attract and retain highly qualified teachers is the most significant problem we face in education today, because without effective teachers, our children cannot receive a quality education.

We believe that teaching is a unique profession filled with the rewards of lasting influence on society. Its responsibilities cannot be taken lightly. It is an art. And like any other art form, it requires not only ability, but patience, dedication, and commitment. Just as a sculptor looks at a block of marble and envisions chipping away to create something extraordinary, a true teacher looks at each student and envisions a masterpiece.

It is imperative that school systems see every new teacher as a professional educator and commit the time and resources necessary to effectively train and support these teachers, in whose hands we so trustingly place our children.

— Annette L. Breaux and Harry K. Wong

Michelangelo's *David*

From 1501 to 1504 Michelangelo worked on a piece of marble that had been left behind by another sculptor. Friends questioned why he would want to work with a piece of discarded marble, a piece that someone else found unsuitable and unusable. "It is not a good piece," they would all say.

Michelangelo worked with it, despite the many protests that he could have selected something much better with which to start. After three years of chipping away at the piece of marble, he had created *David*, which many consider the greatest statue ever sculpted.

With the heart and soul of an artist, Michelangelo knew that *David* existed inside that piece of marble. It was only through chipping away and carving with patience, dedication, and commitment that the work of art he envisioned would be revealed. Michelangelo said that he never created *David*; he simply revealed what was already there.

So it is with each and every child and new teacher. Each is a masterpiece waiting to be revealed.

There is a masterpiece in all of us.

For just as a work of art long outlives the artist, a teacher's influence outlives the teacher.

Highlights of This Book

About Retention

Seventy-five percent to 100 percent of the teachers leaving the profession are "effective" or "very effective" in the classroom. (Page 1)

Districts lose $50,000 when each new teacher leaves the system. (Page 3)

Lafourche Parish schools cut its attrition rate from 53 percent to 15 percent in one year and the attrition rate now hovers around 7 percent. (Page 68)

New York City Public Schools spends $8 million each year (unsuccessfully) on recruiting, yet New Haven Unified School District in California recruits (successfully) at a fraction of the cost over the Internet. (Pages 3 and 96)

About Training

We've given you the step-by-step process for how to structure an induction program in order to train, support, and retain effective teachers. (Page 38)

Select from a list of exemplary induction programs—all replicable. (Pages 58 and 93)

An Illinois district has a four-year induction program that prepares its teachers to apply for national board certification. (Page 98)

A Kansas school district was awarded the NEA-AFT Saturn/UAW Partnership Award for their induction program, which is a cooperative effort between the school district, the National Education Association, and the local university. (Page 98)

A New York non-profit program aggressively recruits and provides rigorous hands-on training for extremely talented people to become urban school principals. (Page 103)

About Support

Louisiana's department of education has adopted Lafourche Parish's very successful induction program as the state's model program. (Page 66)

North Carolina offers high school seniors a $26,000 college scholarship to become teachers. (Page 94)

After reading this *ERIC Digest* article, you'll understand **why mentoring alone does not work.** (Pages 44 and References page 150)

A Las Vegas principal has not lost a teacher in the past seven years. (Page 101)

The No Child Left Behind Act has **$3 billion available <u>for training and for retaining</u>** new teachers and administrators. (Page 133)

Contents

one

The Case for Induction

Prepping the soil

two

There Is Only One Way to Improve Student Learning

Planting the seed

three

How to Structure an Induction Program

Nurturing the seed

seven   Frequently Asked Questions

Collecting the fruits

eight   An Investment in Our Future

Treasuring the harvest

epilogue   Beyond Induction

chapter one

The Case for Induction

*Let us give thanks for this
beautiful day. Let us give thanks
for this life. Let us give thanks
for the water without which life
would not be possible. Let us give
thanks for Grandmother Earth
who protects and nourishes us.*

— Daily Prayer of the
Lakota American Indians

Prepping the soil.

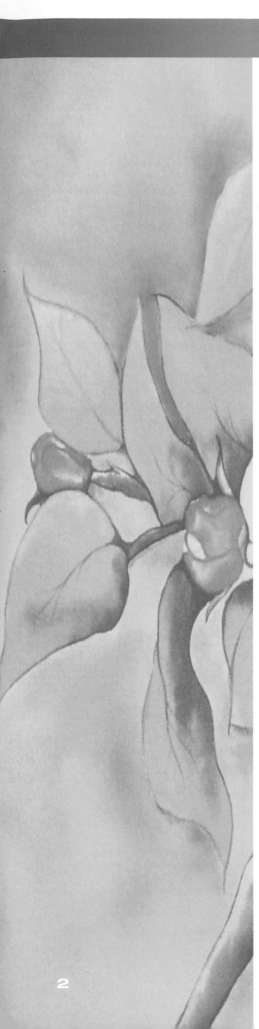

We sincerely thank the many people who have shared with us their research on induction and their induction programs. New teachers are like seedlings, requiring the proper preparation to grow into leaders in education. For those who are dedicated to enriching the lives of new teachers, we present this book.

Sources and Notes for Chapter 1

[1]Johnson, Susan Moore and Susan M. Kardos. (March 2002). "Keeping New Teachers in Mind." *Educational Leadership*, pp. 13-16.

[2]Hare, Debra and James Heap. (May 2001). *Effective Teacher Recruitment and Retention Strategies in the Midwest*. Naperville, IL: North Central Regional Laboratory.

[3]Pawlas, George E. (January 1999). "Help Needed: Mentors for the Next Millennium." *Teaching for Excellence Newsletter*, p. 5.

[4]Recruiting New Teachers, Inc. (1998). *Facts About the Teaching Profession*. Belmont, MA.

[5]Newcomb, Amelia. (October 9, 2001). "Around the Globe, Classrooms in Need." *Christian Science Monitor*.

[6]National Commission on Teaching and America's Future. (1996). *What Matters Most: Teaching for America's Future*. New York.

[7]Resta, Virginia and Leslie Huling. (1998). "Implementing a Campus-Level Support Program for Novice Teachers." Southwest Texas State University. Unpublished.

[8]Gordon, Gary. (Spring 2001). "Retaining Good Teachers." *State Education Standard*, p. 35.

[9]*National Education Goals Panel Weekly*. (February 14, 2001). Available: www.negp.gov.

[10]Goodnough, Abby. (February 17, 2001). "Ad Campaign to Recruit Teachers Draws Fire." *New York Times*.

[11]Jerald, Craig. (January 13, 2000). "Setting Policies for New Teachers." *Education Week*, p. 45.

[12]Moskowitz, J. and M. Stephens. (1997). *From Students of Teaching to Teachers of Students: Teacher Induction Around the Pacific Rim*. Washington, DC: Palavin Research Institute.

[13]North Carolina Teaching Fellows Commission. (1995). *Keeping Talented Teachers*. Raleigh, NC. Available: www.ncforum.org.

[14]Gregorian, Vartan. (July 6, 2001). "How to Train and Retain Teachers." *New York Times on the Web*.

[15]Brooks, Douglas. (May 1985). "The First Day of School." *Educational Leadership*, pp. 76-78.

[16]Public School Forum of North Carolina. (1996). *A Profession in Jeopardy: Why Teachers Leave and What We Can Do About It*. Raleigh, NC. Available: www.ncforum.org.

[17]Heil, Diana. (December 1, 2000). "Plugging the City Teacher Drain." *Albuquerque Journal*.

[18]*The Age*. (January 18, 2001). Available: www.theage.com.au.

[19]Farkas, Steve, et al. (May 2000). "A Sense of Calling: Who Teaches and Why." Available: www.publicagenda.org.

[20]Archer, Jeff. (January 13, 2001). "Competition Is Fierce for Minority Teachers." *Education Week*, p. 33.

[21]Reinhartz, Judy (ed.). (1989). *Teacher Induction: NEA Aspects of Learning*. Washington, DC: National Education Association. (ED313368)

[22]Editors. (January 13, 2000). "Who Should Teach? The States Decide." *Education Week*, p. 8.

[23]Weiss, Eileen Mary and Stephen Gary Weiss. (1999). "Beginning Teacher Induction." Washington, DC: ERIC Clearinghouse on Teaching and Teacher Education. (ED436487)

[24]*Helga* really is her name and this story actually happened. It was reported by Joan S. Schmidt, Seanne Johnson, and Jeffrey Schultz in "Entering Teaching Through the Back Door: Two Alternative Route Teachers Speak" (Fall 1993), *Action in Teacher Education*. If anyone knows the whereabouts of Helga, please ask her to contact the authors at alb24@email.com.

[25]Johnson, Susan Moore and Susan M. Kardos. pp. 13-16.

[26]Wilkinson, Gayle A. (Summer 1994). "Support for Individualizing Teacher Induction." *Action in Teacher Education*, p. 52.

"Your new teacher induction program not only saved my wife as a classroom teacher, but it also saved my marriage. My wife was miserable both at home and at school. Whatever you did at that induction program made her so much more successful as a classroom teacher and a happier person in general."

— Told to Annette L. Breaux

New teacher trainer Liz Yates welcomes the teachers to the profession.

Sue Mangram graduated at the top of her class and was nominated Outstanding Student Teacher. Since high school Sue had wanted to be a classroom teacher thanks to the influence of one of her teachers. In undergraduate school she had invested four years and a substantial amount of money in her future. She wanted, in the best way, to make a difference in the lives of children. Sue thought she was ready to teach. She later said, "I wasn't. Nothing and no one had prepared me for what I was about to face. I had never dreamed that teaching would be so difficult or that I would feel so ALONE. I wanted to abandon the teaching profession after only four weeks in the classroom."

The Sue Mangrams have been the subject of study at the Project on the Next Generation of Teachers at the Harvard Graduate School of Education. Principal investigator, Susan Moore Johnson, describes a new teacher:

"The beginning was awful," Laura recalled, describing her first days of teaching. At the district's orientation meeting for all new teachers, she found nothing there to help her begin her work as a classroom teacher. Laura only learned which classes she would teach when she received the schedule at a faculty meeting the day before school started. She hadn't begun with high

expectations for professional support, but she was still surprised by the lack of organized induction.[1]

It's the Very Effective Who Are Leaving

Current estimates of the proportion of new teachers in urban schools who will not even last their first year as a teacher run as high as 9.3 to 17 percent. Between 40 and 50 percent will leave during the first seven years of their career, and more than two-thirds of those will do so in the first four years of teaching.

Furthermore, evidence suggests that the most academically talented teachers leave in the greatest numbers. A study from the North Central Regional Education Laboratory (NCREL) found that a majority of superintendents in the region indicated that 75 percent to 100 percent of the teachers leaving are "effective" or "very effective" in the classroom.[2]

Studies have identified numerous reasons for exiting early from teaching:
- Lack of support
- Disenchantment with teaching assignments
- Difficulty balancing personal and professional demands
- Excessive paperwork
- Inadequate classroom management
- Inadequate discipline
- High stress[3]

Induction:
Preparing, Supporting, and Retaining
New Teachers

The purpose of this book is to share with you the process used by many schools and school districts that are succeeding with their new teachers. The process of preparing, supporting, and retaining new teachers is called **INDUCTION**.

Teacher Shortages in America

❖ In the next 10 years, America will need to hire 2 million new teachers to meet rising enrollment demands and replace an aging teaching force. Half of our nation's teachers will retire during this period.

❖ Student enrollment is projected to grow rapidly during the next 10 years. By 2006 America will educate almost 3 million more children than it does today—more than 54 million youngsters.

❖ More than three-fourths of urban school districts (77 percent) often must deal with shortages in high-need areas, including science, mathematics, special education, bilingual education, and elementary education.

❖ Nearly two-thirds of urban districts (64 percent) allow noncertified teachers to teach under an emergency license, and 4 in 10 (40 percent) allow for hiring of long-term substitutes.

❖ Most districts (85 percent) say they have an immediate demand for special education teachers, and the majority of districts say they have an immediate demand for teachers in the areas of science (96 percent), mathematics (67 percent), and bilingual education (64 percent).

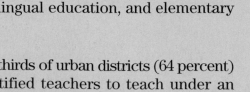

❖ More than half of the districts that responded to a survey (54 percent) reported a need for more elementary teachers and more than 85 percent reported a high need for male teachers.

❖ Nearly all large urban school districts (92 percent) cite an immediate demand for teachers of color.[4]

What Is Induction?

Induction is a structured training program that must begin before the first day of school and continue for two or more years. It has these basic purposes:

1. To provide instruction in classroom management and effective teaching techniques
2. To reduce the difficulty of the transition into teaching
3. To maximize the retention rate of highly qualified teachers

Induction includes all of the things that are done to support and train new teachers and acculturate them to teaching, including the responsibilities, missions, and philosophies of their districts and schools. Results-oriented training is required in order to get new teachers up to speed as fast as possible and maximize their effectiveness. Effective schools know the importance of training and supporting their teachers. Teachers stay with a school where they feel successful and supported.

Teacher Quality, the Top Ten States

Education Week publishes an annual "Quality Counts" issue. The 2002 issue appeared on January 10, and it ranked the states that had the most **Improved Teacher Quality** for the past year.

These are the top ten states in order:

North Carolina
Connecticut
Massachusetts
South Carolina
Arkansas
Oklahoma
Kentucky
Indiana
New Jersey
Vermont

- **The first nine of these ten states are ones that require and finance new teacher induction (not mentoring).**
- **Of the remaining 40 states, only six require and finance new teacher induction.**

Teacher Shortages Around the World

If you think it's hard to find teachers in the United States, consider the plight of schools elsewhere in the world.

The United Nations Educational, Scientific and Cultural Organization (UNESCO) estimates that 15 million more teachers must be hired over the next decade. The problem affects rich and poor nations alike. While the shortage is most severe in southern Asia and Africa, wealthy countries like the United States also face significant shortfalls in key areas.

In some African countries, the number of teachers entering the system is outpaced by those dying of AIDS. In Brazil, Paraguay, the Philippines, and Zimbabwe, between 30 and 50 percent of high-school-age students are enrolled in primary schools as repeaters or late enrollees. More than 80 percent of students in the Russian Federation attend schools that lack teaching materials. Worldwide, 580 million women and children are illiterate.

Never has the need been more apparent, in the US and elsewhere, to give students the tools to gain a better understanding of the world around them.[5]

True, comprehensive induction programs exist in only 15 of 50 states. Data that indicates many more states have induction programs can be misleading. They do not. These reports have included states that hold orientation meetings or provide mentoring only in with the data.

To read what North Carolina is doing to warrant first place in this Quality ranking, see "The North Carolina Plan for Creating Effective Teachers" on page 98.

The results shown in the "Quality Counts 2002" survey are quite obvious. Induction programs train teachers on how to be effective and, thus, improve the quality of their teachers.

> **Schools and school districts that have as their priority the training and improvement of their teachers will have improved student achievement.**

According to the study *What Matters Most: Teaching for America's Future*, **recruiting, preparing, and retaining good teachers is the central strategy for improving our schools.**[6] Study after study has shown that in the next decade, the United States will need to hire more than **2 million teachers** to keep pace with huge enrollment increases, replace an aging workforce as it retires, and respond to the chronic attrition of new teachers that plagues American schools.

The Costs of Low Retention

Per Teacher: $50,000
Human resource specialists in high-performance industries report that a bad hire costs a company nearly 2.5 times the employee's initial salary in recruitment and personnel expenditures and lost productivity. If this is the case, each teacher who leaves the profession during the first three years likely costs taxpayers in excess of $50,000.[7]

Per District: $1 Million
Just how important is retention? Assume that a district has 1,000 teachers, a 5 percent turnover rate (a conservative estimate), and an average teacher salary of $25,000. Commonly accepted figures in the private sector set replacement costs for a professional employee at approximately 1.75 times the average salary. However, let's be conservative again and assume that the direct replacement costs for this district are only one-half this rate, approximately 0.875 times the average salary. The cost for recruiting and replacing 5 percent of the district's teachers (50 teachers) would be $1,093,750—a loss no school board would choose to accept.

The direct costs are often hidden in salaries and spread across human resource, business services, and staff development budgets. As a result, direct costs are invisible. **The indirect costs in extra work for existing employees, reduced teacher effectiveness, and lost student productivity are incalculable.**[8]

Chicago: Almost $6 Million
Chicago officials plan to spend $5.7 million to hire 3,000 teachers for next year. (Officials did not mention any corresponding plan for increasing teacher retention, so will Chicago spend another $5.7 million the following year?)[9]

New York City: $8 Million
Former New York City Schools chancellor Harold O. Levy recruited TBWA\Chiat\Day, a Madison Avenue agency, to create a multimillion-dollar advertising campaign to recruit teachers for the school system. He had originally planned to spend $16 million on the campaign, but the seven-member board of education voted to spend only half that amount.

Randi Weingarten, president of the United Federation of Teachers, said, "It's not honest to have a glitzy marketing campaign, then have teachers end up disillusioned because they don't get the resources or support or salary they need to do the best job."[10]

The fourth annual 50-state report by *Education Week*, "Quality Counts 2000," found that teachers who had **not participated** in an induction program were nearly **twice as likely to leave** after their first three years of teaching as were teachers who had received the benefit of an induction program. The report asked the critical question, **What are states doing to attract, screen, and keep good teachers?** The answer, based on the most exhaustive survey of state teacher policies to date, was—**Not enough.**[11]

Would you fly with a solo pilot in training? Not providing induction for a new teacher is like asking a pilot to learn how to fly while taking a planeload of passengers up for the first time. That would be ludicrous in the airline industry and the public would never allow it to happen; yet it is the prevailing practice in education for most newly hired teachers.

The unspoken message to new teachers is

**figure it out yourself,
do it yourself, and
keep it to yourself!**

Sadly, once they are hired, many new teachers are forgotten and left to fend for themselves. They receive little or no support and soon realize that college preparation and student teaching, no matter how positive those experiences may have been, have not fully prepared them for the realities of the classroom. They need help, and they feel they have nowhere to turn. Many leave teaching very early in their careers. And when they leave, they leave disillusioned and bitter about teaching as an experience and as a profession.

New Teacher Humiliation

The first year of teaching is the most critical.

New teachers feel isolated,
   vulnerable, deeply concerned
   with how they will be perceived,
   and thus afraid to ask for help.

When they are hired,
   they are given a key,
   told which room is theirs, and
   are given no support.

They are given the worst assignments.
   They feel frightened.
   They feel humiliated.
   They are given no assistance, and
      mentoring is not nearly enough.
   They want someone to give them
      hope and tell them when their
      hardships will end.

New teachers require support if they are to succeed.

Beginning teachers rarely make easy or smooth transitions into teaching. Often they are hired at the last moment, left isolated in their classrooms, and given little help. In many cases, a sink-or-swim attitude toward newly hired teachers prevails. Consequently, attrition rates among new teachers often are five times higher than among experienced teachers.[12] It is a lamentable fact of life in our public schools that new teachers are assigned the more-difficult classes and the more-difficult students. Unlike new professionals in other fields, as well as new teachers in other countries, beginning teachers in the United States must work with the toughest clients and take on the most troublesome nonteaching duties.[13]

> *There is a shortage of meaningful advocacy on behalf of new teachers.*[14]
>
> — Vartan Gregorian, President
> Carnegie Corporation

New teachers who are "left to their own devices" feel alone, confused, and inadequate. They often avoid asking for help, fearing the negative perceptions of other teachers. Basically, they're required to perform the same duties, if not more difficult ones, at the same level of skill and competency as their more experienced colleagues.

The Expectations Are Frightening

Beginning teachers are expected to assume the same tasks and responsibilities as the most seasoned teacher on staff.

Beginning teachers are expected to perform the full complement of duties immediately, learning as they go along.

Beginning teachers are expected to be fully prepared to teach on the first day of school and then get better each year.

Whether teachers will choose to remain in teaching depends heavily on their experiences during the crucial initial years in the profession. In fact, Douglas Brooks reports that there is overwhelming evidence that the first two to three weeks of school are critical—they determine how well teachers will succeed for the remainder of the year.[15] According to a report released by the Public School Forum of North Carolina, "Research reveals that teachers who make it past seven years are likely to remain in teaching for a lengthy career. But many do not make it past that point."[16] So what can be done to ensure that these teachers actually do make it past that crucial point?

The answer is a well-organized, sustained new teacher induction program.

Retention and Support: A Critical Link

> *I'm surprised I made it this far in education. When I was hired, I was told to go to my room, to teach, and not to surface until May. I wasn't even given a mentor.*
>
> — Staff developer in Florida
> with over 25 years of experience

Is this the classroom of a new or a veteran teacher? The expectation is the same.

Recruiting Teachers' Aides as Teachers in New Mexico

How do you train a fresh batch of much-needed classroom teachers and then keep them in New Mexico where pay is notoriously low?

Leave it to a former principal to come up with a solution. Debra Carden, who left De Vargas Middle School in October to launch a teacher education program at Santa Fe Community College, faced a packed room of 30 potential teachers.

All of the attendees were teacher assistants—well versed in the ups and downs of school life as employees of the Santa Fe Public Schools. And that, says Carden, is the reason they are desirable teacher recruits.[17]

Luring Support Staff Into Teaching in Australia

Up to 7,300 support staff members in Victorian state schools would be eligible for bridging courses to become qualified teachers under a proposal by the Australian Education Union to tackle "chronic" shortages.

"Among our support staff in schools there is a wealth of experience, knowledge, and understanding of education and it is an untapped resource," said Victoria's union president, Mary Bluett.[18]

Once new teachers are recruited, they must be trained and then receive ongoing support. Otherwise, schools cannot expect to retain them. Consider that if U.S. schools hire 2 million new teachers and continue to allow them to fend for themselves, as has been the case for many new teachers, then at the present rate of attrition, 1 million of those will leave teaching within seven years, and even sooner in urban school districts. Therefore, recruiting these teachers is only one part of the induction process.

"The 100 Best Companies to Work For" was the cover story of the January 10, 2000, issue of *Fortune*. The Container Store, a small retailer of storage and organization solutions, was ranked first (ranked second in the February 4, 2002, issue). Its employees receive 235 hours of training per year. Southwest Airlines (whose employees receive 70 hours of training per year) was ranked second, and Cisco Systems (whose employees receive 80 hours of training per year) was ranked third. Imagine The Container Store, Southwest, or Cisco telling each new employee, "Go to work, don't surface until the end of the day, and if you need help, we'll give you a mentor."

Unlike most dedicated service professions, education fails to support its newly hired teachers from their very first day and through their entire first year. It's little wonder that the teachers don't succeed—and that their students don't succeed either. What happens? Administrators who do not know what to do hire yet more unsupported teachers or just assign teachers a mentor. As a result, many promising new teachers leave the profession after only a few years. The classroom becomes a battlefield, and the solution is to keep sending in fresh troops. The military spends considerably more time training its troops than we do training our teachers.

The issue is support. It is a tragic waste of human resources when dedicated new teachers, full of commitment and energy, leave the teaching profession dejected after only a few years. These new teachers leave with bitterness toward education and they leave not because of poor pay, but because of a **lack of support** from administrators.[19]

Katrina Robertson Reed, a former District of Columbia schools associate superintendent, views her city's induction program as part of its recruitment package. "That's one of the first things candidates ask, before they ask about signing bonuses:

> **'What kind of support am I going to get when I'm there?'"**

Reed says, "We have found over and over that that is really critical."[20]

Training is key to the success of The Container Store.

Induction:
A Necessary Investment

Induction programs are a smart investment in the ongoing training, support, and retention of beginning teachers, who, as a result of the programs, become more qualified, capable, and effective teachers. Successful induction programs go a long way toward improving the quality of teaching and ensuring student achievement.

Despite the importance of teacher induction, inducting new members into the profession in any systematic way is more the exception than the rule, at least in the United States.[21] Though many more school districts are developing programs in an attempt to support and retain new teachers, far too many districts continue to provide little, if any, support for their new teachers. Typically, beginning teachers do not engage in anything more than school orientations. And although 28 states

The induction process welcomes and supports the new teachers.

have laws that require or encourage districts to offer induction programs, only 15 states require districts to provide induction programs to all beginning teachers. Of the states that require it, only 10 foot some or all of the bill.[22]

The purpose of a multiyear induction process is to help new teachers become successful, effective, professional educators who will stay with the school or district. **Induction programs have proved to be very successful in training and retaining effective teachers.**

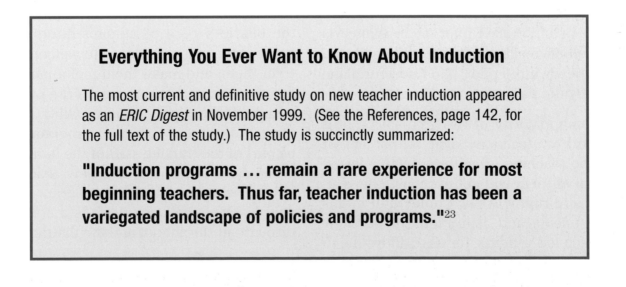

Everything You Ever Want to Know About Induction

The most current and definitive study on new teacher induction appeared as an *ERIC Digest* in November 1999. (See the References, page 142, for the full text of the study.) The study is succinctly summarized:

"Induction programs ... remain a rare experience for most beginning teachers. Thus far, teacher induction has been a variegated landscape of policies and programs."[23]

Structured workshops greet the new teachers.

A Typical First-Year Teaching Experience

When a new teacher, whether novice or veteran, is hired, three things may happen to orient the new employee to the district and school:

1. The Teacher Is Given an Assignment.

In an all too common scenario, the teacher is simply given an assignment and told to go and teach. No support person or structured plan of assistance is available for the new teacher. This would be like an airline telling a newly hired pilot, "Go find your plane at Gate 17 and fly the passengers to Memphis."

The overwhelming majority of research says that if this happens to new teachers, over 50 percent of them will not be teaching after three to five years. Up to 17 percent of them will not even last one year. (See "She Left as Abruptly as She Came" later in this chapter.) The talents and aspirations of our new teachers are much too valuable for us to allow one to

five years of their lives to be wasted and to render the education they pursued useless.

2. The Teacher Is Given a Mentor.

The research is clear on this point: Simply giving a new teacher a mentor does not work. (See "No Research to Support Mentoring Alone" on page 55.) Just giving a new teacher a mentor to contact if help is needed is not enough—teaching is much too complex for such a simplistic approach. With luck, a mentor may be trained, compensated, accessible, knowledgeable, and willing to help. Moreover, the beginning teacher is often at the mercy of the mentor's philosophy, schedule, competence, and training. Imagine an airline telling a newly hired pilot, "There is no company training program, but here's your mentor's number to call if you get into trouble at 35,000 feet."

In a system of individual mentors, there is no consistent mission. Twenty new teachers plus 20 different mentors equals 20 people teaching in 20 different ways, which means that the school is populated by a group of "loose cannons" and a school culture is nonexistent.

3. The Teacher Goes Through an Induction Program.

In this case, newly hired teachers are part of a systematic, integrated, multiyear plan formulated by the district's core of administrators, teachers, and perhaps the union, designed to welcome the teachers, train them, and make them feel a part of the school and the district. As one part of the process, they are assigned a trained mentor, who has also been through the same induction program and may even be part of the training staff of the induction program. When help is needed, the new teacher can go to anyone who is part of the program—even a fellow new teacher—because there is a consistent culture throughout the school and the district.

She Left as Abruptly as She Came

For Helga, who was called into service the week school began, the introduction to her school was abrupt. **No one noticed her when she entered the office, and no one offered to assist her.** When she asked to speak to the principal, the secretary spoke to her sharply.

"After a few minutes," Helga explains, "Mr. Smith [the principal], whom I'd met on one other occasion when I came to see the school, came flying out of his office like a whirlwind. The scene that followed was almost comical. Everyone was vying for his attention. Children were calling to him to tell of the wrongs they'd suffered at the hands of some 'unjust' teacher, teachers were questioning or complaining about scheduling of children and even about the time of the assembly on Friday. One secretary was trying to relay phone messages, while another secretary was traipsing along behind Mr. Smith trying to remind him of the combination for the safe. All the while, Mr. Smith barked out instructions on things the secretaries needed to do so he could get certain things accomplished that day. Chaos."

Helga called to Mr. Smith, but it was obvious that he did not know who she was. After Helga introduced herself, the principal introduced her to the secretaries, gave her the key to her room, and wished her luck. **She experienced instant immersion into her teaching assignment, with no orientation to the school, the students, or the community**.

"I walked to the other building in a daze," she says. "Wasn't somebody going to walk over with me and tell me a little bit about what to expect? Wasn't anyone going to show me where the bathroom was or tell me what the other teachers do for lunch? Wasn't I going to get a few words of encouragement, or, for heaven's sake, an idea of what time the first period started? I felt very alone. I kept mentally patting myself on the back for having come the week before so I'd know where my room was.

"I started to really understand that I was totally on my own. I started using my lunches and prep periods to walk around to the other teachers and get acquainted and find out where to get materials and who I needed to 'get in good with.' One day during my second week, a man … came down and introduced himself as my new mentor. He told me to see him if I had any questions. That was of some comfort but a little too open-ended. The seeming lack of structure made me uncomfortable.

Part of Helga's discomfort and problem stemmed directly from starting so abruptly, with no induction process. Within a few weeks, Helga says, she was beginning to feel overwhelmed: "I was feeling so overwhelmed, and I had no time. I couldn't get everything done. I still had no reading books. 'Getting by' is what I felt like I had been doing. If I stayed one day ahead, I felt prepared. There wasn't even any time for me to prepare my classroom before the kids arrived.

"It is like realizing you are asleep and having a nightmare, knowing that you can stop the dream or wake up, and yet you continue on with the horror because this is a TEACHING JOB. This is what you've supposedly been trained for. You ask yourself—why am I not happy? It wounds [you] deeply when you step into a job that is supposed to be rewarding and fulfilling, and it turns out to be a nightmare filled with horror and despair."

The experience began taking its toll on Helga. She lost weight, began having nightmares, had difficulty sleeping, and her mental health was in jeopardy. She felt a sense of isolation from the other teachers. Helga felt as though she had failed. **After three months, Helga left as abruptly as she had come.**

Helga could have been saved if her district had offered an induction program.[24]

Robert...when he was informed about the school's orientation meeting, thought, "Wonderful. They'll introduce me to everything. I'll know what's going on." He had hoped to learn about the school, his colleagues, the school's technology, and anything else he might need to know to do his job well. Instead, he said he got "none of that," only a series of meetings about general topics, without any focus on "the way [this school] actually does things." He said flatly that it was "a joke." [25]

Induction: The Key to Helping New Teachers Succeed

In the fall of 1991, the superintendent of the Port Huron School District in Michigan (which services 12,000 students) foresaw that a great many older teachers in his district would be retiring within five years and that the district would be forced to fill those vacancies with new, inexperienced teachers. The district began a new teacher induction program in 1991. The program is a cooperative effort between the district's staff development department and the teachers' union. William Kimball, who was responsible for initiating the program and who became the district superintendent in 1998, says,

After seven years, there are more induction-bred teachers than veteran teachers in our system and you can see it today by the change in our culture.

Induction Increases Retention

- **33 percent** of qualified new teachers leave within the first three years.
- **50 percent** of qualified new teachers leave within the first seven years.
- **95 percent** of beginning teachers who experience support during their initial years **remain in teaching after three years**.
- **80 percent** of the supported teachers **remain in teaching after five years**. [26]

The key to student achievement is a staff of effective teachers.

What Induction IS and IS NOT

Induction is the systematic process of training and supporting new teachers, beginning **BEFORE** the first day of school and continuing throughout the first two or three years of teaching. Its purposes include, but are not limited to, the following:

1. Easing the transition into teaching
2. Improving teacher effectiveness through training in effective classroom management and teaching techniques
3. Promoting a district's culture—its philosophies, mission, policies, procedures, and goals
4. Maximizing the retention rate of highly qualified teachers

The multiyear process begins with four or five days of initial training prior to the first day of school. During this initial training, new teachers are instructed in the rudiments of effective classroom management, first-day procedures, discipline, instructional strategies, and more.

The term *induction* is often mistakenly used synonymously with the terms *mentoring* and *orientation.* Mentoring is only one component of an induction program. Orientation is another. Many school districts only provide their new teachers with mentors or provide a day of orientation and call it "induction." In these cases, teachers have not been inducted. They have received mentors and orientation. **Mentoring and orientation by themselves will do little to aid in the retention of highly qualified new teachers.** However, as integral components of a structured induction program, they are valuable. The induction process is ongoing and systematic. It provides information, assistance, support, feedback, coaching, guidance, modeling, and much more. It unfolds in progressive stages, following a teacher's development over a period of time.

Teacher induction programs provide beginning teachers the support they need during the often-difficult transition from preservice education to actual classroom teaching—the transition from being students of teaching to being teachers of students. Clearly, the research supports not only the success of induction programs, but also the importance of developing such programs for **all new teachers.**

Therefore, the question is no longer whether or not to provide induction, but rather, HOW to develop an induction program that will help ensure the success and retention of highly qualified teachers in every classroom.

This book is about how to develop a successful induction program.

The Case for Induction

Summary and Implementation

Planting the Seeds
Information We've Shared

- The most academically talented teachers leave in the greatest numbers.
- New teachers cite lack of support and training as main reasons for exiting the teaching profession.
- Teachers who do not participate in induction are nearly twice as likely to leave teaching.
- The states showing the most improvement in teacher quality have something in common—Induction.
- Mentoring is only one component of an ongoing, highly structured training process known as INDUCTION.

Nurturing Growth
What You Can Do to Make a Difference

- Recognize that *knowing* something and *doing* something are not the same. The knowledge you gain is meaningless if you don't put it to good use.
- Resolve to *do* something—to take the necessary steps in order to train, support, and retain the best teachers for your school or district. The remaining chapters will guide you on your journey toward making a difference.

Reaping the Harvest
Benefits to Your School System

- Quality training produces quality teaching.
- Quality teachers improve student achievement.

chapter two

There Is Only One Way to Improve Student Learning

There is no experience better for the heart than reaching down and lifting people up.

— John Andrew Holmer

Planting the seed.

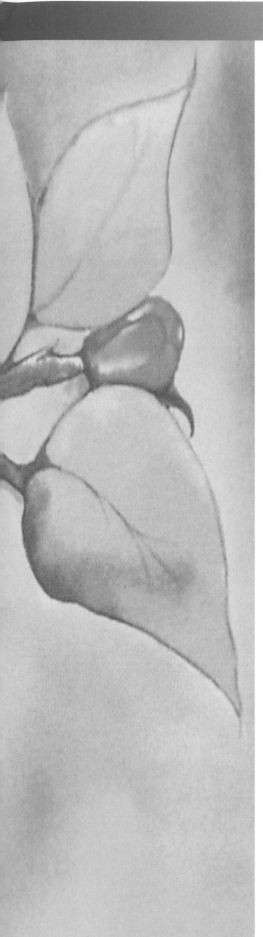

Sources and Notes for Chapter 2

[1] Jerald, Craig D. (August 2002). "All Talk, No Action." Washington, DC: Education Trust. Available: www.edtrust.org.

[2] Roza, Marguerite. (April 19, 2001). "It's the Teachers, Stupid." *Christian Science Monitor.*

[3] Greenwald, R., L. Hedges, and R. Laine. (1996). "The Effect of School Resources on Student Achievement." *Review of Educational Research*, 66, pp. 361-396.

[4] Resta, Virginia and Leslie Huling. (1998). "Implementing a Campus-Level Support Program for Novice Teachers." Southwest Texas State University. Unpublished.

[5] Chase, Bob. (April 25, 2001). "To Hire and to Hold." *Education Week*, p. 48.

[6] For more information on Florida Fund for Minority Teachers, contact Iana Baker, FFMT Inc., 100 Norman Hall, P.O. Box 117045, Gainesville, FL 32611.

[7] Ferguson, Ron. (1996). "Paying for Public Education." *Harvard Journal on Legislation*, 28, pp. 465-498.

[8] Johnston, Robert. (April 5, 2000). "In a Texas District, Test Scores for Minority Students Have Soared." *Education Week.*

[9] Sanders, William L. (1996). *Cumulative and Residual Effects of Teachers on Future Student Academic Achievement.* Knoxville, TN: University of Tennessee Value-Added Research & Assessment Center.

[10] Haycock, Kati. (March 2001). "Closing the Achievement Gap." *Educational Leadership.*

[11] Archer, Jeff. (May 5, 1999). "Sanders 101." *Education Week on the Web.* Available: www.edweek.org.

[12] National Commission on Teaching and America's Future. (1996). *What Matters Most: Teaching for America's Future.* New York.

[13] Archer, Jeff. (February 18, 1998). "Students' Fortunes Rest with Assigned Teacher." *Education Week on the Web.* Available: www.edweek.org.

[14] Fetler, Mark. (March 26, 1999). "High School Staff Characteristics and Mathematics Test Results." *Education Policy Analysis Archives.* Available: http://epaa.asu.edu/epaa/v7n9.html.

[15] Sack, Joetta. (May 5, 1999). "Class Size, Teacher Quality Take Center Stage at Hearing." *Education Week.*

[16] Sanders, William L. (1996).

[17] National Commission on Teaching and America's Future. (1996).

[18] Archer, Jeff. (February 18, 1998).

[19] Killion, J. and S. Hirsh. (March 18, 1998). "A Crack in the Middle." *Education Week on the Web.* Available: www.edweek.org.

[20] National Commission on Teaching and America's Future. (1996).

[21] Minner, Sam. (May 30, 2001). "Our Own Worst Enemy." *Education Week,* p. 33.

[22] National Commission on Teaching and America's Future. (1996).

[23] Olson, Lynn. (January 13, 2000). "Finding and Keeping Competent Teachers." *Education Week,* p. 12.

[24] Grace, Melissa. (January 17, 2001). "Principal Shortage Is a Crisis, Panel Told." *New York Daily News.*

[25] Pappano, Laura. (December 3, 2000). "Catholic Schools Struggle to Keep Teachers: Job Openings and Higher Pay Lure Many Away to Public Classrooms." *Boston Globe Online.* Available: www.boston.com/globe.

[26] *Hartford Courant* (January 4, 2001). Headline.

[27] *BBC News.* (January 18, 2001). "Teacher Shortage a 'National Crisis'." Headline.

[28] *Toronto Star.* (October 15, 2000). "Teacher Shortage May Worsen."

[29] Merrow, John. (October 6, 1999). "The Teacher Shortage: Wrong Diagnosis, Phony Cures." *Education Week on the Web.* Available: www.edweek.org.

[30] National Commission on Teaching and America's Future. (1996).

The fact that school districts are plagued with the problem of attracting and retaining highly qualified teachers for their classrooms is a major issue in education. We believe that this is the most significant problem we face in education today, **because without effective teachers, our children cannot receive a quality education.**

The least qualified teachers—those with no credentials and little or no formal training—are ending up in schools with the neediest students, seriously undermining attempts to improve student achievement. According to the latest Schools and Staffing Survey, classes in high-poverty and high-minority schools were much more likely to be assigned to a teacher lacking minimal academic qualifications in the subject being taught.[1]

Nationally, one out of four secondary classes in core academic subjects (24 percent) are assigned to a teacher lacking even a college minor in the subject being taught. In the nation's high-poverty schools, that rate skyrockets to over one third of classes (34 percent), compared with about one out of every five classes (19 percent) in low-poverty schools. Similarly, 29 percent of classes in high-minority schools are assigned to an out-of-field teacher, compared with 21 percent in low-minority schools.

These are the very schools where students are in the most desperate need for good teaching, yet they are twice as likely as other children to receive an inexperienced teacher and an uncertified teacher.

Worse yet, these teachers receive little or poor on-the-job training.

It's teachers who make the difference. In the 1960s educators began uncovering the connection between poverty and low student performance. At first, people thought it was the poverty itself that caused the poor performance. In later years researchers realized that poor students in predominantly middle-class or wealthy schools outperformed their peers in high-poverty schools. Thus researchers began to realize that it was not only the students, but also the educational experience that was different in poor schools. The real cause of the achievement gap between poor and wealthier students is the uneven distribution of teachers that districts have allowed. **Poor schools are staffed by teachers with the least experience and the lowest qualifications.**[2]

> **"Substantial evidence shows that teacher qualification is tied to student achievement."**[3]

Student Achievement and Teaching Experience

Virginia Resta and Leslie Huling report that as compelling as the financial costs related to new teacher attrition are, an even more important cost is related to student achievement.[4] Imagine a scenario in which a novice teacher resigns and is replaced by a second novice teacher who is also unsuccessful and is replaced by yet a third novice teacher. It is easy to see that, at the end of this three-year scenario, the instruction being provided in that classroom is not as effective as it would likely be with a teacher who had three years of teaching experience. When children fail to achieve over a period of years, one has to wonder about the quality of the teaching they have received through the years, compared with the quality of instruction received by other children who have fared better.

Dr. John Pedicone, superintendent of the Flowing Wells School District, is an active participant in the new teacher induction process.

Resta and Huling further report that **few districts have begun to analyze the correlation between student achievement and teaching experience.** However, one urban district in Texas has done just that and has indeed found a significant correlation between teaching experience and student scores on the Texas Assessment of Academic Skills (TAAS) (SBEC Panel Data Request, 1998). When this district compared the TAAS pass rates of students who had first-year teachers with those of students who had teachers with five or more years of teaching experience, it found a statistically significant difference in favor of experienced teachers.

In reading, for example, teaching experience accounted for more variance than ethnicity of the teacher, gender of the teacher, or highest degree held by the teacher. The one factor accounting for more variance than teaching experience was prior reading achievement. The point is that there are serious academic consequences to not providing novice teachers with the induction support needed to help them become successful teachers. **If administrators are truly serious about student achievement, they must also be serious about induction support for novice teachers.**

"A recent RAND study shows that teachers are transferring out of poor and minority schools in growing numbers. In some schools, the teacher turn-over rate is as high as 50 percent."[5]

Florida Fund for Minority Teachers

The Florida Fund for Minority Teachers (FFMT) awards scholarships biannually to minority students who wish to teach in Florida's public elementary and secondary schools. FFMT coordinates a collaborative, performance-based scholarship program for African American, Hispanic, Asian American, Pacific Islander, American Indian, and Alaskan Native students. The primary purpose of this program is to attract community college graduates who are capable and promising minority students to pursue teaching careers in Florida public schools. The scholarship is offered to Florida residents who are newly enrolled as upper-division undergraduates or graduates in a state-approved teacher preparation program and who will become full-time teachers in a K–12 Florida public school.

An annual recruitment and retention conference is held for all students who receive the scholarship. In addition, community college minority students are invited to attend this conference to learn more about the advantages of entering the teaching profession. Placement fairs are held periodically to match graduating scholars with Florida school districts.[6]

Student Achievement
At a Fraction of the Cost

**A large-scale study found that
every dollar spent on raising teacher
quality netted greater student
achievement gains than with any
other use of school resources.**[7]

We need to stop spending billions of dollars in constant pursuit of the quick fix, the "program on a white horse" and start investing in our teachers and their effectiveness. This can be done at a fraction of the cost of the programs we are currently investing in—and with far better results. **Effective schools and school districts invest in improving the pedagogical practices of their teachers.**

New educational technologies and programs can be tremendous assets—provided that the teachers using them have the basic skills necessary to use them effectively. However, we challenge you to consider the possibility that the market for most of these programs would collapse if an effective teacher were placed in every one of America's classrooms.

Though we are not suggesting that all of the problems in this country's schools and classrooms are teacher-related, we do firmly believe this:

**If well-trained, competent, caring teachers
were present in every classroom,
we would witness a staggering
INCREASE in student achievement, motivation,
and character improvement,
along with a marked
DECREASE in discipline problems.**

Programs do not teach; teachers teach. We can look to Worsham Elementary School in Houston, Texas, for an example. Holly Fisackerly is principal of Worsham Elementary, where 86 percent of the students are Hispanic, 88 percent are economically disadvantaged, and 50 percent have limited English skills. Yet in 1999, 98 percent of her Hispanic third and fourth graders passed the TAAS reading test, compared with 97 percent of white students and 84 percent of Hispanic students statewide.[8]

Fisackerly did not accomplish this with any programs, but rather, she focused her efforts on producing effective teachers. Each year she trains all of her rookie teachers after school for 90 minutes per day, two to three days per week. "I must get my new teachers and students, who need help, to be the best they can be as fast as possible," Fisackerly says. In addition, there are weekly grade-level meetings to discuss student assessment and intervention. The 230 students who required intervention in 1999 were given skills-development classes after school two days per week. Fisackerly is acting on what William Sanders, formerly of the University of Tennessee, has discovered:

**As teacher effectiveness increases,
lower-achieving students are the first to benefit.**[9]

Student Achievement and Teacher Effectiveness

We take the students who have less to begin with and then systematically give them less in school. What schools do matters enormously. And what matters most is good teaching.[10]

— Kati Haycock

Researchers at the University of Tennessee, Knoxville, have concluded that the harmful effects of a poor teacher can linger well into the future and that a string of bad teachers can leave students at a huge academic disadvantage. The effects of **one bad teacher** were still reflected in test scores **two years later**. Research from Tennessee, Dallas, and Boston indicates that students placed with one ineffective teacher emerge a full year behind peers taught by an effective teacher. If students subsequently have ineffective teachers three years in a row, the effects on the students' performance are catastrophic. Many of these children never recover.

In 1996 William Sanders used data from two Tennessee districts and divided their teachers into five groups, from least effective to most effective. He found that, on average, students who had been taught by less-effective teachers three years in a row scored below the 50th percentile in mathematics by the third year. By contrast, those who had been taught by highly effective teachers three years in a row scored above the 80th percentile. Sanders concluded that **teachers are the single most important influence on student progress**—even more important than socioeconomic status.

Simply put, Sanders found that the effects of a bad teacher, or two consecutive bad teachers, can stick with a child for years. Conversely, the influence of a good teacher can still be seen years down the road. At the same time, he found that highly effective teachers can push students to make significant gains regardless of school location.[11]

Everything You Need to Know About Student Achievement

• Two hundred studies have shown that the only factor that can increase student achievement is a knowledgeable, skillful teacher.[12]

• Researchers in the Dallas School District have shown that having a less-effective teacher can significantly lower a student's performance over time, even if the student gets more-competent teachers later on.[13]

• Schools with more-experienced and more highly educated mathematics teachers tend to have higher-achieving students. Even in very poor schools, student achievement is higher if students have a well-prepared teacher.[14]

• The most important factor, bar none, is the teacher. Having a single ineffective teacher can affect student learning for years, and having an ineffective teacher for two years in a row can damage a student's entire academic career.[15]

• As teacher effectiveness increases, lower-achieving students are the first to benefit.[16]

There is only one way to improve student achievement, and the research is very specific on this point:

The teacher—and what the teacher knows and can do—is the determining factor in student achievement.

Teacher Qualifications

• More than 12 percent of all newly hired "teachers" enter the workforce without any training at all. Another 15 percent or more enter without having fully met state standards.

• More than 50,000 people who lack the training required for their jobs have entered teaching annually on emergency or provisional licenses.

• Only 500 of the nation's 1,200 education schools meet common professional standards.

• Fewer than 75 percent of all teachers have studied child development, learning, and teaching methods; have degrees in their subject areas; and have passed state licensing requirements.

• Nearly 25 percent of all secondary teachers do not even possess a college minor in their main teaching field. This is true for more than 30 percent of mathematics teachers.

• School districts spend only 1 to 3 percent of their resources on teacher development, in contrast to much higher expenditures in most corporations and in other countries' schools.[17]

GOALS OF THE FIRST PROGRAM:

* Reduce the intensity of the transition into teaching

* Improve teacher effectiveness

* Increase retention of more highly qualified teachers

Lafourche Parish posts the goals of its new teacher induction program.

Researchers in Dallas, building on the work of Sanders, determined that having a less-effective teacher can significantly lower a student's performance over time, even if the student later gets more-competent teachers.[18]

Study after study has shown that student achievement is directly related to teacher effectiveness. **Yet only a small percentage of most school districts' budgets are earmarked for training teachers to be better teachers.**

The Consortium for Policy Research in Education found that roughly 1 percent of education spending goes toward staff development. It recommended tripling that figure, which would still come in short of the private sector average for training, which is about 7 percent of total budgets. The National Staff Development Council advocates spending 10 percent of school dollars on staff development.[19]

A study comparing high-achieving and low-achieving elementary schools with similar student characteristics found that differences in teacher qualifications accounted for more than 90 percent of the variations in student achievement in reading and mathematics.[20]

The bottom line is that highly qualified teachers mean improved student achievement! With that in mind, let us take a look at some national statistics on teacher qualifications.

Teacher Quality—It Is THE ISSUE

Teacher quality . . . is the most powerful predictor of student success.

Teacher quality is not just an important issue facing our schools. It is THE ISSUE.

Much time and many resources will continue to be lost if we don't begin to focus on the variable that matters most: teacher quality.[21]

— Sam Minner

Although hundreds of studies have shown that fully prepared teachers are more effective than those who are unqualified, the practice of hiring untrained teachers continues. More than 12 percent of all newly hired "teachers" enter the classroom without any training at all, and another 15 percent or more enter without having fully met state standards. Although no state will allow a person to fix plumbing, guard swimming pools, style hair, write wills, design a building, or practice medicine without completing professional training and passing an examination, more than 40 states allow school districts to hire, on emergency licenses, teachers who have not met basic examination or training requirements.[22]

Even teachers who are fully licensed may not be fully prepared to teach. The alarming attrition rates of certified new teachers bear evidence to that fact. Though much criticism has been aimed at district hiring practices and preservice preparation programs, there are still far too many teachers, with or without the proper qualifications, who are not adequately prepared to teach. And without adequate preparation, they cannot be effective. It is that simple.

Therefore, it seems ludicrous not to put our efforts into providing ongoing training and support for teachers in an attempt to ensure that each and every one of our children will be taught by highly qualified teachers. **Again, the answer lies not in seeking out the latest educational innovations, but in training teachers to teach effectively!** The research confirms what common sense has suggested all along:

A skilled and knowledgeable teacher can make an enormous difference in how well students learn.[23]

There's a Teacher Shortage, Really

New York Schools Face a Critical Shortage

The New York City Board of Education estimates that over the next five years, it will lose 55,000 of its 79,000 teachers to retirement. And union officials say as many as 500 veteran principals out of 1,100 could retire or quit by the end of this school year. New York City schools are facing not only a massive teacher shortage, but also a "crisis in leadership," according to District 30 superintendent Angelo Gimondo.[24]

Catholic Schools in Massachusetts Are Losing Teachers

With as many as 28,000 public school teachers over the next five years eligible to retire under the state's new teacher retirement plan, Catholic schools—which have the same teacher certification requirements as public schools—are seeing their teaching ranks raided.[25]

Two Headlines

"A Shortage Is Expected in Connecticut"[26]

Nearly half of Connecticut's 45,000 teachers are expected to retire in the next decade.

"The United Kingdom's Teacher Shortage Is Dubbed a 'National Crisis'"[27]

Canada's Teacher Shortage Is Getting Worse

According to a recent survey, Canada's school boards no longer can find enough qualified teachers for the country's 5 million schoolchildren and are bracing themselves for the shortage to get worse. More than two-thirds of the 272 school boards surveyed said they fear they will have trouble hiring the teachers they need next year.[28]

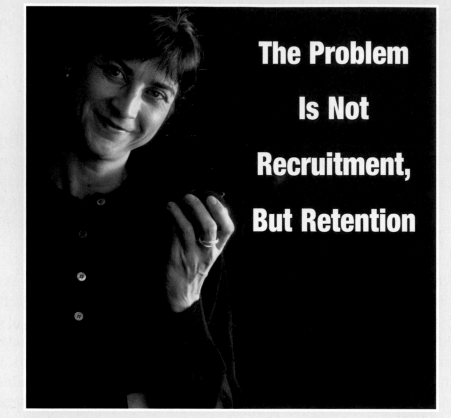

The Problem Is Not Recruitment, But Retention

John Merrow argues that **"we're misdiagnosing the problem as 'recruitment' when it's really 'retention.'"** "Merrow explains the essence of the problem this way: "Simply put, we train teachers poorly and then treat them badly—and so they leave in droves." He suggests that "where shortages exist, these are often what should be labeled 'self-inflicted wounds.' They fall into three categories: Schools underpay and mistreat teachers and eventually drive them from the profession; inept school districts cannot find the qualified teachers living under their noses; and substandard training ill prepares young men and women for the realities of classroom life."

He likens the problem to a swimming pool with a serious leak: "You wouldn't expect that pouring more and more water into the pool would in time fix the leak, but that's precisely the approach we are taking toward the so-called teacher shortage. . . . The response has been to recruit more people into teaching, using a variety of strategies including public-service-announcement campaigns, $100 million in federal money, hiring bonuses, help with mortgages, and recruitment trips to Spain and other distant lands."

Merrow reminds us that "almost every U.S. president since Harry Truman has warned of teacher shortages and large-scale recruitment efforts have followed. Yet the pool keeps leaking water because no one is paying attention to the leak."

"The fact remains," says Merrow, "that **our nation's 1,300 schools and colleges of education already produce more than enough teachers**. But about 30 percent of those newly minted teachers don't go into classrooms. Some never intended to; they were majoring in education because it's an easy way to get a degree or to have a 'fallback' option. Others found they couldn't get teaching jobs in their home towns and so they found other work; that is, staying home was the goal, not becoming a teacher."

"Many who become teachers don't stay long," Merrow points out. **"An estimated 30 percent leave the field within five years; in cities, the exit rate is an astonishing 50 percent."**

Moreover, as Merrow states, "Of every 100 new graduates with licenses to teach, 30 do not. Of the remaining 70, at least 21 will have left teaching within five years. At the very least, that is an inefficient use of human and material resources."

So how do we fix the leak? It's really quite simple. We fix the leak by **providing adequate training and support for beginning teachers, thereby increasing the retention** of more competent, qualified, and satisfied professionals for America's classrooms.[29]

(Emphasis added to original text by authors.)

How an Induction Program Can Help

As a central office staff developer,
I truly believe in the induction process.
If you do not transmit a district's culture, mission,
and beliefs as employees join the family,
then when do you?

— Joan Hearne
Wichita Public Schools, Kansas

A handshake and a smile are just some of the many ways the new teachers are welcomed to Lafourche Parish.

All new teaching employees need to be formally welcomed and introduced to the district's mission, philosophies, procedures, and culture. They need to receive initial training in classroom management in order to ensure their success from the very first day of school. They need to understand exactly what will be expected of them and receive the necessary ongoing training and support in order to carry out those responsibilities and duties. They need the guiding hands of mentors, along with the understanding and support of administrators, faculty, and staff. They need to feel accepted as vital contributors to the overall effectiveness of their schools.

> **There is truly no better experience**
> **for the heart than helping people.**
> **By helping new teachers to succeed,**
> **we help students to succeed.**

At a time when all students must meet higher standards for learning, access to good teaching is a necessity, not a privilege or something to be left to chance. And competent teaching depends on educators who deeply understand subject matter and how to teach in ways that motivate children and help them learn. Like doctors, engineers, and other professionals, teachers must have access to high-quality education and careerlong opportunities to update their skills if they are to do their jobs well.[30]

- **The bottom line is that there is no way to create good schools without good teachers. It is the administrator who creates a good school. And it is the teacher who creates a good classroom.**

- **The best way to have effective teachers is to create a culture of effective teaching and to train your new teachers with an induction program.**

By implementing an induction program in your school or district, you will be able to meet all the critical needs of teachers and students and you will be able to affect the future of education dramatically by increasing teacher confidence and competence. An induction program will also foster a culture of effective teaching.

Without effective teachers,
we cannot and will not have effective schools.

There Is Only One Way to Improve Student Learning

Summary and Implementation

Planting the Seeds
Information We've Shared

- The least qualified teachers often end up with the most difficult teaching assignments.
- The less qualified the teacher, the lower the student achievement.
- As teacher effectiveness increases, lower achieving students are the first to benefit.
- Every dollar spent on raising teacher quality nets greater gains in student achievement than any other use of school resources.
- Effective teachers build effective schools.
- The best way to create a culture of effective teachers is to train new teachers with an induction program.

Nurturing Growth
What You Can Do to Make a Difference

- To improve student achievement, improve the quality of your teaching force.
- Put highly qualified, competent teachers in your lowest performing schools and those schools will no longer be your lowest performing schools.
- Allocate a significant amount of funding in your budget for teacher training.
- Design and implement an induction program for new teachers—today. The next chapter will walk you through the process.

Reaping the Harvest
Benefits to Your School System

- The impact on student achievement is immediate when monies and efforts are put into teaching teachers to be more effective.
- Induction is simple, productive, and cost-effective.

chapter three

How to Structure an Induction Program

*When you truly believe in
something, and you carry it in
your heart, you accept no excuses,
only results.*

— Ken Blanchard

Nurturing the seed.

Sources and Notes for Chapter 3

[1]Garet, Michael, Andrew Porter, Laura Desmoine, Beatrice Birman, and Kwang Suk Yoon. (Winter 2002). "What Makes Professional Development Effective?" *American Educational Research Journal,* pp. 915-946.

[2]Liebermann, Ann and Diane R. Wood. (March 2002). "The National Writing Project." *Educational Leadership,* pp. 40-43.

[3]Watanable, Ted. (March 2002). "Learning from Japanese Lesson Study." *Educational Leadership,* pp. 36-39.

[4]Wong, Harry K. and Rosemary T. Wong. (January 2002). "A Most Effective School." Available: http://teachers.net/gazette/JAN02/.

[5]Wong, Harry K. (March 2002). "Induction: The Best Form of Professional Development." *Educational Leadership,* pp. 52-54.

[6]The Gaston County New Teacher Induction Program can be viewed at www.effectiveteaching.com. Look for Gaston County New Teacher Induction Program in the product listing and click on it to watch the 5 minute program.

[7]Hendrie, Caroline. (June 12, 2002). "Annenberg Challenge Yields Lessons for Those Hoping to Change Schools." *Education Week,* p. 6.

[8]The Southeast Center for Teaching Quality. (January 2002). "Recruitment and Retention Strategies in a Regional and National Context," p. 2. Available: www.teachingquality.org.

[9]Cross, Christopher T. and Diana Wyllie Rigden. (April 2002). "Improving Teacher Quality." (Reporting on the work of Jane L. David and Patrick M. Shields. (2001). *When Theory Hits Reality: Standards-Based Reform in Urban Districts. Final Narrative Report.* Menlo Park, CA: SRI International.) *American School Board Journal.*
Available: www.asbj.com/2002/04/0402coverstory2.html.

The new teacher induction program was my lifesaver! The techniques I learned in the new teacher induction program have proved to be vital to my students' success in the classroom and in the community. I have attended all three years of the induction program and have continued to improve because of it.

— Phyllis Prince,
Special Education Teacher
West Thibodaux Middle School, Louisiana

The American Educational Research Association (AERA) reported in their Winter 2002 journal the following:

Teachers learned more in teacher networks and study groups than with mentoring and in traditional classes and workshops.[1]

The study asked the question,

"How do teachers increase knowledge and skills?"

Responses came from a nationally representative sample of 1,027 public school math and science teachers in kindergarten through grade 12.

People like Antoinette Kellaher, Supervisor of New Teacher Programs for the Prince George's County Schools, affirmed the study's findings when she said,

I just returned from a school visit and watched a second-year teacher work her magic with a group of active middle schoolers. It made me feel that running a long-term induction program is the absolute way to go.

(See Chapter 5, page 89, for the Prince George's Program.)

The theme of the March 2002 issue of *Educational Leadership* was "Redesigning Professional Development." Two significant articles in this issue, "The National Writing Project"[2] and "Learning from Japanese Lesson Study,"[3] confirm the findings of the AERA and the observation of Antoinette Kellaher. They both say this:

- Networks create learning communities that teachers need.

- Colleagues treat each other as potentially valuable contributors.

- Students benefit when teachers share their best ideas and strategies with each other.

- Learners are responsible for the learning.

- Teachers generate, as well as gain, knowledge created by learning communities.

- Lesson study is a shared professional culture, not just a professional development activity.

- Quality teaching becomes, for teachers, not just an individual but also a group responsibility.

Mentoring, typically, does not create learning communities, because mentoring is an individual activity, whereas induction is a comprehensive and sustained group process. Induction is a process that teaches the social and cultural practices that center on learning, what it means to be a learner, and what it means to help others learn.

> Teachers learn and acquire skills not from disarticulated, one-shot mentors or workshops, but from collegial learning communities where new and veteran teachers develop respect for each other and their respective contributions.

Teachers are grouped in learning communities for the Flowing Wells School District induction program.

An Exemplary On-Site Induction Program

The best induction programs are those that are on-site and on-time programs. Bridget Phillips, principal of Goldfarb Elementary School in Las Vegas, Nevada, typifies this. The attrition rate at the school for the past six years has been zero.

Mentors are no longer really used at Goldfarb. Instead, student teachers and new teachers are surveyed as to their needs. The list is publicized and "tons" of teachers respond with willingness to answer, help, or present sessions at in-house training meetings. This is a true learning community of educators sharing with and helping fellow educators.[4]

When the National Elementary Schools Principal Association published its latest book, *Leading*

Learning Communities: Standards for What Principals Should Know and Be Able to Do, they must have been thinking of Bridget Phillips. The book says that, first and foremost, a principal is to be an instructional leader, which means having the competency to build a family or culture that is a learning community.

Goldfarb Elementary School builds on the two-year induction program of the Clark County School District. Bridget Phillips takes all of her first year teachers through an in-house induction training program for one semester. A cadre of administrators and teachers teaches the new teachers. The purpose of this training is two-fold:

1) to train, support, and retain effective teachers, and

2) to acculturate the new teachers to how things are done at Goldfarb and continue to ensure a vision of student achievement.

Bridget Phillips acknowledges that her staff is an A+ staff. **Effective schools are learning communities, places where teachers and administrators study, work, and learn together with the mission of improving student achievement.**

> New teachers need more than mentors; they need induction programs that acculturate them to the school and equip them for the classroom.[5]

Bridget Phillips (left) stands with one of her former students, Rebecca Dehner, who is now part of her A+ teaching staff at Goldfarb.

Elements of Successful Induction Programs

No two induction programs are exactly alike; each caters to the individual culture and specific needs of its unique school or district. However, there are several common components that underlie the most successful induction programs.

Successful induction programs do the following, and we highly recommend that you include all of these components in your own school or district induction program.

- Start with an initial four or five days of induction before school begins.

- Offer a continuum of professional development through systematic training over a period of two or three years.

- Provide study groups where new teachers can network and build support, commitment, and leadership in a learning community.

- Incorporate a strong sense of administrative support.

- Integrate a mentoring component into the induction process.

- Present a structure for modeling effective teaching during in-services and mentoring.

- Provide opportunities for inductees to visit demonstration classrooms.

What New Teachers Are Taught

In the schools in Port Huron, Michigan, new teachers are taught the kind of techniques shown in the following checklist during their new teacher induction program. Imagine the success your new teachers could achieve if on the first day of school, they had already taken, or had prepared to take, the steps listed in the "Start-of-School Checklist."

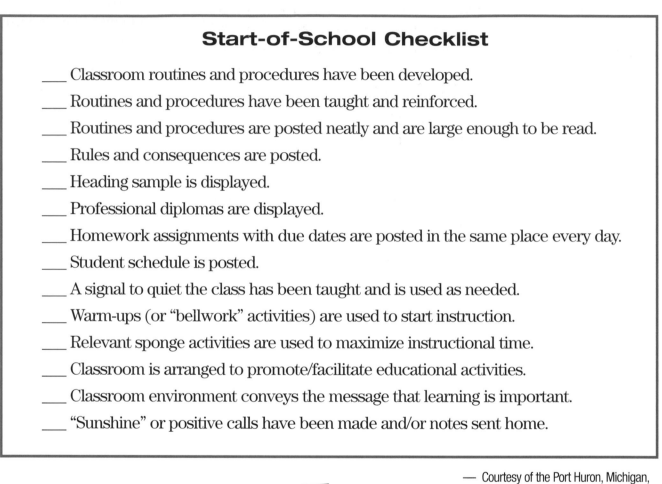

Start-of-School Checklist

___ Classroom routines and procedures have been developed.

___ Routines and procedures have been taught and reinforced.

___ Routines and procedures are posted neatly and are large enough to be read.

___ Rules and consequences are posted.

___ Heading sample is displayed.

___ Professional diplomas are displayed.

___ Homework assignments with due dates are posted in the same place every day.

___ Student schedule is posted.

___ A signal to quiet the class has been taught and is used as needed.

___ Warm-ups (or "bellwork" activities) are used to start instruction.

___ Relevant sponge activities are used to maximize instructional time.

___ Classroom is arranged to promote/facilitate educational activities.

___ Classroom environment conveys the message that learning is important.

___ "Sunshine" or positive calls have been made and/or notes sent home.

— Courtesy of the Port Huron, Michigan,
New Teacher Induction Program

Procedural signs
are posted for the students
on the first day of school

First Day of School Script

Melissa Pantoja scripted—yes, *scripted*—her first day of school, and she learned how to do this from the El Reno, Oklahoma, new teacher induction program. She is like a coach who scripts the first 25 plays of a game. A teacher would not "wing it" in a classroom any more than a coach would on a football field or a pilot would on a flight from New Orleans to Kansas City. The successful and effective teacher goes in with a plan and modifies that plan if conditions change. The details of Melissa's script can be found at http://teachers.net/gazette/JUN00/covera.html.

Melissa began the first day of her first year of teaching with a plan. She scripted the first day of school with a plan for each of the following:

First Day Script Plan

- Greeting each student at the door
- Welcoming students to class and introducing herself
- Explaining procedures for arriving in and leaving class
- Explaining rules and daily procedures
- Numbering assignments
- Respecting the classroom and the art supplies
- Designating areas for the teacher's belongings and students' belongings
- Explaining thematic and other lessons
- Using the art centers
- Maintaining portfolios
- Organizing notebooks

At the end of her first year as a teacher, Melissa Pantoja wrote,

> **"My first year of school was a success."**

Effective teachers organize and structure the classroom for their own success and, most importantly, for the success of their students. **Melissa's success is a tribute to her school district's new teacher induction program.**

Research Induction First

My advice to anyone planning an induction program is this: Don't just jump right in. Research induction first and understand that there is a lot of planning involved. We found out what the best districts around the country were doing, and we decided to build on that, developing a "best of the best" program.

We visited the "mother of all induction programs," in the Flowing Wells School District in Tucson, Arizona. It has been in existence for almost 20 years. They receive so many requests for information that they now host an annual workshop where participants can learn and see firsthand how to conduct a successful induction program.

— Annette L. Breaux

For information on the Flowing Wells program, contact

Institute for Teacher Renewal and Growth
Susie Heintz
Flowing Wells School District
1556 West Prince
Tucson, AZ 85712
520-690-2200

How to Start Your Own Induction Program

The Governor's Award for Excellence in Education was given to Gaston County Schools in North Carolina for their new teacher induction program. They have produced a short video that succinctly explains their program goals, mission, and day-by-day agenda. To help other school districts plan their own induction programs, this video can be viewed at www.effectiveteaching.com.[6]

The Components of Induction

Teachers can be trained to be effective. Once they are trained, a good administrator will retain them and build a culture that reflects effective teaching for the school. For this to happen, the induction process must have three components:

1. **Training:** New teachers are taught and shown effective classroom strategies through a series of workshops, demonstration classrooms, observations, and debriefing sessions.

2. **Support:** A cadre of mentors, administrators, and staff developers work with new teachers personally, in regularly scheduled sessions, to support and assist the teachers.

3. **Retention:** Administrators build a learning community where the contributions of all teachers are respected and shared. Effective administrators must retain effective teachers, creating a culture that values teaching and learning.

The Induction Process

In an induction process the emphasis is on training and the pace is steady. The trainers assume the roles of classroom teachers and the new teachers become their "students." Early training concentrates on classroom management and instruction. **The primary focus is on instructing teachers in techniques that ensure student success.**

A major role of trainers is to immerse new teachers in their district's culture and to unite them with everyone in the district in order to form a cohesive, supportive instructional team. New teachers should quickly be made a part of the district "family."

An essential component of early training is the use of demonstration classrooms at appropriate grade levels and in appropriate subject areas. Master teachers, often mentor teachers, simulate the way their rooms are arranged and managed for the first day of school. New teachers invariably sit in awe as they learn from the experts how to start school successfully.

At the end of the initial induction week, there is usually an awards ceremony and a civic function where new teachers receive certificates and welcome packages from community supporters. Because the induction process stresses lifelong learning, the best new teacher induction programs continue for several years.

Demonstration classrooms are visited by beginning teachers in Flowing Wells.

Training is one of the best ways to send a message to your teachers that you value them and want them to succeed and stay.

It is much worse to not train teachers and keep them than to train them and lose them!

How to Structure an Induction Program

Induction programs, of course, cater to their own culture and specific needs. However, they all use some common steps which you can use as a guide to plan your own induction program.

Seven Steps for Structuring an Induction Program

▶ ### Step 1: Gather Information on Successful Programs

Your very first step in structuring an induction program for your school or district is to gather information on successful induction programs. You have already begun this process by purchasing this book, which will provide you with valuable information on structuring a program of your own. As you develop an induction program, do not "reinvent the wheel." There is no need. Many schools and school districts across the country have already implemented very successful induction programs and would be happy to share information on these programs. Contact these schools and districts to obtain information on their programs. Read through the information you receive and then pick and choose the components of each program that you feel could be implemented successfully in your own school or district. (In Chapters 5 and 6, several successful programs are profiled, along with contact information, to assist you with this first step.)

Checklist for Step 1

Check each task as it is completed.

___ *Information has been requested from several schools and districts with successful induction programs.*

___ *Information has been received from the schools and districts contacted.*

___ *Information received has been reviewed.*

List all components of other schools' and districts' programs that you would like to include in your own program.

_____

_____

_____

_____

_____

_____

_____

_____
_____
_____
_____
_____

List any other components that you would like to include in your own program.

_____
_____
_____
_____
_____
_____
_____
_____
_____
_____
_____
_____
_____
_____

Note: *All of the items listed under "Elements of Successful Induction Programs" should be included in your program. (See page 33.) However, though the entire induction process typically lasts two or three years, in the first year of a program's implementation, a school or district need only plan for the first year. If a first-year program is already in place, you should consider adding a second-year component.*

> ### Step 2: Determine What Your District Already Has to Offer

The next step in structuring an induction program is to assess the status of your own school or district with regard to what, if anything, is already in place for supporting new teachers. Is there a state assessment program that offers assistance to new teachers? Is there any type of structured orientation for new teachers? Is there a mentoring program already in existence? Does the school or district offer any professional development opportunities for new teachers? What resources are available for funding an induction program? These resources might include general funds, special education funds, Title 1 funds, Federal funds, staff development funds, or professional development grants.

The information you have gathered from other school districts should provide further insight into the best ways to use all available resources and coordinate all efforts for new teacher development.

Checklist for Step 2

Check any of the following that already exist in your school or district.

___ *Statewide assessment program*

___ *Statewide mentoring program*

___ *Districtwide mentoring program*

___ *Schoolwide mentoring program*

___ *Districtwide orientation for new teachers*

___ *Schoolwide orientation for new teachers*

___ *Other:* _____

___ *Other:* _____

Describe the types of professional development activities for new teachers, if any, that already exist in your school or district.

_____

_____

_____

_____

_____

_____

_____

_____

_____

_____

_____
_____
_____
_____
_____
_____
_____
_____
_____
_____

Check each source of funding available for your induction program and list the amount of funding available from each source.

___ *General funds*   *Amount:* _____

___ *Special education funds*   *Amount:* _____

___ *Title 1 funds*   *Amount:* _____

___ *Federal funds*   *Amount:* _____

___ *Staff development funds*   *Amount:* _____

___ *Grant funds*   *Amount:* _____

___ *Other:* _____   *Amount:* _____

What is your estimated budget? _____

Check each item that is included in your budget. (All of these items should be considered.)

___ *Stipends for attendees (based on days or hours of the entire induction process)*

___ *Stipends for presenters*

___ *Days added to contracts of new teachers*

___ *Materials for attendees*

___ *Refreshments or meals*

___ *Resources used to develop the program*

___ *Presentation equipment (computers, overhead projectors, etc.)*

___ *Presentation materials*

___ *Other*

➤ **Step 3:**
Establish a Program Structure

Next, you will have to decide how the induction process will be structured. Where will the induction take place? Will there be four or five days of initial induction before school begins? Will there be a second induction program offered for those hired after the initial induction at the start of the school year? Will all inductees attend one general session, or will there be grade-level- or subject-area-specific induction? Who will attend the induction—all first-time teachers or all teachers new to the school or district? If all teachers new to the school or district will be attending, will they all attend the same sessions, or will sessions be different for teachers with no teaching experience? How many participants are expected? The number of participants will determine whether all can attend a general session or not. If the group is larger than 50 or 60 people, they should not all be inducted together. Districts that typically hire 300 new teachers a year usually have several induction sessions occurring simultaneously.

Sample Program Structure

Attendees for initial induction in August: All teachers new to the district.

Number of participants: 50 first-time teachers and 30 experienced teachers new to the district.

Presentation structure: All first-time teachers will attend the same sessions. Experienced teachers new to the district will attend a separate set of sessions. There will not be grade-level- or subject-area-specific instruction. However, the new teacher support groups and some of the ongoing training sessions will be grade-level-specific.

Year 1 ••••••••••••••••••••••••••••••••

- Four days of training in early August for first-time teachers
- Two days of training in early August for experienced teachers new to the district*
- One day of training in August for administrators
- Two days of training in September for late hires
- Three days of further training during the year for first-time teachers: one in October, one in January, and one in April
- Three days of mentor training in August and one day of mentor training in January
- One hour of new teacher support group meetings per month for nine months
- Four informal observations of new teachers by their mentors
- Two informal observations of new teachers by the induction coordinator
- One day of visits to demonstration classrooms

*Experienced teachers new to the district receive two days of initial induction. After that, they may attend any of the other sessions during the three-year process, based on principals' requests. Also, all teachers new to the district are assigned a mentor for one full year.

Year 2 ••••••••••••••••••••••••••••••••

- One day of training in early August
- Three days of further training during the year: one in October, one in January and one in April
- One hour of teacher support group meetings per month for nine months
- Two informal observations of teachers by the induction coordinator
- One half-day of visits to demonstration classrooms

Year 3 •••••••••••••••••••••••••••••

- Four half-days of training during the year: one in September, one in November, one in January, and one in March (which includes a graduation ceremony)

- One informal observation of teachers by the induction coordinator

Checklist for Step 3

Where will the induction be held? _____

What are the dates of the August induction? _____

How many days will the initial induction in August last?
___ *Four days*
___ *Five days*
___ *Other:* _____

How long will the induction process last?
___ *One year*
___ *Two years*
___ *Three years*
___ *Other:* _____

What will be provided for teachers hired after the initial induction?

_____

_____

_____

_____

_____

_____

_____

_____

_____

_____

Outline the program structure:

Attendees for initial induction in August: _____

Number of participants:

_____

Presentation structure:

_____

_____

_____

_____

_____

_____

_____

Year 1 Process Structure:

❑ _____

❑ _____

❑ _____

❑ _____

❑ _____

Year 2 Process Structure:

❑ _____

❑ _____

❑ _____

❑ _____

❑ _____

Year 3 Process Structure:

❑ _____

❑ _____

❑ _____

❑ _____

❑ _____

Step 4: Choose the Topics to Be Covered

Once you have determined how the process will be structured, determine what topics will be discussed during each component of the initial induction that will take place before school begins. Topics for future training sessions can be developed at a later time. (The specific needs of your teachers will help determine future in-service topics.)

Typical topics for the initial four or five days of induction include the following:

- **Classroom management**
- **Lesson planning**
- **Instructional strategies**
- **Discipline**
- **Local policies and procedures**
- **The first days of school**
- **Time management**
- **Working with parents**
- **Accommodating individual differences**

Classroom management should be the main focus throughout the initial days of induction because without effective classroom management, teaching and learning cannot take place. You should not attempt to cover "everything a new teacher needs to know" in the initial induction. Rather, you should provide training that will prepare new teachers for the first days and weeks of school.

Checklist for Step 4

Check each topic you will address during the initial four or five days of induction.

___ *Classroom management*

___ *Lesson planning*

___ *Instructional strategies*

___ *Discipline*

___ *Local policies and procedures*

___ *The first days of school*

___ *Time management*

___ *Working with parents*

___ *Accommodating individual differences*

___ *Other:* _____

___ *Other:* _____

___ *Other:* _____

___ *Other:* _____

___ *Other:* _____

___ *Other:* _____

> ## Step 5:
> ## Select Effective Presenters

In determining who will give the presentations during the initial days of induction, it is of utmost importance to remember that ANY program is only as good as the people teaching it. If your mission is to train teachers to teach effectively, then you MUST select presenters who are highly effective teachers! Possible presenters might include instructional coordinators, principals, classroom teachers, mentor teachers, or supervisors.

Tips for Selecting Presenters

- The number of presenters should be kept to a minimum.
- Presenters should be people who will continue to work closely with the new teachers throughout the induction process.
- Presenters should share a common philosophy about the purpose of induction and about teaching in general.
- Presenters should be highly effective teachers and excellent motivational speakers.

Checklist for Step 5

How many presenters will you have for the initial induction process? _____

List the names and positions of the presenters.

Presenter _____ *Position* _____ *Topic* _____

Presenter _____ *Position* _____ *Topic* _____

Presenter _____ *Position* _____ *Topic* _____

Presenter _____ *Position* _____ *Topic* _____

Presenter _____ *Position* _____ *Topic* _____

Presenter _____ *Position* _____ *Topic* _____

Presenter _____ *Position* _____ *Topic* _____

Presenter _____ *Position* _____ *Topic* _____

Presenter _____ *Position* _____ *Topic* _____

Presenter _____ *Position* _____ *Topic* _____

Step 6: Create a Presentation Format

The setting for the four or five days of initial induction should be a simulated classroom. In this type of setting, the **presenters are the "classroom teachers"** and the **inductees are the "students."** Everything that is taught should be modeled. The physical environment should resemble a typical classroom. On the first day, the "students" should be welcomed by their "teachers." The atmosphere should be comfortable and informal yet structured, with specific procedures. These procedures should be taught, modeled, practiced, and practiced again. The teaching and learning that are modeled during induction should resemble the types of teaching and learning that will be expected to occur in the inductees' own classrooms.

Noelee Brooks models for induction participants how <u>not</u> to dress on the first day of school.

Tips for Structuring the Initial Induction

- Be organized. Have everything in place before the inductees arrive.
- Greet the inductees as they arrive.
- Provide refreshments.
- Set up a system of "bellwork" so that inductees have assignments awaiting them each morning and after breaks.
- Implement procedures for getting the students' attention, moving into cooperative groups, speaking during the presentation, entering and leaving the room, getting materials, getting the teacher's attention, and so on.
- Provide ongoing feedback and praise.
- Keep the inductees actively involved in their learning.
- Model effective teaching at all times.
- Provide useful resource materials for inductees on all topics addressed.
- Have fun! Prove, through your own modeling, that active, meaningful learning is much more effective than the traditional lecture-and-note-taking method.

Also, the classrooms of several effective teachers should be used as demonstration classrooms for inductees to visit at some time during the initial induction. This way, inductees can see how successful teachers prepare their classrooms before school begins. They can also receive instruction from these classroom teachers on first-day procedures.

The final day of induction should include a closing ceremony where inductees receive certificates for having completed the initial phase of induction.

Checklist for Step 6

Check each task as it is completed.

___ *Banners welcoming new teachers have been made.*

___ *Facilities for the presentation have been reserved.*

___ *Presentation equipment has been obtained.*

___ *Materials for the new teachers have been prepared.*

___ *Materials for the presenters have been prepared.*

___ *Arrangements have been made to provide refreshments.*

___ *Certificates of completion for inductees have been printed.*

___ *Demonstration classrooms have been selected and prepared.*

➤ **Step 7:**
Keep Everyone Informed

One of the most important components of a successful induction program is good communication—making sure everyone involved knows about the upcoming induction and its importance. First, send out letters of invitation and agendas to participants well in advance of the induction so that they can plan to attend. (Some districts add extra days to new teachers' contracts in order to ensure that they attend.) Also, send letters of invitation and agendas to administrators, community leaders, school board members, mentor teachers, and anyone else involved. Many of the most successful induction programs have some type of social gathering during the initial week of induction where new teachers meet mentor teachers, principals, members of the supervisory staff, school board members, and community leaders. This sends a message of support to the new teachers. It says that you welcome them to the district, that you value them, and that you want to help ensure their success in the classroom.

Checklist for Step 7

Check each task as it is completed.

___ *Agendas have been prepared.*

___ *A letter of invitation has been written for inductees.*

___ *A letter of invitation has been written for school board members, community*

   leaders, and others involved in the process.

___ *Agenda and letter has been sent to each new teacher.*

___ *Agendas and letters have been sent to administrators, community leaders, and others.*

___ *The media have been notified of the upcoming event.*

___ *Other:* _____

___ *Other:* _____

What a Half-Billion Dollars Found Out

Known as the Annenberg Challenge, former U.S. ambassador and publishing magnate, Walter H. Annenberg gave a half-billion dollars—the largest grant ever to education—and put forth a challenge in 1993. Using this money, local school districts developed an eclectic mix of different and dissimilar approaches to improving schools. Many of these five-year projects have been completed and evaluated.

The conclusion: **Professional development of teachers was identified as the best use of Mr. Annenberg's money.**[7]

In a 1999 survey conducted by the Washington State Institute for Public Policy on beginning teachers, 75 percent of mentors observed their beginning teachers only two times or fewer last year, and almost half never saw their novices teach.[8]

A study of seven urban districts reported that "the only reform effort that clearly resulted in student achievement gains had clear instructional expectations, supported by extensive professional development, over a period of several years."[9]

$500,000,000.00

Using the funds Boston tried whole-school change, Chicago tried small learning communities, Houston tried class size reduction, Los Angeles tried improving literacy, New York tried creating small schools of choice, and Philadelphia tried citywide learning standards.

The conclusion: **The money that delivered the best return was when it was invested in giving teachers SUSTAINED opportunities to improve their classroom skills. This activity was the most productive.**

Mentoring is not sustained. It is a short term, one-shot buddy system.

Induction is sustained, especially if it is an organized, structured, and multiyear process.

Effective school districts produce effective teachers with an organized, SUSTAINED, and multiyear staff development program that begins with new teacher induction.

It is the teacher, what the teacher knows and can do, that is the most significant factor in student achievement.

Just think what we could have done with the half-billion dollars if we had spent it originally on the SUSTAINED professional development of teachers.

Why There Must Be Structure

Look at any successful organization and you will see structure. Look at any successful school district, such as the New Haven Unified School District described on pages 106 and 107, and you will see structure. In the Flowing Wells School District in Tucson, Arizona, there has been a series of administrative changes. (See "Research Induction First" on page 36.) Yet the success of their program and the culture of the district continues year after year because of their very effective and successful new teacher induction program.

People like structure because it provides information on how things should be done. Students like a classroom with structure because they feel secure in knowing how things are going to be done. New teachers like structure because it fulfills their needs for safety, security, and belonging, and reduces anxiety. The alternative to structure is confusion or, at worst, chaos.

Thus, all good schools and districts need an organized new teacher induction program.

The purpose of having an organized, structured induction program is to pass on from group to group the structure and culture of how things are done.

**People not only like structure,
they like successful results.**

**An induction program is structured as
a results-oriented staff development process.**

How to Structure an Induction Program

Summary and Implementation

Planting the Seeds
Information We've Shared

- The three components of induction are training, support, and retention.
- Components of successful induction programs include pre-school year training, ongoing training for two or more years, teacher networking, administrative support, mentoring, modeling effective teaching, and demonstration classrooms.
- There are seven simple steps to structuring an induction program.

Nurturing Growth
What You Can Do to Make a Difference

- Follow the seven simple steps to develop your own induction program.
- Do not reinvent the wheel. Emulate what the most successful school districts are already doing. Read more about these programs in Chapter 5 and 6.
- Successful induction goes far beyond mentoring.

Reaping the Harvest
Benefits to Your School System

- An induction program is an investment in the future of your school system.
- Inducted teachers are well-trained teachers. Well-trained teachers affect student achievement.

chapter four

Mentoring the New Teacher

*The greatest crime in the world is
not developing your potential.
When you do what you do best,
you are helping not only yourself,
but the world.*

— Roger Williams

Supporting the fruits.

Sources and Notes for Chapter 4

[1]Wong, Harry K. (March 2002). "Induction: The Best Form of Professional Development." *Educational Leadership*, pp. 52-54.

[2]Schmoker, Mike. (2001). *The RESULTS Fieldbook: Practical Strategies from Dramatically Improved Schools.* Alexandria, VA: Association for Supervision and Curriculum Development.

[3]Little, J. W. (1990). "The Mentor Phenomenon and the Social Organization of Teaching." In Cazden, C. (ed.). *Review of Research in Education,* vol. 16. Washington, DC: American Educational Research Association, pp. 297–351. As quoted in Feiman-Nemser, Sharon. (1996). "Teacher Mentoring: A Critical Review." Washington, DC: ERIC Clearinghouse on Teaching and Teacher Education. (ED397060)

[4]Huffman, G. and S. Leak. (January-February 1986). "Beginning Teachers' Perceptions of Mentors." *Journal of Teacher Education,* pp. 22–25. As quoted in ERIC Clearinghouse on Teaching and Teacher Education. (1986). "Teacher Mentoring." Washington, DC: ERIC Clearinghouse on Teaching and Teacher Education. (ED271477)

[5]Johnson, Susan Moore and Susan M. Kardos. (March 2002). "Keeping New Teachers in Mind." *Educational Leadership,* pp. 13-16.

[6]Feiman-Nemser, Sharon. (1996). "Teacher Mentoring: A Critical Review." Washington, DC: ERIC Clearinghouse on Teaching and Teacher Education. (ED397060)

[7]Saphier, Jon, S. Freedman, and B. Aschheim. (2001). *Beyond Mentoring: How to Nurture, Support, and Retain New Teachers.* Newton, MA: Teachers 21.

[8]North Carolina Teaching Fellows Commission. (1995). *Keeping Talented Teachers.* Raleigh, NC: The Public School Forum of North Carolina. Available: www.ncforum.org.

[9]Wong, Harry K. (August 8, 2000). "Mentoring Can't Do It All." *Education Week.* Available: www.NewTeacher.com.

[10]Weiss, Eileen Mary and Stephen Gary Weiss. (1999). "Beginning Teacher Induction." Washington, DC: ERIC Clearinghouse on Teaching and Teacher Education. (ED436487)

[11]Canfield, Jack and M. V. Hansen. (1993). *Chicken Soup for the Soul: 101 Stories to Open the Heart and Rekindle the Spirit.* Deerfield Beach, FL: Health Communications.

[12]Wong, Harry K. and Rosemary T. Wong. (April 2001). "How to Recognize Where You Want to Be." Available: http://teachers.net/gazette/APR01/covera.html.

[13]Whitaker, Susan D. (September-October 2000). "What Do First-Year Special Education Teachers Need? Implications for Induction Programs." *Teaching Exceptional Children.*

On the last day of our induction program, I felt that I had definitely made the right choice of a career. I have seen the joy that teaching can bring to both teachers and students, and I can't wait to begin what I know will be a very rewarding career.

— Carla Holzer
Thibodaux High School, Louisiana

Beyond Mentoring

"If we hope to redesign professional development, we must go beyond mentoring to offering comprehensive induction programs.

"You don't prepare lifelong learners—much less leaders—simply by giving them a mentor."[1]

Mentors are a very important component of the induction process and we believe in the value of mentors. But some misconceptions need to be addressed. Mentoring and induction are not the same.

- A mentor is a person who serves as support.
- Induction is an organized process designed to train, support, and retain new teachers.

You can have an induction program without mentors, but you cannot have effective mentoring without a formal induction program.

Mistakenly, many use the terms *mentoring* and *induction* synonymously. These school districts employ mentoring alone and then wonder why they must continue to fight to retain competent teachers. Sadly, they have been misled or misinformed.

Some people are calling their new teacher programs "mentoring-induction programs," which is incorrect and confusing. You either have a mentoring program or an induction program (possibly with a mentoring component).

No Research to Support Mentoring Alone

So-called "mentors" are everywhere these days, but they aren't often given release time or a clear, compelling charge.[2]

— Mike Schmoker

Since the early 1980s, mentoring has received increased attention as part of the local, state, and national teacher reform agenda. However, actual research on the benefits of mentoring is scant. To date, **much of the research on mentoring has tended to focus on things such as how meaningful mentoring activities should be designed, what components mentoring programs should include, what criteria should be used in the selection of mentors, and what types of training should be provided for prospective mentors.**

Of the research conducted on the benefits of mentoring for new teachers, most conclusions use vague phrases such as "mentoring may," "mentored teachers are likely to," or "in most cases the mentors and the new teachers felt that the program was beneficial." There have been few comprehensive studies well informed by theory and designed to examine in depth the context, content, and consequences of mentoring.[3]

Susie Heintz, Our Teacher

On a sunny day in Tucson in February 2000, Susie Heintz, director of the Flowing Wells new teacher induction program, was escorted to the high school auditorium, where the best-kept secret in town had been concealed from her for over six months. Administrators, teachers, parents, students, and her husband had been planning a day to honor "Susie Heintz, Our Teacher."

For over 16 years, Susie has been watching over this "mother of all induction programs," along with all the other programs that the Flowing Wells School District's **Institute for Professional Growth and Renewal** comprises. The Flowing Wells new teacher induction program is a five-year program that guides novice teachers, helping them become experts, leaders, and problem solvers.

When Susie is asked if the program has mentors, she says shyly, "Well, yes, I'm everybody's 'mentor.'" In her humility, what she hesitates to tell you is that she really is everyone's "teacher." She "teaches" in a large classroom provided by the district strictly for professional development.

So on that surprising day in February, teachers from the past 16 years came back to honor their "teacher" and thank her for the success they owe to "Susie School." Susie Heintz has trained everyone in the district—administrators and teachers alike.

The success of the Flowing Wells School District can be traced to the efficacy of its induction program, where there is a master teacher who teaches teachers, who in turn go out and teach children and other teachers.

Although there are occasional stories of how one person has been a successful mentor, the success of mentoring programs has been documented largely by opinion surveys. Long-term objectives, including the retention of new teachers and development of experienced ones, have had insufficient time to be realized.[4]

Susan Moore Johnson of the Project on the Next Generation of Teachers at the Harvard Graduate School of Education describes the frustration of two new teachers:[5]

Laura was assigned a mentor who might have helped her answer questions over time. He taught a different grade and subject, however, and they met "zero times." Many new teachers in our study went through their first months of school believing that they should already know how their school works, what their students need, and how to teach well.

Having no access to clear answers or alternative models compromised the quality of their teaching, challenged their sense of professional competence, and ultimately caused them to question their choice of teaching as a career.

Katie found herself isolated from her veteran colleagues, who seemed to know how to teach. Despite the high skill and good intentions of her first mentor, Katie did not get what she knew she needed:

I'm very isolated from her.... I met with her a few times and I was always welcome to go in her room and take a look at her materials and borrow anything that she had. But she just didn't have the time to come in and observe me and really talk with me practically about the things that I could do in here.

She and her colleagues had no access to experienced teachers to guide them in their difficult work. Although she acknowledged that things began to get better in her second year, she explained that, in her first year, "We felt like we were just kind of drifting along in our own little boat."

Mentoring may be fine during the new teachers' initial year, but teaching is a lifelong learning experience. Because mentoring is a one-to-one process, mentoring stops after the mentor leaves, whereas induction is a district's and school's organized, cultural process designed to encourage a dual commitment for teachers to teach each other.

We know that people learn best when they learn from and support each other in a learning community.

Everything You Want to Know About Mentoring

The most current and definitive study on teacher mentoring appeared as an *ERIC Digest* in July 1996. (See the References, page 150, for the full text of the study.) The study's main conclusions on mentoring were as follows:

1. The lack of clarity or purposes of mentoring have not been matched to the enthusiasm shown for mentoring.
2. Claims about mentoring have not been subjected to rigorous empirical scrutiny.
3. Few comprehensive studies exist that have examined in depth the context, content, and consequences of mentoring.
4. More direct studies are needed about mentoring and its effects on teaching and teacher retention.[6]

Mentoring Is Like a Blind Date

Jon Saphier, Susan Freedman, and Barbara Aschheim have written a book, *Beyond Mentoring*.[7] Inherent in the title is the direction teacher-leaders and well-informed administrators are moving. If we are to train, support, and retain new teachers, we need to move beyond mentoring. This is what they say:

❖ For too many teachers, the mentoring pairing process results in a "blind date." The teachers do not know each other and neither partner has input into the pairing.

❖ Mentors alone cannot hope to provide the range of input, feedback, and support beginning teachers need.

❖ The ad hoc, informal nature of traditional mentoring scenarios relies heavily on the initiative, instincts, and good will of the veteran teacher and the protégé.

❖ A comprehensive induction program involves more than just mentors. We need to go beyond mentoring.

❖ A well-designed induction program is essentially excellent staff development.

❖ Effective induction programs inherently work to transform the culture of a school.

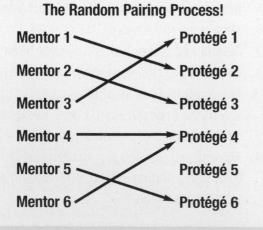

The Random Pairing Process!

The personal computer has been on the market for the last 20 years. It now pervades our lives and is a major factor in the world's intellectual, political, social, and financial communities. Yet after 20 years of experimenting with mentoring as a process for helping new teachers,

1. there are no data to validate the effectiveness of mentoring;
2. no programs can be cited to demonstrate the success of mentoring; and
3. we still can't decide if mentoring works!

My brother-in-law is a first-year teacher and was having a horrible time. The district provided no induction program, and when he asked for help, he was told to contact his mentor. He didn't even know he had a mentor. So he called this teacher and informed her that she was his mentor. She said, "I am?" He said, "Thanks, but no thanks," and hung up.

— Name withheld to protect the innocent

The North Carolina Teaching Fellows Commission says, "Giving a teacher a mentor 'only' is a convenient and unconsciously foolish way for an administrator to divorce himself or herself from the leadership required to bring a beginning teacher up to professional maturity level."[8] The commission has found that principals and new teachers rated mentoring the least-effective way to help new teachers. One out of four new teachers claimed that they received either "poor support" or "no support" from their mentors. Simply assigning a mentor does little to remedy the situation of new teachers becoming discouraged and leaving the profession.

We cannot jeopardize an entire generation of new teachers with a process that has not produced any results in 20 years and still needs "more direct studies." **In contrast to mentoring, induction has proved effective beyond any doubt.**

Mentoring—One Component of Induction

Simply assigning a mentor teacher does little to remedy the situation of teachers becoming discouraged and leaving the profession. Induction and mentoring must go hand-in-hand. You cannot do one without the other.

— Leslie Huling

The term *mentoring* implies a trusting, supportive relationship between a more-experienced member and a less-experienced member of an organization. In any profession most new members, early in their careers, seek the advice, counsel, and support of more-experienced colleagues. Many organizations provide "mentors" for new members as part of a formalized, structured induction process. The key word here is part. Any organization relying SOLELY on the concept of "mentoring" to train and support its junior members CANNOT and WILL NOT survive.

Million Dollar Players Are Coached, Not Mentored

When a professional football organization drafts new team members, these new members, though already versed in the rudiments of the game, are not simply provided with "mentors" to ensure their success and ongoing development. Instead, ALL members of the organization provide structured training and ongoing support to foster optimal skill development in the new member during the overall "induction" process. And much of this training takes place BEFORE the season begins.

A major league baseball team signed Bill Carpenter, a newly retired elementary school principal, when he graduated from high school. At training camp, he recalls, the camp was crawling with coaches. They had coaches for pitching, hitting, catching, base running, outfield play, infield play, sliding, base stealing, taking signals, and warming up drills, just to name a few.

They did not have mentors or facilitators to lead them in a forum for reflection. Baseball, like a school, is a team function, and everyone needs to know the culture of the team and how it operates in harmony and unison.

This same concept of induction can be applied to almost any profession. Doctors, lawyers, engineers, and other professionals must all prove their abilities BEFORE they are allowed to practice their professions independently. They are not placed in professional settings and told to rely on their "mentors" if they have any questions. Tragically, many new recruits in a school district receive little or no training as classroom teachers. Giving them only a mentor exacerbates the problem.

Mentoring can't do it all. New teachers learn best from systematic induction programs.[9]

Mentors must not replace or be the only form of formal or informal induction assistance. If this is not taken into account, there is the danger that mentors will be viewed incorrectly as substitutes for the school community whose professional responsibility it is to assist teachers in becoming successful in their new work setting.

Any educator seeking to enhance the success and retention of new teachers must understand that mentoring is only one component of a successful induction program. Without all of the components in place, mentoring by itself will be of little benefit to new teachers.

What's Really Scary

In the working world no one talks about mentoring "alone"—except in education. What's really scary is that the idea of mentoring as a stand-alone cure-all has become institutionalized in education.

McDonald's has an attrition rate of 300 to 400 percent a year. That translates into an employee staying for two months. In addition, they hire immigrants, senior citizens, school dropouts, and disabled people. Yet, they are successful and are the world's most recognized brand. How do they do it? First, they do not give each new employee a mentor. Rather, they have a well organized and comprehensive training program. Every employee goes through a "station observation checklist," which comprises a list of tasks that are to be done at each station or job, such as cashiering, grill work, preparation, and dish washing. Employees are systematically trained in the skills and procedures that promote the culture of McDonald's.

Home Depot has "Home Depot University," where employees receive three days of training for cashier work. Then, if they want to advance, they can attend different training sessions for other departments, such as customer service, plumbing, electrical supplies, hardware, and gardening, as well as sessions on management. Employees grow and advance as they receive more training and become cross-trained.

Mervyn's stores (a division of Target) and Domino's Pizza each have two-week training programs for their new employees.

Football and baseball teams have training camps. Even million-dollar athletes participate in training programs every year.

Airlines all have training facilities, where new employees are trained and to which most permanent employees return for training on a regular basis.

But in **Education** many schools and school districts do not provide training. A definitive study on new teacher induction describes the sorry situation:

Although shown to be valuable, induction programs that include sustained feedback in collaborative environments remain a rare experience for most beginning teachers. Thus far, teacher induction has been a variegated landscape of policies and programs.[10]

The Real Needs of New Teachers

Some educators believe that a new teacher should be given a "forum for reflection" with a mentor, whatever that means. Yet it is a well-known fact that new teachers will not reveal their weaknesses. Their students walk in late, won't sit down, steal the paintbrushes, yell and throw chairs, and talk back. And these frightened new teachers, who go home in utter frustration and emotional turmoil each night, get nothing more than a "mentor for reflection?" Get real.

Maslow's theory of motivation postulates that individuals' needs are arranged in a hierarchy. The needs of the lowest level must be satisfied before the individual can progress to the next higher level. According to this theory, the following are an individual's needs with the lowest need on the bottom working up to the highest need at the top of the stack:

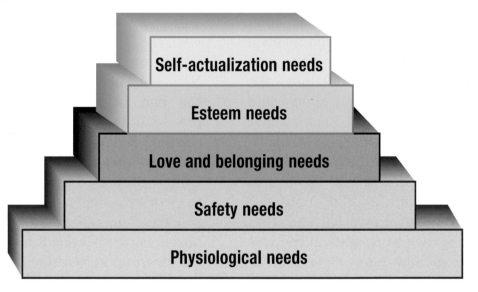

Those who promote only "a forum for reflection" are obviously viewing education through rose-colored glasses. New teachers are neither ready nor able to reflect effectively. Rather, a new teacher's first needs are the first four just listed:

1. Physiological needs: Where is my classroom? Why doesn't someone show me where my classroom is? Where do I eat lunch and what will it cost? When do I get paid and how do I make sure that I have health insurance? Isn't anyone going to show me where the bathroom is or tell me what the other teachers do for lunch? When

does first period begin? Can someone help me with setting up telephone and utility service in my new home? (See the story of Helga, a new teacher whose basic needs went unmet, under "She Left as Abruptly as She Came," page 13.)

The Clark County Schools in Nevada have a "welcome center" for their new teachers. The center helps new teachers find housing and set up utilities, provides maps, recommends banking facilities, and assists with all the other physiological needs of teachers who are new in town. Held before school begins, there is a "community day" where the new teachers can come to meet Geographic Buddies (people from the same home town or state), Teaching Buddies (others who share the same grade level and/or subject), and Hobby Buddies (people who share the same interests). Local merchants are there also sharing their services and products and, of course, breakfast and lunch are served.

2. Safety needs: Where do I park, and will it be safe to park there? Can I stay after school or come here during the weekend? What do I do if I need to call for help? Whom do I call?

Jodee Brentlinger, a principal in San Juan Capistrano, California, personally introduces each new teacher to the office staff, custodians, and other staff members. After introductions, she walks them into the workroom and lounge and then takes them to their classrooms. Each teacher is provided with appropriate teacher manuals, district objectives, and so on. (A complete handbook is provided at the first staff meeting to all staff members.) At the official preopening staff meeting, all new staff members are introduced to their teams and then the entire staff introduces themselves so that all new hires meet veteran teachers and veteran teachers meet the new hires. Once every two months throughout the course of the year, Brentlinger takes the classes of an entire grade level, thus freeing their teachers, to the multipurpose room and conducts a directed drawing lesson. This allows the teachers to work together in order to connect both personally and professionally—ultimately, for the benefit of their students.

3. Love and belonging needs: Who is in my grade level or department? Does anyone care about me? I haven't met anyone at the school. It's so lonely here.

Clark County's new teacher welcome center introduces new hires to the community and to each other in a most efficient way.

Cathy Lozen, director of the Port Huron, Michigan, New Teacher Induction Program, reports that at the end of one of the program's four-day pre–school year induction workshops, the coordinators of the program returned to their office to find flowers from all the participants, along with a card thanking those responsible for the workshop and a note saying, "We now feel like welcomed members of the Port Huron family." Lozen says, "We had become a cohesive and caring group in four days. We all bonded and our district is truly better for it. What a feeling!" There are no estranged new teachers, working unsupported and in isolation, in Port Huron.

4. Esteem needs: Is there nothing but the four walls and me here? The homeless shelter where I volunteer has better facilities. There's nothing in the halls. Isn't anyone proud of anything around here? When will I hear a few words of encouragement? What can I do to help so that I feel I have some significance around here? I feel so useless and so alone. Won't someone tell me about the "unwritten rules" in the school?

In the Lafourche Parish Public Schools in Louisiana, much effort goes into making new teachers feel welcome. On the fourth and final day of the initial induction training in August, there is a very moving slide presentation recapping all that has been learned and all that has been gained over the past four days. "We really bond with these new teachers," says Liz Yates, an induction team member, "and none of us wants to see it end. The good news is that it's only the beginning of a three-year journey with these teachers, hopefully leading to a lifelong career." Following the slide presentation, there is a candlelight ceremony where new teachers gather in a circle and listen to the poem "I Am a Teacher."[11] There is rarely a dry eye in the room as the inductees come forward to receive their certificates of achievement along with hugs and well-wishes from their teachers. This is followed by a luncheon at which new teachers meet mentor teachers, principals, school board members, and administrative staff members. On the afternoon of the fourth day, the new teachers visit demonstration classrooms specific to their grade levels and receive advice and instruction from successful veteran teachers.

Yes, a new teacher can reflect. But if these first four basic human needs are not met, the teacher will not stay with a school. If these needs are met—and, most importantly, if there is a structured induction program—then, and only then, we can expect a new teacher to become a self-actualized individual who is secure, comfortable, and able to reflect effectively.

The Original Mentor—a Teacher, Not a "Mentor"

New secretaries do not receive a mentor. They are trained and assisted. Doctors, factory workers, actors and actresses, chefs, electricians, and dental hygienists do not receive a mentor. They are trained and assisted. Even million-dollar-per-year athletes are trained, every day, all year long, every year. In every aspect of the working world, people are trained and assisted.

New teachers, on the other hand, often receive no training. Typically, they are thrown into a classroom and left to survive as best they can. They may be lucky enough to receive an effective and caring mentor who has the time to help and who may even be compensated. The problem is that giving a new teacher ONLY a mentor is impractical and ineffective. Perhaps the problem exists because the term mentoring and its concept are incorrectly used in education.

In Greek legend, Mentor was the faithful friend of Odysseus ("Ulysses" in Latin), the hero of the Odyssey. When Odysseus went to fight the Trojans, he asked Mentor to be the guardian of his son, Telemachus. He instructed Mentor to be a teacher and adviser to his son. Thus Mentor was Telemachus's teacher and adviser, not his mentor. Unfortunately, much of the educational literature on mentoring describes a mentor as a facilitator or support person. **What a new teacher needs is a teacher or a tutor—much more than a support person.**

We take issue with the word *only*, not the word *mentor*. Commendations are certainly due to those who have promoted the concept of mentoring, as it is certainly better than the former method of not giving a new teacher any help. However, it is time to move beyond mentoring into a comprehensive, sustained induction program.

Mentors Are Part of a Team

In order to be fully functioning, skillful classroom teachers, new recruits must go through a structured training program and receive ongoing support from ALL members of their organization—an induction process, tailored to the needs of the individual. A skilled mentor may be used as one means of support, but the mentor is only ONE member of the team. Administrators, staff developers, and effective, experienced classroom teachers constitute the rest of the team.

We fully believe in the efficacy of mentors, but what a new teacher needs and deserves is a tutor, a master teacher, or—ideally—a group of teachers, staff developers, and administrators who will teach the new teachers and get them up to speed quickly. New teachers need tutors who will teach them how to teach and show them what to do. A mentor, on the other hand, is someone who can serve as a support person to a new teacher or, later in a teacher's professional life, as an inspiration to an experienced teacher.

What has proven to be effective with new teachers is a comprehensive, structured, organized induction program where the central office leaders, site administrators, teachers' union, school board, and all veteran teachers are involved. Just as it takes a village to raise a child, the success of new teachers is the vital responsibility of the entire educational community. **Everyone is a stakeholder in the nurturing, training, and retaining of new teachers.**

In the Hopewell, Virginia, school district's induction program, each new teacher is provided with three support people, all in the same building.

Mentor: This is an assigned teacher to whom the novice teacher can turn for immediate, simple assistance, such as answers to school procedural questions or quick advice.

Coach: Teachers who are coaches are experts in classroom management and instructional skills. There are presently four in each school and that number may increase to five if the number of new teachers increases proportionally.

Lead teacher: This is a teacher who can help with subject matter questions. There are five on each campus, each specializing in one of five areas—English, math, science, social studies, and technology.

The roles of the three people are strictly supportive and nonevaluative. All of the mentors, coaches, and lead teachers receive training, teach in the same building, and receive release time to observe and assist. Lead teachers are financially compensated for attending conferences. They then conduct workshops on what they have learned.

Each New Teacher Has Three Support People

In addition, the new teachers receive support from staff developers and administrators from both the central office and the building site. Principals are the instructional leaders and evaluators. The central office staff provides coordinators to assist at each school site, and the assistant superintendent, Linda Hyslop, structures and coordinates the new teacher induction process.

In the 1998-99 school year, Hopewell hired 47 teachers and lost only 1.[12]

What new teachers need is a useful induction program. **They require pragmatic, practical, and tangible training and guidance.** Can you imagine a restaurant that does not train its workers, but provides them each with a mentor and tells them that if the kitchen is on fire or the customers are suffering from food poisoning to call their mentor for reflection?

Exit Stats

The attrition rate reported for special education teachers is consistently higher than the attrition rate reported for general education teachers.[13]

E-Mentoring 24/7

In less than 24 hours she had a mentor. A new teacher, who did not want her school to be identified because she was getting no help, asked if someone could help her find a mentor. She was advised to go to www.teachers.net and the Mentor's Center or Beginning Teachers' Chatboard (http://teachers.net/mentors/beginning_teachers/). Within 24 hours she had a mentor, which speaks well of the professional caliber of teachers out in cyber space. People are willing to help—just ask. Two other places to find experienced and friendly teachers are

"Golden Apples" at http://teachers. net/mentors/golden

and

"Retired Teachers" at http://retired.teachers.net/chatboard

In Illinois, new teachers can turn to the Novice Teacher Support Project, run by the University of Illinois in Urbana-Champaign. Using a special password, new teachers can get e-mentoring from over 40 veteran teachers statewide. You just reach out and someone will respond. Typically, the person who posts a query will get many different responses from which a choice will need to be made, not a pat answer from one mentor. And it operates 24/7 with confidentiality.

In Texas, Judi Harris at the University of Texas started WINGS Online, an Internet bulletin board for new and student teachers. The program can be seen at http://emissary.ots.utexas.edu.

E-mentoring is a valuable resource for new teachers. However, the question to be asked is, "Why is there e-mentoring?" This is because school districts are not offering their new teachers any form of organized, comprehensive support. E-mentoring will help many new teachers, but e-mentoring has a major short-coming. It only offers short-term, temporary help to a teacher in an isolated situation. This help is needed. However, it does not create a culture or local learning community.

The research is clear. Teachers and administrators who work together create effective schools where students succeed and achieve.

How Lafourche Parish Trains Its Mentors

The mentoring component of Lafourche Parish's FIRST (Framework for Inducting, Retaining, and Supporting Teachers) program is tied in with Louisiana's assessment program for new teachers. Mentors are paid by the state and the training is dictated by the state. However, the state strongly recommends that the mentoring process be intertwined with induction.

In Lafourche Parish members of the induction team provide training to mentors to ensure that a consistent message is carried to all new teachers. There are criteria designed to promote careful selection of mentors and only the very best teachers receive consideration. Mentors attend a highly structured three-day training session in September and receive ongoing follow-up training. Also, all school-based instructional facilitators are trained in mentoring. These facilitators oversee the mentoring process at each school site to ensure that mentoring remains structured and consistent for every new teacher.

The Lafourche Parish induction team of Liz Yates, Annette Breaux, Noelee Brooks, and Debbie Toups provides training for mentors and for the new teachers.

The actual mentoring process is in no way haphazard. During the first semester, the mentor focuses on basic classroom management with the new teacher. During the second semester, the mentor begins to prepare the new teacher for the assessment process, on which certification decisions are based. During the first semester of the new teacher's second year, the mentor and the new teacher focus on successful completion of the assessment process. And during the second semester of the second year, the mentor works with the new teacher on developing a professional portfolio.

Consistency is the key and mentors are just that— mentors. They do not in any way replace the administrators, curriculum specialists, or other support personnel involved in the induction process. **Rather, mentors are members of a supportive team.**

Mentor Roles and Responsibilities

Despite a lack of conclusive research, most educators will agree that new teachers do benefit from the support, encouragement, and knowledge of more-experienced colleagues. However, many mentoring programs are set up haphazardly, giving little consideration to pairing new teachers with qualified, well-trained mentors who have compatible teaching responsibilities, personalities, ideologies, and so on. It is important to understand a crucial principle:

The success of any mentoring program hinges largely on the quality and preparedness of its mentors.

Though the roles and responsibilities of mentors will vary somewhat from school to school, district to district, or state to state, the conventional beliefs about mentoring roles and responsibilities are as follows:

A MENTOR IS

- ✔ A teacher
- ✔ A friend
- ✔ A guide
- ✔ A coach
- ✔ A role model

A MENTOR IS NOT

- ✘ An administrator
- ✘ A supervisor
- ✘ An evaluator
- ✘ A "spy" for the principal

A MENTOR PROVIDES

- ✔ Support
- ✔ Encouragement
- ✔ A listening ear
- ✔ A welcoming shoulder
- ✔ Constructive feedback
- ✔ Suggestions for improvement

A MENTOR MUST EXHIBIT

- ✔ Professionalism
- ✔ A positive attitude
- ✔ The ability to plan and organize
- ✔ A love of children and teaching
- ✔ Excellence in teaching
- ✔ Good communication skills
- ✔ Good coaching skills
- ✔ Good conferencing skills

A MENTOR IS RESPONSIBLE FOR

- ✔ Maintaining confidentiality
- ✔ Sharing knowledge, skills, and information with the new teacher
- ✔ Meeting frequently with the new teacher
- ✔ Observing the new teacher
- ✔ Providing demonstration lessons
- ✔ Familiarizing the new teacher with school policies, procedures, and culture
- ✔ Participating in ongoing mentor-training activities

A MENTOR MUST BE

- ✔ Understanding
- ✔ Supportive
- ✔ Trustworthy
- ✔ Empathetic
- ✔ Innovative
- ✔ Knowledgeable
- ✔ Open-minded
- ✔ Reform-minded
- ✔ Committed

OUR MENTORS . . .

- ✔ _____
- ✔ _____
- ✔ _____
- ✔ _____
- ✔ _____
- ✔ _____
- ✔ _____

How to Develop a Mentoring Component for Your Induction Program

When developing a mentoring component for your induction program, careful consideration must be given to several important issues:

✔ Determining the goals for your mentoring program, which might include the following:

- ❏ Easing new teachers' transition into the classroom
- ❏ Increasing retention of qualified new teachers
- ❏ Improving the skills of new teachers
- ❏ Revitalizing the skills of mentor teachers
- ❏ Providing an on-site support system for new teachers
- ❏ Assisting teachers participating in a statewide assessment program

✔ Securing adequate funding for the mentoring program

✔ Appointing a team of "mentor trainers" and determining the amount of initial and ongoing training that will be provided for mentors, which might cover such topics as the following:

- ❏ Teaching strategies
- ❏ Classroom management techniques
- ❏ Coaching techniques
- ❏ Stages of teacher development
- ❏ Needs of new teachers
- ❏ Conferencing skills
- ❏ Observation techniques
- ❏ Policies and procedures of the mentoring program
- ❏ Roles and responsibilities of the mentor teacher
- ❏ Reflective teaching
- ❏ Development of professional improvement plans
- ❏ Communication skills

✔ Defining the roles and responsibilities of the mentor

✔ Determining criteria for mentor selection, which might include the following:

- ❏ A minimum of five years of successful teaching experience
- ❏ Evidence of excellence in teaching
- ❏ A valid teaching certificate
- ❏ A willingness to commit to ongoing professional development
- ❏ A willingness to meet frequently with the new teacher
- ❏ A willingness to share knowledge, skills, and information with others

❐ A willingness to provide demonstration lessons for the new teacher

❐ A sincere love of children and of teaching

✔ Determining criteria for pairing mentor teachers with new teachers, which might include the following:

❐ Grade level or content area

❐ Common planning periods

❐ Proximity of the mentor teacher's classroom to the new teacher's classroom

❐ Compatibility of the mentor teacher and the new teacher

❐ Needs of students

✔ Making provisions for mentor stipends, release time for observations, supplies, and other items unique to the process

✔ Devising a system for evaluating the success of the mentoring component

A Final Word on Mentoring

The old equation **"LESS = MORE"** can be altered slightly here. In this case, it is clear that

MORE = LESS = MORE:

MORE qualified, caring mentors = IMPROVED support for new teachers

IMPROVED support for new teachers = MORE successful new teaching experiences

MORE successful new teaching experiences = LESS teacher turnover

LESS teacher turnover = MORE capable, well-trained, effective teachers

MORE capable, well-trained, effective teachers =

Improved Student Achievement!

> **There is nothing more important than to develop the potential of people. Thus, mentors must be more than just buddies; they must be trained to bring out the best in people.**

A well-planned, structured mentoring component will enhance the success of the overall induction process. But it is the induction process that fosters a culture of effective teaching, ensuring the high-quality education our children so deserve.

Mentoring the New Teacher

Summary and Implementation

Planting the Seeds
Information We've Shared

- Mentoring is not enough.
- Any organization relying solely on providing a mentor for new teachers will not succeed in training and retaining effective teachers.
- A strong mentoring component may enhance the overall success of the induction process, but it is the INDUCTION process that fosters effective teaching.

Nurturing Growth
What You Can Do to Make a Difference

- Do not allow mentoring to be the sole means of support for new teachers.
- Move beyond mentoring into a comprehensive, sustained induction program.

Reaping the Harvest
Benefits to Your School System

- Induction, not mentoring, creates a culture of effective teachers.
- Fostering a culture of effective teaching ensures high quality education for all students.

chapter five

Exemplary Induction Programs

Choose a job you love, and you will never have to work a day in your life.

— Confucius

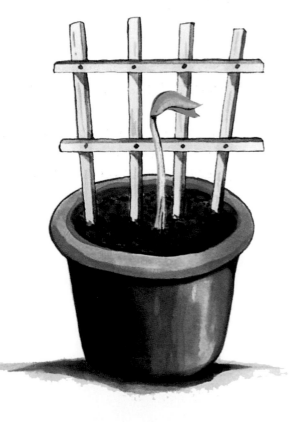

Sprouting.

Sources and Notes for Chapter 5

[1]Bennett, William J., et al. (July-August 1998). "A Nation Still at Risk." *Policy Review*, p. 23.

[2]Johnson, Susan Moore and Susan M. Kardos. (March 2002). "Keeping New Teachers in Mind." *Educational Leadership*, pp. 13-16.

[3]DePaul, Amy. (2000). *Survival Guide for New Teachers: How New Teachers Can Work Effectively with Veteran Teachers, Parents, Principals, and Teacher Educators*. Jessup, MD: U.S. Department of Education, Education Publications Center.

[4]Wong, Harry K. and Rosemary T. Wong. (2001). *The First Days of School: How to Be an Effective Teacher*. Mountain View, CA: Harry K. Wong Publications.

[5]Futtrell, Mary, Dean of the Graduate School of Education. George Washington University.

[6]Senge, Peter M. (1990). *The Fifth Discipline: The Art and Practice of the Learning Organization*. New York, NY: Doubleday.

[7]Schmoker, Mike. (1996). *Results: The Key to Continuous School Improvement*. Alexandria, VA: Association for Supervision and Curriculum Development.

[8]Schmoker, Mike. (2001). *The RESULTS Fieldbook: Practical Strategies from Dramatically Improved Schools*. Alexandria, VA: Association for Supervision and Curriculum Development.

[9]"Rate Your School: Here's How to Do It." (October 2000). *Catalyst*. Available: www.catalyst-chicago.org/10-00/1000rate.htm.

[10]From Canfield, Jack and M. V. Hansen. (1993). *Chicken Soup for the Soul: 101 Stories to Open the Heart and Rekindle the Spirit*. Deerfield Beach, FL: Health Communications.

[11]Wong, Harry K. and Rosemary T. Wong. (2001).

[12]Heintz, Susie. (1997). *National Training Seminar Manual*. Tucson, AZ: Flowing Wells School District.

[13]Wong, Harry K. and Rosemary T. Wong. (2001).

[14]Wong, Harry K. (1996). *The Effective Teacher*. Mountain View, CA: Harry K. Wong Publications. Videotape series.

[15]Ingersoll, Richard M. (June 2002). "The Teacher Shortage: A Case of Wrong Diagnosis and Wrong Prescription." *NASSP Bulletin*. Available: www.nassp.org/news/bltn_teachshort0602.html.

[16]Wong, Harry K. and Rosemary T. Wong. (2001).

Our new teachers became more successful and they were all coming back the following year. This had never happened until we implemented an induction program.

— Elmo Broussard
Superintendent
Lafourche Parish Public Schools
Thibodaux, Louisiana

There is a need for a structured, systematic, sustained instructional training system for beginning teachers in order to help them become effective professionals.

If this can happen in one school district, it can happen in yours and thousands of others. This is truly not rocket science. Nor is it a mystery. What is mysterious is that we continue to do what doesn't work.[1]

For systematic training and support to occur, the Project on the Next Generation of Teachers at the Harvard Graduate School of Education says what is needed is **sustained** School-Based Professional Development. They state:

The questions and uncertainty that new teachers bring to school require far more than an orientation meeting, a mentor in the building, and a written copy of the school's discipline policy.

What new teachers want in their induction is experienced colleagues who will take their daily dilemmas seriously, watch them teach and provide feedback, help them develop

instructional strategies, model skilled teaching, and share insights about students' work and lives.

*Therefore, what new teachers need is **sustained, school-based professional development** guided by expert colleagues, responsive to their teaching, and continuous throughout their early years in the classroom.*

Principals and teacher leaders have the largest roles to play in fostering such experiences.[2]

We know that inadequately prepared, poorly supported teachers leave the profession at staggering rates. The reason is obvious: lack of training, lack of support, and lack of success. We know that well-prepared, supported teachers remain in teaching and enjoy rewarding, successful careers, making a positive impact on the lives of countless children.

New teachers who are trained and supported are less likely to leave the profession than those who are left to fend for themselves.

We know that highly successful schools and school districts are successful because they TRAIN, SUPPORT, and RETAIN the most effective teachers. The first and most important step they take is to provide a structured induction program for their new teachers.

The Induction Process

Although induction programs differ because they cater to the unique cultures and communities they serve, all have some commonalties. They all teach the following:

- Effective classroom management procedures and routines
- Effective instructional practices
- Sensitivity to and understanding of the school community
- Lifelong learning and professional growth
- Unity and teamwork among the entire learning community

The primary focus of the induction process is on instructing teachers in techniques that will help them to help their students be successful. Thus classroom management and instruction take center stage.

The focus is on training and the major role of the trainers is to immerse new teachers in a district's culture and to unite them with everyone in the district to form a cohesive, supportive instructional team. New teachers quickly become a part of the district "family."

A major feature of the induction process is the use of demonstration classrooms in appropriate grade levels or subject areas. A master teacher, many times one of the mentor teachers, simulates the way a

classroom should be arranged and managed for the first day of school. The new teachers invariably sit in awe as they learn firsthand, from the experts, how to start school successfully.

At the end of the induction week, there is usually an awards ceremony and a civic function where all the new teachers receive certificates along with welcome packages from community supporters. Because the induction process stresses lifelong learning, the best new teacher induction programs continue for several years.

The Port Huron Program—Typical Yet Elegantly Effective

The **New Teacher Induction Program** in Port Huron, Michigan, has been in existence for 10 years. It is a basic yet elegantly effective program because it does its job uncommonly well, which is what all new teachers want. **New teachers do not want fads; they want solutions.** Training new teachers is not brain surgery. It's actually quite "doable." Just do it!

The director of the Port Huron program during all of these years has been Cathy Lozen, and she says,

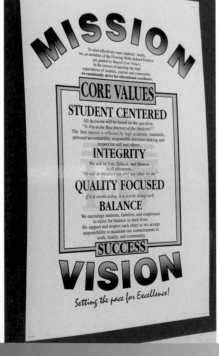

One-shot staff development meetings do not work. We wanted a sustained program, one where we could keep new teachers close to us for a year, nurture them, and take them step-by-step through the year—and beyond. Then they'd have a really solid foundation about the district, about teaching, and about our expectations. We're kind of a "no-excuses" district; the job of the teacher is to help all students succeed.

The culture of a school district is transmitted during the induction process.

The Need for Demonstration Classrooms

In demonstration classrooms, new teachers see firsthand what organization is needed for an effective school year.

Many new teachers receive little more than a quick orientation on school policies and procedures before they begin teaching. And there is often no time in the day—or week, for that matter—allotted for sitting down with colleagues to discuss pedagogical methods, daily dilemmas such as time and classroom management, and coping strategies. Worse yet, new teachers never see another classroom.

"I never sat in anyone else's classroom even once," laments first-year teacher Gail A. Saborio of Wakefield, Rhode Island. "Mine is the only teaching style I know. I felt that sometimes I was reinventing the wheel."[3]

Their actions back their philosophy. To start, they have a four-day orientation with the following components:

Day 1

- New teachers enjoy a welcome breakfast with balloons, flowers, and gifts. This is mostly a day to get acquainted with key staff members.
- A resource notebook is provided for each teacher.
- The district hosts a bus tour for the new teachers with a stop at one of the middle schools and tours of three demonstration classrooms.

Day 2

- The teachers receive *The First Days of School*[4] along with instruction on classroom management and the importance of classroom procedures, rules, and routines.

Day 3

- Trainers continue the instruction and then lead a "hot topics" discussion of some of the issues that teachers might encounter in the local schools.

Day 4

- New teachers visit demonstration classrooms. Selected teachers at appropriate grade levels and in appropriate subject areas share their reasoning for certain classroom arrangements.

The four-day training concludes with a discussion of professionalism, professional attire, making a good impression, and the importance of calling parents with positive news. Each teacher is awarded a certificate, a mug, and a "teacher start-up kit" in a tote bag filled with bulletin board borders, letters, a chalk holder, notepads with an apple design, and posters on which classroom procedures can be written. Cathy Lozen

reports, "The seminar ends with an emotional 'pep talk,' which really makes you proud of who you are and what career you've chosen."

Port Huron's training and nurturing do not stop after the initial pre–school year four-day training. "Support teachers" are provided and "special-topic seminars" are held monthly during the school year.

A favorable aspect of the Port Huron program is that it was developed in conjunction with the Port Huron Education Association, the area teachers' union. The involvement of the education association with the administration is beneficial for students, colleagues, and administrators. "We model teamwork as a way of achieving mutually desired goals," says Lozen.

At the end of one of the four-day, pre–school year workshops, Lozen returned to her office to find flowers from all the participants and a card thanking those responsible for the workshop. The card read,

"We now feel like welcomed members of the Port Huron family."

Lozen says, "We had become a cohesive and caring group in four days. We all bonded and our district is truly better for it. What a feeling!"

In contrast to the many new teachers who feel helpless and alone, there are no novice teachers working in isolation or unsupported in Port Huron. (See the example of Helga under "She Left as Abruptly as She Came," page 13.) Through its investment in an induction program, Port Huron has reaped unforeseen benefits that have exceeded the expectations of all involved. The district was able to change its culture in about five years. For information contact

Cathy Lozen
Port Huron Area Schools
1925 Lapeer Avenue
Port Huron, MI 48060

Induction and Culture

Induction brings order and vision to a very valuable process. Mentoring does not.

- Mentoring benefits the individual.
- Induction benefits the group by bringing people together.

An induction program acculturates each new teacher who joins the district "family" so that the culture of the district is continuously nourished. Teachers stay with such a school district because they are part of a common culture where everyone is working toward the same goals.

You MUST Have a Culture

We need to understand that we all have a common agenda. That agenda focuses on a system-wide plan to guarantee that every child will have the optimum opportunity to learn and to be successful. So the school board, the central administrators, the teacher educators, the students who are preparing to be teachers, and classroom teachers must work together to develop programs and strategies that improve the quality of teaching.[5]

Their Culture—It's Huge

Southwest Airlines is the only airline that has consistently made money. How does Southwest succeed when others fail? They have a huge competitive advantage. It is the company's culture, an esprit de corps, that is central to its success. Competitors can buy all of the same physical things. But the things they cannot buy are dedication, devotion, and loyalty, which promote the feeling of participating in a worthwhile cause or crusade.

Once hired, employees go through rigorous people-skills courses at the University for People, Southwest's training center in Dallas. To protect Southwest's tradition out in the field, the company has set up "culture committees" at each of its airports. These committees are responsible for ensuring that each site carries on the spirit of Southwest. This is what Southwest is about, their culture—it's huge!

Results of an Effective Induction Program

> **Mentors Don't Align—Induction Aligns**
>
> *Unaligned teams produce very little; whereas "alignment" is the necessary condition for effective teaming. Team learning is the process of aligning the capacity of a team to create the results its members truly desire.*[6]

The ultimate purpose of an effective induction program is student achievement. On student achievement we can look at two books written by Mike Schmoker. The first book, *Results: The Key to Continuous School Improvement*, reports that **three characteristics exemplify continuous school improvement:**

- **Ensuring meaningful teamwork**
- **Setting clear, measurable goals**
- **Regularly collecting and analyzing performance data**[7]

In his second book, *The RESULTS Fieldbook: Practical Strategies from Dramatically Improved Schools*, he shares the "eminently replicable and adaptable" core practices of five school districts that have produced short- and long-term, measurable achievement results.[8]

"A rapidly growing number of schools have made a momentous discovery: When teachers regularly and COLLABORATIVELY review assessment data for the purpose of improving practices to reach measurable achievement goals, something magical happens," says Schmoker. And that magic is student achievement.

How? By having people working collaboratively as a team.

Schmoker further says, "Cultivating and capturing teacher expertise is one of the most grossly underused assets in education." Accordingly, he dedicates his book "to the day when we regard TEACHERS and their <u>organized</u> expertise as the center of school improvement."

The staffs of the five school districts he profiles have three common characteristics:

1. They are goal-oriented.
2. They function in data-driven collaboration.
3. They conduct ongoing assessment.

For this to happen, mentoring ALONE will not produce the desired results. Mentoring is concerned with supporting an individual teacher. **Induction is a group process, one that organizes the expertise of educators.** When you have a collaborative culture, people will climb mountains, move mountains, and do whatever it takes—for the sake of the students.

Mentoring is caring for an individual, whereas induction is caring for the group. Teaming mentoring with the induction process will yield student achievement.

When Teachers Work as Teams

The Consortium on Chicago School Research found that in schools where teachers worked as teams, students were taught math above their grade level. In schools where teachers worked alone, instruction lagged behind. In these schools eighth-grade math teachers typically taught math at a fifth-grade level.[9]

Three Highly Effective Induction Programs

In this section we will take a detailed look at several school districts that provide exemplary induction programs for new teachers in rural, suburban, and urban settings. Though each program is tailored to meet the unique needs of its population, all possess the basic components and structure common to successful induction programs.

Framework for Inducting, Retaining, and Supporting Teachers (FIRST)
Lafourche Parish Public Schools

Program Goals

The Lafourche Parish Public Schools with its central office in Thibodaux, Louisiana, has instituted the **Framework for Inducting, Retaining, and Supporting Teachers (FIRST)** program. The primary purpose of the program is to **improve student achievement**. To accomplish this, the FIRST program has the three main goals:

- Reducing the intensity of the transition into teaching
- Improving teacher effectiveness
- Increasing the retention rate of highly qualified teachers in the school district

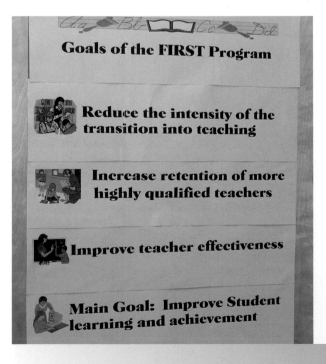

Inception of the FIRST Program

When the program was originally being developed, the Lafourche Parish schools researched some of the most successful induction programs and used these programs as models. In doing so, they looked first to what has been called the "mother of all induction programs," that of the Flowing Wells School District in Tucson, Arizona. (See further on in this chapter on page 86.)

A Cooperative Effort

Lafourche attributes much of the success of its FIRST program to the combined efforts of the following people: teachers, students, and administrators in all of its 27 schools, central office administrators, curriculum coordinators, site-based instructional facilitators, parents, school board members, community members, and the faculty members of the education department at Nicholls State University, who work closely and collaboratively with the school system to ensure top-quality preservice teacher preparation.

The program goals are posted for all new teachers to see during their training.

Program Description

Lafourche typically hires between 40 and 60 first-time teachers in August to fill positions in its 27 schools. The highly acclaimed success of its induction program has become one of the district's main attractions for new teachers. The program consists of three years of ongoing training and support. It commences with a highly structured four-day training session for all new teachers in early August, before school begins. New teachers receive stipends to attend. Even though participation is voluntary, 99 percent of new teachers participate eagerly.

On the first day, new teachers are greeted and welcomed by the superintendent, the assistant superintendent, supervisors, principals, coordinators, school board members, and experienced teachers. Welcome banners adorn the training arena, and refreshments are served. Each participant's picture is taken and placed on a map of the district next to the school where that participant will be teaching. The new teachers are seated in cooperative groups and they immediately begin their first "bellwork" assignment, which allows everyone to get to know one another.

The superintendent officially welcomes everyone, sharing the district's philosophy, goals, and culture. The three curriculum coordinators are the main presenters throughout the four days. Other presenters include a Title 1 coordinator, a special education coordinator, a principal, experienced teachers, and a second-year teacher.

Elmo Broussard, superintendent, welcomes the new teachers to the school system.

Chronicle of a New Teacher

I am a new teacher in Thibodaux, Louisiana. . . . Upon signing my contract, I am invited to participate in the FIRST program, a three-year journey toward effective teaching. I attend a four-day training in early August. On

Day 1 we are welcomed by administrators, school board members, coordinators, principals, and experienced teachers. There are refreshments, handshakes, welcome banners, cameras flashing, and an overall atmosphere of people who are happy to have us as members of their organization. We immediately get started with "bellwork," an assignment that we will receive each morning as we arrive. The atmosphere is that of a "model classroom," where we are the students and the induction team members are our teachers. They model exactly what we need to do during our first days and weeks of school.

The superintendent and the induction team introduce themselves. Everyone is smiling, everyone is expressing confidence in our future success as teachers, everyone shares a common philosophy, and I begin to understand what is meant by a "shared culture" of beliefs that must guide any successful

school district. We are assured that the next four days will help alleviate our fears, answer many of our questions, and provide the basic tools we need in order to become effective classroom teachers. I like this place already!

The very first things we learn are the classroom procedures—procedures for securing attention, working in groups, taking breaks, passing out materials, and so on. These procedures are modeled and practiced. They

remain consistent throughout the four days and help our "classroom" run as smoothly as a well-oiled machine. I learn that establishing procedures from day one is crucial to good classroom management and I receive explicit instructions on how to establish routines, procedures, and rules for my classroom.

The four days are highly structured; the pace is steady; the environment is very positive and work-oriented. We are actively involved in all lessons. Though classroom management remains the focus, we also learn about district policies and procedures, positive discipline, lesson planning, instructional strategies, students with special needs, and more. On Day 3 a second-year teacher talks to us about first-year experiences and the value of induction. It helps to hear from someone who was in our shoes just one year ago. On Day 4 soft music echoes in the distance as we all stand together listening to a poem titled "I Am a Teacher."[10] There are very few dry eyes in the room as we receive certificates of achievement along with hugs and well-wishes from our "teachers." Next, we are treated to a luncheon, where we meet mentor teachers, principals, school board members, and more of the administrative staff. Following lunch, we visit demonstration classrooms, where the district's most successful veteran teachers show us how they have prepared for the first day of school.

I head for home, much more confident than I was just four short days ago. With so many people helping to ease my transition into teaching, I am confident that I will become a well-trained, highly effective, and successful classroom teacher. And the children I teach will be the ultimate winners.

Each participant receives a copy of *The First Days of School*[11] along with a new teacher binder that includes the following:

- A letter of welcome from the superintendent
- The district's philosophy and mission statements
- Staff and faculty rosters for each school
- A place for posting daily schedules and duty schedules
- A guide for developing a classroom management plan
- A place for posting classroom or schoolwide discipline plans
- Checklists of things that must be in place before school begins
- Sheets for recording individual student data
- Interest inventories for students
- Tips on parent communication and teacher-parent relations
- Tips on classroom management
- A "success journal" for teachers' daily classroom experiences

The atmosphere is comfortable, pleasant, and work-oriented. The setting replicates a model classroom. The curriculum coordinators are the "teachers" and the new teachers become the "students." Participants remain actively involved in all lessons. Procedures and routines are immediately established, modeled, and practiced in order to set the stage for a well-managed classroom.

Day 1 focuses on classroom management and local policies and procedures.

Days 2 and 3 address the first days of school, discipline, instructional strategies, assessment techniques, working with parents, and meeting individual learner needs. Though a variety of topics are addressed during the four days, the primary focus remains on **classroom management**.

On **Day 3** a second-year teacher talks to the new teachers about the value of the induction process.

This teacher entertains questions from the inductees and shares personal first-year experiences.

On **Day 4,** after a general review, there is an awards ceremony, where new teachers receive certificates of achievement for completion of the initial phase of the induction process. A luncheon follows, where new teachers meet mentor teachers, principals, school board members, and administrative staff members. On the afternoon of Day 4, the new teachers visit demonstration classrooms specific to their grade levels and receive advice and instruction from some of the district's most successful veteran teachers.

In January the school district hires between 30 and 40 more first-time teachers. For those new teachers hired in January, a "streamlined" two-day initial induction session is conducted.

Mentor Teachers

At each school site new teachers are paired with mentor teachers, who offer guidance and assistance during the first two years of teaching. Mentor teachers are paid for their services. The mentoring component is state-funded. The new teacher's particular needs, grade level, and assignment, as well as the location of the new teacher's classroom, are all considered in matching mentors with new teachers. These mentor teachers, selected for their excellence in teaching, receive three days of intensive training conducted by the curriculum coordinators and they continue to receive ongoing training throughout their tenure. They remain classroom teachers but receive release time to work with the new teachers.

The mentor teachers work collaboratively with the district curriculum coordinators and site-based instructional facilitators in conducting informal observations of the newly-hired teachers. These observations are not used for evaluation; the intent is to provide new teachers with specific, immediate, nonthreatening feedback on their teaching performance. Individual improvement plans are developed in order to enhance each new teacher's present skills.

Instructional Facilitators

Lafourche has instructional facilitators in each of their K–8 schools. They hand-select their most effective teachers to spend their days in classrooms conducting demonstration lessons, observing and providing feedback, assisting teachers in setting up classroom management plans, and lending their ears, shoulders, and expertise to new teachers. It's so much more effective than their mentoring component—not because the mentors aren't doing excellent jobs, but because they have their own classrooms and can't always provide immediate assistance and feedback. These facilitators are in the classrooms daily, reinforcing all of the things taught to the new teachers during induction.

The instructional facilitators receive training from the school system. Lafourche also conducts monthly support group meetings for them and the facilitators in turn, go back and host monthly meetings for the new teachers and provide ongoing training for their entire staffs.

Additional Resources

Another component of the induction process involves monthly district-level new teacher support group meetings. During these meetings new teachers share their experiences, voice concerns, and cooperatively seek solutions to problems. The curriculum coordinators facilitate these meetings.

New teachers are also required to participate in the Louisiana Teacher Assistance and Assessment Program, with formal observations determining certification decisions. All teachers participating in this program receive two additional days of training in September on the Louisiana Components of Effective Teaching. The FIRST program has recently been adopted as a statewide induction model, as induction has become an integral component of the state's assistance and assessment program. The new statewide program is now known as "Louisiana FIRST."

In April new teachers return for a one-day induction review. On this day new teachers address ongoing concerns, share first-year teaching experiences, and receive additional training.

During the second and third years of the induction process, the curriculum coordinators and instructional facilitators continue to work closely with the new teachers. Classroom observations are ongoing. In addition, second- and third-year teachers attend four half-day sessions to receive further training in classroom management, authentic assessment, the Louisiana Components of Effective Teaching, high-stakes testing, instructional strategies, positive discipline techniques, and instructional decision making. During one segment of each session, participants pose questions, voice concerns, seek solutions to common classroom problems, and share personal classroom experiences. Again, participants are paid stipends to attend. Second- and third-year teachers also have the option of participating in monthly support group meetings.

Another means of support for the new teachers is the Prescriptive Inservice Program. The program consists of successful veteran teachers providing monthly in-service training for participants and conducting ongoing, informal prescriptive observations with feedback. Participation is voluntary and any teacher requiring additional support may participate.

Role of the Principal

At each school site the role of the principal in the induction process is an important one. To ensure consistency between what is promoted during the initial induction training and what will be promoted in the schools, principals receive awareness training before the actual induction process begins. At each school the principal provides orientation, support, encouragement, and guidance for the new teachers, along with opportunities for ongoing assistance and staff development.

During the initial induction training in early August, one of the principals provides some of the actual training. New teachers hear—from a principal's viewpoint—what will be expected of them regarding professional attire, attitude, responsibilities, and professionalism in general.

Program Results

Data collected since 1993 indicate a dramatic decrease in the rate of new teacher attrition in the Lafourche Parish school system. Just a few short years ago, the Lafourche Parish school system had a vision. The goal: to implement an induction program that would ease the way for new teachers by providing ongoing training and support. The results: **overwhelming enthusiasm** on the part of new teachers, mentors, administrators, school board members, and the community, a **drastic decrease** in new teacher attrition rates, and a **culture of more confident, competent, qualified new teachers** influencing the lives of thousands of students.

And all within a budget of $50,000 a year. Compare this investment with "The Costs of Low Retention" in Chapter 1, page 6. This a small price to pay for an endeavor on which no dollar amount could possibly be placed: the children, our future.

For information on the Lafourche Parish Public Schools' FIRST program, contact

Annette Breaux,
Curriculum Coordinator
Lafourche Parish Public Schools
110 Bowie Road
Thibodaux, LA 70301

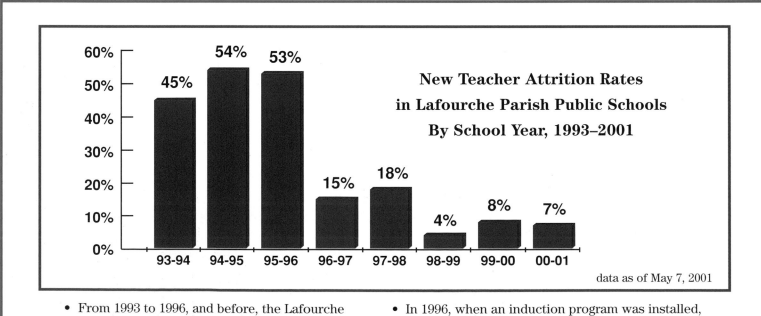

New Teacher Attrition Rates in Lafourche Parish Public Schools By School Year, 1993–2001

data as of May 7, 2001

- From 1993 to 1996, and before, the Lafourche Parish school system typically experienced a 51 percent rate of attrition.
- In 1996, when an induction program was installed, the attrition rate dropped to 15 percent.
- Today it hovers around 7 percent.

How Successful Is Lafourche's FIRST Program?

FIRST is so successful that Louisiana has adopted it as a statewide model for all school systems.

One can't argue with their success and the Lafourche schools have made some tremendous strides. Since implementing an induction program, their attrition rate has dropped an astounding 80 percent!

The Louisiana FIRST program is designed to equip school system teams with knowledge, skills, and dispositions to significantly improve the assistance opportunities available to new teachers. Information on Louisiana FIRST is available at

www.doe.state.la.us/DOE/OQE/certification/
LaFirst_r1.pdf

Teacher Induction Program for Success (TIPS)
Flowing Wells School District

Located in Tucson, Arizona, Flowing Wells is a small suburban school district that achieves big results. Though not a wealthy community (over 50 percent of the students are eligible for free or reduced-rate lunches), Flowing Wells gives education top priority. Achievement scores are well above the national average, and seven of the district's eight schools have received national academic recognition awards. **The Flowing Wells Teacher Induction Program for Success** was one of the first of its kind in the United States and, since its inception in 1985, has continued to receive national recognition as an exemplary staff development program.

TIPS emphasizes five critical attributes that are the cornerstones of the district's vision:

1. Effective instructional practices
2. Effective classroom management procedures and routines
3. A sensitivity to and understanding of the Flowing Wells community
4. Teaching as a reflection of lifelong learning and ongoing professional growth
5. Unity and teamwork among administration, teachers, support staff, and community members[12]

Program Goals

TIPS is designed to transmit the district and community culture. The major goals of this program are to build a sense of culture and to articulate the district's mission and philosophy. It involves a structured training program for all teachers new to the district. This training provides not merely an orientation to the district's organizational pattern, but also a framework of the district's vision for student learning and success.

Program Description

In Flowing Wells it is difficult to determine where one aspect of professional development ends and another begins. The transition is that smooth. Professional development is ongoing and careerlong, with training that is very specific to the stages of teacher growth. Therefore, induction has no clear-cut timelines. New teachers are inducted during their initial years in teaching and the training and support simply meld into ongoing careerlong professional development. This is the way induction should be and it is one of the main reasons that Flowing Wells is one of the most effective school districts in the United States.

TIPS begins with four days of intensive training in early August before the school year begins. Participation is mandatory for first-time teachers, and extra days are added to their contracts so that they can participate in induction. On the morning of **Day 1**, new teachers are greeted by the induction team, the superintendent, and members of the supervisory staff. The feelings of teamwork and collegial support are immediately evident as the new "team members" are welcomed aboard. Refreshments are served, pictures are taken, new teachers are organized into cooperative groups, and the instruction begins. The setting is that of a model classroom, with the induction team representing the teachers and the new teachers representing the students.

The focus for the next four days is on classroom management and instructional strategies. No time is wasted as new teachers delve into instructional practice and learn on **Day 1** how to introduce a lesson, how to teach objectives, and how to engage their students in active participation. Procedures and routines for the induction classroom are established, modeled, and practiced from the very beginning. Materials provided to new teachers include the following:

- A copy of *The First Days of School*[13]
- A letter of welcome from the superintendent
- A copy of the district's mission and goals
- Information on each of the schools in Flowing Wells
- Information on "what induction looks like" throughout the first year of teaching and beyond
- Information on the Flowing Wells ongoing career development program
- Classroom management tips
- A glossary of education terms
- Sample first-day checklists

Day 2 continues with instructional practices. New teachers, in their cooperative groups, actually write instructional objectives and plan sample lessons.

On Day 3 new teachers learn about insurance, health care, the culture of the Flowing Wells School District, and the unique needs of the population. They view a video titled *The Flowing Wells Community in Action*. Then, new teachers board a bus with the superintendent for a guided tour of the Flowing Wells community. A luncheon is sponsored by the Flowing Wells Education Association. That afternoon new teachers report to their respective schools for planning time with principals. Curriculum, texts, and school procedures are discussed.

On Day 4 the instruction shifts to classroom

Teachers work together to hone their skills.

management. New teachers learn the importance of structured bellwork, routines, procedures, and more, including a segment on the importance of professional attire. They also learn to formulate effective discipline plans with clearly stated rules and consequences. For this segment of the training, new teachers view parts of *The Effective Teacher*[14] video series.

Next, the new teachers visit the classrooms of some of the district's master teachers in elementary, junior high, and high schools. These master teachers have their rooms ready for the first day of school and new teachers tour the classrooms and receive instruction from the veterans on "how it's done." Finally, on the afternoon of **Day 4**, the new teachers report to their own classrooms to begin first-day preparations.

Of course, this is not the end of induction. Three days of further training in instructional strategies and classroom management are scheduled throughout the school year. The final seminar in March includes an awards ceremony, where the superintendent presents new teachers with framed certificates.

Throughout the year the staff development coordinator serves as a "mentor" to all new teachers, observing each new teacher five times. The purpose of these observations is to help the new teachers focus on strengths, weaknesses, and professional development. Also, each school site has a volunteer site coordinator who meets bimonthly with new teachers to offer support.

During a teacher's second year with the Flowing Wells School District, instructional coordinators mentor the new teachers. These coordinators are master teachers who receive stipends and release time in order to work with the teachers they are mentoring. Instructional strategies, professional skills, classroom management techniques, assessment techniques, and policies and procedures receive continued emphasis.

In the third and fourth years, teachers receive advanced training in instructional strategies, cooperative learning, higher-level thinking, and more. Instructional coordinators continue to observe and support these teachers.

Again, the staff development program in Flowing Wells is careerlong. There are five levels of career development progressing from "novice" (first-year teachers), to "advanced beginner" (second-year teachers), to "competent" (third- through fifth-year teachers), to "proficient," to "expert." (A chart showing the five-year program is in the References section, page 173.) At each level there is structured training, along with formative and summative observations and evaluations. In Flowing Wells there's something for everyone at all levels of teaching and professional growth.

Induction Training Seminar

Each year, Flowing Wells holds a two-day national induction training seminar for educators interested in learning how to implement an induction program. Topics and activities include, among other things, the following:

- A simulation of the first day of induction
- Sessions with the superintendent, supervisors, and principals
- School visits
- Sessions with mentor teachers
- Sessions with first-year teachers
- Training with the staff development coordinator
- A training manual

Program Results

The success of TIPS sends a clear message to any school district interested in training, supporting, and retaining highly qualified teachers: **Induction is a MUST!**

The following program outcomes of TIPS are typical of any school district implementing structured induction:

- Reduced anxiety for first-year teachers
- A higher-quality teaching force
- A reduced attrition rate for new teachers
- Increased student achievement
- A common culture throughout the district
- A common mission and set of goals
- A common professional dialogue among teachers, support staff, and the community
- A willingness to participate in careerlong staff development

For information on TIPS contact

Susie Heintz, Staff Development Coordinator
Flowing Wells School District
1556 West Prince Road
Tucson, AZ 85705

Induction eases the anxiety felt by first year teachers.

Numbers and Definitions

Richard Ingersoll, leading authority on teacher turnover, reports that teacher turnover is due to two factors:

Attrition—teachers who leave the occupation of teaching altogether
Migration—teachers who move to teaching jobs in other schools

Teacher migration does not change the overall supply of teachers as retirement and career changes do. Migration does not contribute to teacher shortages.

The most recent attrition data based on surveys conducted by the National Center for Education Statistics shows 11 percent of teachers leave in their first year of teaching. This data is from 1996. At press time, the 1999-2000 data had not been released.

After 1 year	11% attrition
After 2 years	21% attrition
After 3 years	29% attrition
After 4 years	33% attrition
After 5 years	39% attrition[15]

New teachers learn from master teachers how to organize and manage a classroom for success.

Professional Educator Induction Program
Prince George's County Public Schools

If you think induction programs are only feasible for smaller rural and suburban school districts, think again. The Prince George's County public school system, bordering Washington, DC, is the largest K–12 school district in the state of Maryland and the nineteenth largest school district in the United States. It includes 183 schools with 137,000 students. Between 1,000 and 1,500 new teachers are hired annually, and **all are inducted**.

Both the student and teaching populations are extremely diverse and highly mobile and, historically, attrition rates have been high. Therefore, in 1998, as part of its efforts to better train, support, and retain new teachers in order to increase student achievement, Prince George's County Public Schools implemented the **Professional Educator Induction Program**. Prior to this, teachers new to the school district received only basic orientation.

Program Goals

The primary mission of the Professional Educator Induction Program is to facilitate teachers' professional development during their two-year induction period. As a result of this process, new teachers can better promote student achievement in a culturally diverse environment by successfully implementing the goals, objectives, policies, procedures, and research-based best practices required by the school system. The assistance this program provides helps ensure the development of a community of learners committed to remaining in the district as professional educators.

These are the goals of the program:

- To provide new teachers with the opportunity to become familiar with the district's employees, resources, and support services

- To provide new teachers with an introduction to the curriculum and instructional program for which they are responsible
- To assist new teachers with lesson planning
- To assist new teachers in acquiring classroom organization and management skills
- To provide new teachers with an opportunity to build a network and support system

Program Description

There is evident support of the induction process from the superintendent, directors, supervisors, principals, mentors, classroom teachers, parents, students, and community leaders. All participate in welcoming the more than 1,000 new teachers as they enter the doors of Eleanor Roosevelt High School early on a Monday morning in August to begin **four days of highly structured training.**

On Day 1, upon entering the training site, new teachers sign in and receive a "welcome bag" including a wealth of information about Prince George's County Public Schools, a copy of *The First Days of School*,[16] various information on first-year teaching and classroom management, several welcome gifts, a resource binder, and more. The resource binder includes these items, among others:

- Mission and goals of the school district
- Highlights of key programs and initiatives
- Information on scope and sequence frameworks, curriculum materials, and support resources
- Summaries of policies and procedures
- Information on professional development opportunities
- Information on certification requirements
- Tips on classroom management and instructional delivery
- Tips on successful communication with parents

- *Standards for Excellence in Teaching* document
- Information on teacher observations and evaluations
- A copy of the school system's yearly calendar

After signing in and gathering materials, participants are treated to breakfast in the school's cafeteria. In the main hallway a variety of booths are set up to provide general information, along with information on special programs, the local credit union, the local teachers' union, mentoring, and other issues that concern beginning teachers. Participants have access to these booths during morning registration, break times, and lunchtime.

Following registration and breakfast, new teachers enter the main auditorium, where they are greeted with music by the high school's string quartet. The director of staff development welcomes everyone, and an elementary student officially begins the general session by singing "The Wind Beneath My Wings," dedicated to all the new teachers in Prince George's County. New teachers then hear from one of the district's principals, who speaks about providing a positive environment for the urban learner. The principal's foremost message is that every child is a vessel of untapped potential and that the most important job of the teacher is to find ways to nourish the seeds of strengths and talents that lie within each student.

During the opening general session, the staff development team members are introduced and the superintendent welcomes the new teachers to the district.

After receiving a general overview of the next four days, the new teachers are assigned to demonstration classrooms specific to their grade levels, content areas, or specialty areas. These classrooms are used as models of what the classroom should look like prior to students' arrival on the first day of school. Here the new teachers spend the next two and a half days with instructional supervisors and some of the district's most successful veteran teachers, receiving instruction on such topics as classroom management, instructional strategies, curriculum programs, lesson planning, and first-day procedures. Lunch is provided daily.

On **Day 2** there is another brief general session. After a musical performance by the high school's choir, a local television instructional specialist shares his film following the progress of five new teachers through their first year of teaching. The video piece titled *The First Year: A Teacher's Odyssey* captures the essence of what a new teacher typically experiences—the anticipation, the frustration, the workload, the questions, the successes, the occasional downfalls, and the daily reminders that theirs is the greatest job of all. Following the general session, the instructional program continues in the demonstration classrooms. This program continues through the afternoon of **Day 3**.

On the evenings of Days 2 and 3, new teachers have the option of participating in computer classes or visiting the "Make-N-Take Center," where participants make bulletin boards and visuals for their classrooms. The department of staff development supplies this center with ideas and materials for duplication, creation, and classroom use. It is open to teachers throughout the year.

On the afternoon of Day 3, there is a general closing session, where new teachers evaluate the program, hear further words of encouragement, and view a slide show capturing the events of the week.

On Day 4 all new teachers meet by "clusters"— groups of high schools and their elementary and middle feeder schools. Here they receive further training from mentor teachers and instructional specialists before going on to their individual schools for a basic orientation.

In October new teachers participate in a fifth-day follow-up session, where they receive further support and training. For teachers hired after August, induction training is offered on several Saturdays throughout the school year.

The initial four-day induction session marks the beginning of a two-year commitment from the school district to provide ongoing training and support to all of its newly hired teachers.

Support Services for the New Professional

In Prince George's County there are many services to assist the new professional:

- A comprehensive induction program including a series of intensive training workshops
- A formal mentor teacher program at 30 schools
- A voluntary teacher-coaching program at 18 schools
- A "buddy system" set up at individual schools, with assistance provided by one or more of the following: a fellow practitioner, the grade-level chairperson, the department chairperson, a teacher coordinator, a team leader, or the school administrator
- Networking classes as part of the certification process, taught by grade-level and content-area master teachers and dealing with specific concerns, instructional tasks, and other content-appropriate issues
- The professional library
- The instructional resource center
- The Make-N-Take Center
- Certification courses through area universities
- State-Approved Workshops–Modulated Experiences (SAW-ME) courses
- On-line professional development
- "At the Center" professional development programs

Program Results

The Professional Educator Induction Program has met with eager support and enthusiasm from administrators, mentor teachers, classroom teachers, students, parents, the community, and, of course, induction participants. The success of the induction process is evidenced by a higher retention rate of competent and confident new teachers committed to making a difference in the lives of the students they teach.

For more information about the Professional Educator Induction Program, contact

Antoinette Kellaher
Supervisor of New Teacher Programs
Prince George's County Public Schools
William Irwin Buck Staff
    Development Center
3901 Woodhaven Lane
Bowie, MD 20715

> **Turn teaching from a job into a profession you love, and you will never have to work a day in your life.**

It is through an induction program that new teachers begin with an attitude of lifelong learning, of working collegially, and of being part of a family that cares for each other's success. With this new culture firmly established it is realistic to believe that people in this profession will love it so much that they believe they are not coming to work each day!

Comparison of Induction Programs

	Lafourche Parish Public Schools (Louisiana)	Flowing Wells School District (Arizona)	Prince George's County Public Schools (Maryland)
Title of program	Framework for Inducting, Retaining, and Supporting Teachers (FIRST)	Teacher Induction Program for Success (TIPS)	Professional Educator Induction Program (PEIP)
Type of district	Rural	Suburban	Urban
Number of schools	27	8	188
Number of students	16,000	6,500	137,000
Age of program	7 years	18 years	5 years[A]
Approximate number of first-time teachers hired annually	80	18	1,200
Approximate number of newly hired teachers with experience	35	14	600
Yearly budget	$50,000	$200,000 total staff development budget $120,000 for induction (Varies year-to-year depending on number of new teachers.)	$750,000 (Varies year to year, may fluctuate based on budget.)
Funding sources	District	District	District
Duration of initial induction	4 days in August	4 days in August for all, 1 additional day for High School teachers	6 days in August
Total in-service days during first year	7	4 full days after initial induction	7

[A]Current mandatory program in existence for 2 years was revised 4 years ago from a program first developed in 1992.

	Louisiana (continued)	**Arizona** (continued)	**Maryland** (continued)
Participants	First-time teachers (Experienced new teachers are inducted separately.)	Everyone new to the school district	Everyone new to the school district
Length of support for new teachers	3 years	4+ years	2 years
Primary focus	Classroom management and instructional strategies	Classroom management and instructional strategies	Classroom management and instructional strategies
Use of demonstration classrooms	Yes	Yes	Yes
Induction team	Coordinators, administrators, classroom teachers	Coordinators, administrators, classroom teachers	Coordinators, administrators, classroom teachers
Type of payment for induction participation	Stipends	Extra days added to contract for all new teachers to the district.	Stipends
Voluntary or mandatory participation in induction	Voluntary (99 percent attendance)	Mandatory (100 percent attendance)	Mandatory
Mentoring component	Yes (state-funded)	Yes (district-funded + grant)	Yes (state and local-funding)
Statewide assistance and assessment program	Yes	No	Yes
Most recent attrition rate of certified new teachers (those leaving the school district)	7 percent	11 percent[B]	7.2 percent

[B]Of the four teachers who left out of 34 (11 percent), two relocated to pursue additional education and two relocated for marital reasons. No one left because of dissatisfaction with teaching. Thus, the attrition rate could be considered zero.

Exemplary Induction Programs

Summary and Implementation

Planting the Seeds
Information We've Shared

- Successful induction programs stress effective classroom management, effective instructional practices, acculturation to the school community, lifelong learning, and teamwork.
- The primary goals of induction are: 1) reduce the intensity of the transition into teaching, 2) increase retention of highly qualified teachers, 3) improve teacher effectiveness, and most importantly, 4) improve student achievement.
- Lafourche's FIRST program has been adopted as a statewide model.
- Flowing Wells offers an annual training seminar on how to implement a successful induction program.
- Prince George's County hires 1200 new teachers a year and all are inducted.

Nurturing Growth
What You Can Do to Make a Difference

- Recognize that no matter the size of your district, it is easy to implement a successful induction program.
- Use the information from the programs featured in this chapter to create your own induction program.
- Don't put induction off one more minute. Take a step. Begin it.

Reaping the Harvest
Benefits to Your School System

- Induction doesn't cost money. It saves money.
- Induction training helps ensure reduced anxiety for new teachers, increased retention of a higher-quality teaching force, a shared culture throughout the district, and improved student achievement.

chapter six

More Induction Programs

It's a funny thing about life; if you refuse to accept anything but the best, you very often get it.

— Somerset Maugham

Blossoming.

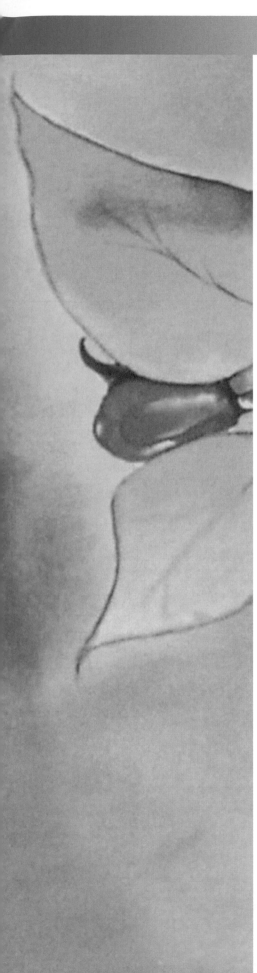

Sources and Notes for Chapter 6

[1] Public School Forum of North Carolina. (1996). *A Profession in Jeopardy: Why Teachers Leave and What We Can Do About It.* Raleigh, NC. Available: www.ncforum.org.

[2] Wong, Harry K. (1996). *The Effective Teacher.* Mountain View, CA: Harry K. Wong Publications. Videotape series.

[3] Albert, Linda. (1996). *Cooperative Discipline.* Circle Pines, MN: American Guidance Service.

[4] Marcuzzo, Trish. (1998). "That Noble Title Teacher." Mountain View, CA: Harry K. Wong Publications.

[5] Wong, Harry K. (1996). "Teacher Induction, Mentoring, and Renewal." *The LPD Video Journal of Education.* Linton Professional Development Corporation.

[6] Killion, Joellen. (2002). *Assessing Impact: Evaluating Professional Development.* Oxford, OH: National Staff Development Council.

[7] Hassel, Emily. (2002). *Professional Development: Learning from the Best.* Naperville, IL: North Central Regional Educational Laboratory.

[8] National Commission on Teaching and America's Future. (1996). *What Matters Most: Teaching for America's Future.* New York.

[9] Snyder, Jon. (1999). *New Haven Unified School District: A Teaching Quality System for Excellence and Equity.* New York: National Commission on Teaching and America's Future.

[10] Available: www.ctc.ca.gov/cstppublication/cstpreport.html.

[11] Available: www.ctc.ca.gov/cstppublication/cstpreport.html.

[12] Wong, Harry K. and Rosemary T. Wong. (2001). *The First Days of School: How to Be an Effective Teacher.* Mountain View, CA: Harry K. Wong Publications.

[13] Danielson, Charlotte. (1996). *Enhancing Professional Practice: A Framework for Teaching.* Alexandria, VA: Association for Supervision and Curriculum Development.

[14] Lindberg, Peter Jon. (August 2000). "Behind the Scenes on Singapore Airlines," *Travel + Leisure.*

[15] Jack Raines is now the county's Assistant Superintendent and can be contacted at the high school address.

[16] Mrozowski, Jennifer. (February 21, 2002). "Study Links Teacher Quality and Student Progress." *Cincinnati Enquirer.*

[17] Keiffer-Barone, Susan and Kathleen Ware. (May 2001). "Growing Great Teachers in Cincinnati," *Educational Leadership,* pp. 56-59. Additional information can be obtained from Kathleen Ware, Cincinnati Public Schools, Education Center, P.O. Box 5381, Cincinnati, OH 45201.

[18] Pierce, Milli. (May 26, 2001). "Bay Area Faces Shortage of Principals; Schools Struggling to Find Qualified, Willing Candidates." *San Jose Mercury News.*

[19] Gilman, D. and R. Lanman-Givens. (May 2001). "Where Have All the Principals Gone?" *Educational Leadership,* p. 23.

[20] Available: www.theschooldaily.com. (April 5, 2002).

[21] *The News & Observer* of Raleigh, NC. (February 22, 2002).

[22] Blackboard information available: www.blackboard.com.

[23] *EducationNews.org.* (July 9, 2001). "Triage for the Teacher Shortage: A Guide to Helpful Organizations." Available: www.educationnews.org.

Our induction program has proved to be one of our best investments. Every district should absolutely be doing it.

— Kathryn Robbins, Superintendent
Leyden High School District 212
Franklin Park, Illinois

Support for new teachers comes in many forms.

Next to testing, the hottest issues in education today **are the shortage of teachers and new teacher training.** Go to www.educationnews.org each day and you will see this is true. The most effective schools and districts recognize these critical issues and do something about them—they induct, more than mentor, their new teachers. Their results are **increased retention of more highly qualified, capable, competent new teachers.** Kathryn Robbins is only one of many who willingly and proudly shares her districts' induction successes.

This book has been very simple to write yet extremely difficult to finally produce. Examples of promising new induction programs appear daily. Thus we have not lacked for material in writing this book. The problem is that we constantly encounter new examples of induction programs with exciting improvements and new twists. Here are just a few examples:

- Clark County Schools of Nevada have a new teacher **welcome center** that assists teachers in securing car loans and finding housing or other needs.
- New Haven Unified Schools of California do most of their **recruiting over the Internet.**

- Blue Valley Schools of Kansas won the NEA-AFT Saturn/UAW Partnership Award for their program, which is a **cooperative effort** between the school district, the National Education Association, and the University of Kansas.
- Community Consolidated School District 15 of Illinois has a four-year induction program that prepares its teachers to apply for **national board certification.**
- When tiny Glades County, Florida, with less than 100 teachers, started a new teacher induction program, they invited the **veteran teachers to attend**, and almost all of them came.
- Jack Raines, a high school principal, started an induction program and saw his **referral rate drop** from 133 students to 2 after the first grading period.
- CalStateTEACH sends a mentor and college instructor to your school. **House calls?**
- North Carolina offers high school seniors a $26,000 **college scholarship** to become teachers.
- New Leaders for New Schools aggressively recruits and provides rigorous **hands-on training** for extremely talented people to become urban school principals.

On the other side of the coin, far too many school districts either are doing nothing for their new teachers or are just giving them a "buddy" or "mentor." Is this sufficient support? Hardly! For this reason, it was important to produce this book, with the intention of helping even more new teachers succeed with the help of an induction program.

If by chance you are a novice teacher and are reading this book, use this chapter to discover the exemplary school districts who truly want you to realize your potential and succeed. Apply for employment to these districts as they will nurture you, care for you, and train you.

The North Carolina Plan for Creating Effective Teachers

- **Teaching Fellows Program:** This program offers $26,000 four-year college scholarships to 400 graduating North Carolina high school seniors.

- **District induction:** The state provides three days of pay for all new teachers to attend an induction program before school begins. Stipends for mentors are also provided for one year.

- **Teachers' union:** The North Carolina Education Association sponsors programs for new teachers and works in concert with school district induction programs to help new teachers succeed.

- **University support:** At the University of North Carolina at Chapel Hill, professors from the university's education department provide problem-solving support to graduates during their first years on the job. This program, the Lighthouse Project, fosters on-line discussions that assist young teachers while keeping education professors up to date on the realities of today's classrooms.

- **Public School Forum:** This is a public organization that helps shepherd the Teaching Fellows Program, providing summer conferences for the fellows. The Public School Forum has produced a highly recommended publication that offers practical, proven suggestions for induction programs—*A Profession in Jeopardy: Why Teachers Leave and What We Can Do About It.*[1]

- **Teacher Academy:** Funded by the North Carolina General Assembly, continuous learning for professional development is provided on 10 campuses. The curriculum is organized by teachers, for teachers and administrators. http://www.ga.unc.edu/NCTA/

- **National board certification:** The state pays each candidate's $2,000 fee, provides up to three days of release time for candidates to prepare, and gives a 12 percent annual pay increase to those who achieve certification. As a result of this commitment, the state now leads the nation in the number of national board certified teachers. North Carolina has 2,377 national board certified teachers, about one-fourth of the nation's total.

- **The Southeast Center for Teaching Quality:** Housed at the University of North Carolina, the center engages in research and publications designed to enhance opportunities for all students to have competent, caring, and qualified teachers. They are available at www.teacherquality.org and their publication, *Recruiting Teachers for Hard-to-Staff Schools*, is highly recommended.

List of Induction Programs

We have chosen to present in this chapter a selection of programs that represent a diversity of communities, all sharing a common mission of training, supporting, and retaining new teachers, and all experiencing remarkable success. For each program listed, there is a brief description followed by contact information. We respectfully share their information with you and gratefully acknowledge these schools and school systems for allowing us to include them in this listing.

**North Carolina
Gaston County Schools
Teacher Induction Program for Success**

The district's **Teacher Induction Program for Success (TIPS)** consists of a weeklong seminar for all teachers new to the school district, with monthly follow-up sessions on Saturdays throughout the year. This program has received the Governor's Award for Excellence in Education.

Linda Rader
Gaston County Schools
236 Eighth Avenue
Cramerton, NC 28032

**Kansas
Blue Valley School District 229
Alliance for Educational Excellence**

This induction program is an alliance between the Blue Valley School District, the Blue Valley National Education Association, and the University of Kansas. The program is designed to induct new teachers into the school district and provide an option to work toward a master's degree, with all classes taught in Blue Valley facilities for the convenience of the new teachers. Training consists of sessions held five days prior to the scheduled return of all district teachers, with three additional training sessions during the first year. This is paid training and is part of each new teacher's contract. Three master teachers are assigned to observe, confer with, and support each beginning teacher. Besides a mentor—a fellow teacher in the same grade or content area—the beginning teacher receives a trained peer assistant who is part of the Blue Valley Peer Assistance Program. Peer assistants have release time to instruct and support new teachers and to assist with the assessment process. This program received the NEA-AFT Saturn/UAW Partnership Award in 2001.

Sandy Chapman
Blue Valley School District 229
15020 Metcalf Avenue
Overland Park, KS 66283

**Oklahoma
El Reno Public Schools
New Teacher Assessment Program**

As part of the El Reno **New Teacher Assessment Program (N-TAP)**, all teachers new to the school district attend an initial induction training session—the Program for the Effective Teacher (PET)—just prior to the beginning of the school year. PET consists of a full week of orientation to the school district, training in classroom management and instructional strategies, and an introduction to the district's philosophy, mission, and procedures.

N-TAP enlists the ongoing support of staff development personnel, principals, coordinators, mentor teachers, school board members, and supervisory staff in order to ensure that new teachers are highly trained and adequately supported, increasing the likelihood that these new teachers will remain in the profession.

Sue Pennington
El Reno Public Schools
P.O. Box 580
El Reno, OK 73036

Illinois
Community Consolidated School District 15
Helping Teacher Program

The **Helping Teacher** program is a mandatory four-year induction program with a strong mentoring component that helps prepare new teachers for national board certification. A full-time teacher induction facilitator-trainer coordinates the program, which satisfies and surpasses state-mandated requirements for induction and certification.

Carole Einhorn
Community Consolidated School District 15
580 North First Bank Drive
Palatine, IL 60067

Florida
Manatee County
Teacher Induction Program for Success

Starting with a four-day pre–school year training session, new teachers in Manatee County begin the **Teacher Induction Program for Success (TIPS)**—a three-year program to prepare them to be effective teachers. There are periodic support group meetings and strong support from peer groups and administrators. Study cadres are organized with peer teachers, who help the new teachers prepare

documentation of the professional competencies that beginning teachers must demonstrate in order to be certified in Florida. Participants must create portfolios that clearly demonstrate evidence of competencies in each of 15 areas. Manatee County also has the Alternative Certification for Teachers (ACT) program.

To recognize his efforts, Steve Zickafoose was awarded the 2001 National Staff Development Council's (NSDC) New Staff Developer Award.

Steve Zickafoose
Manatee County Board of Education
215 Manatee Avenue West
Bradenton, FL 34205

New York
Islip Public Schools
Induction Program

The Islip School District has a comprehensive, three-year induction program, which begins with an orientation program before the inductees' first year and continues as ongoing professional development throughout the initial, tenure school years. Teachers proceed through their three-year tenure-track program as cohorts—building relationships and support groups.

Year-1 teachers have a three-day orientation, facilitated by Linda Lippman, the director of human resources. Meetings combine basic procedural information, introductions, a bus tour through the community, team-building activities, food, first-day advice, icebreakers, organizational strategies, and meetings with central office administrators, the payroll account clerk, building principals, and the union president. This group of new teachers meets monthly with the director of human resources and focuses on *The Effective Teacher*[2] video series as a catalyst for conversation and discussion. Collegial circles meet informally in between formal monthly meetings. Additionally, workshops are given on parent-teacher conferencing strategies, open house, and more.

Year-2 teachers have a one-day orientation with an introduction to *Cooperative Discipline*,[3] which becomes the focus of monthly meetings. This philosophy deals with classroom management techniques and interventions for encouraging appropriate behaviors along with understanding that "to discipline" means "to teach." Team-building activities are conducted to promote a sense of cohesion and belonging. And yes, there's food!

Year-3 teachers have a one-day orientation facilitated by the director of human resources which focuses on reviewing the intervention strategies espoused by *Cooperative Discipline*.

Linda Lippman, standing, works with new teachers Patricia Raben, Kim Pittsley, and Rick Magale. Notice the start-of-class "Do Now" activity that's on the board for the teachers to do!

Year-3 teachers also meet monthly, but each meeting is shaped by needs assessments, with appropriate workshop presenters invited to each meeting. Past workshops have included cooperative learning strategies, multiple learning styles, study skill techniques, stress management, time management, self-esteem for educators, and more. And, of course, there's more food!

A newsletter is distributed three times throughout the school year to new staff members. *TIPS (Teacher Induction Program Stuff)* is the newsletter, which includes information about teaching strategies, cooperative learning, and district information. A new teacher is featured in each issue.

At the end of the year, after the board of education has approved tenure for eligible teachers, a celebration is held. A multimedia presentation is the focal point where newly tenured teachers are featured. The theme one year was "I Believe," based on Nancy Sifford Alana's poem from *The Effective Teacher* video series. Each teacher was asked to create an "I Believe" statement, and with it their picture was presented to the community as they received their "diploma" of "That Noble Title Teacher"[4] by Trish Marcuzzo. And yes, food was included in the celebration!

The Islip New Teacher Induction Program is growing and succeeding. They are proud of the vision of their superintendent, who originated the program, and of the response of the participants to the training. It is the district's intention that the program will continue to grow and will support the investment in their new staff, affording them the opportunity to become the teachers that, as Christa McAuliffe said, "will touch the future."

Linda Lippman
Islip Public Schools
215 Main Street
Islip, NY 11751

Michigan
Port Huron Area Schools
New Teacher Induction Program

The Port Huron **New Teacher Induction Program** is designed to acquaint newly hired teachers with the people, polices, and resources of the district as well as provide them with the procedural and instructional strategies to ensure their success in the classroom. The program includes a four-day induction training session for new teachers in early August, monthly professional development seminars held throughout the first year of district employment, and the assignment of an in-building Support Teacher to lend ongoing direct assistance at the building level.

Cathy Lozen
Port Huron Area Schools
1925 Lapeer Avenue
Port Huron, MI 48060

Arizona
Glendale Union High School District
New Teacher Induction Program

Started in 1993, the Glendale **New Teacher Induction Program** is a joint creation of the district administration and the local education association. It is designed to train first-, second-, and third-year teachers new to the district. Staff development begins two weeks before the school year with 10 days of instruction for first-year teachers. The emphasis is on Essential Elements of Instruction (Madeline Hunter) and classroom management (Harry Wong). District workshops include one workshop each semester followed by local inservice meetings.

Each school has a skilled mentor whose role is to train and support the new teachers. Lessons and teaching strategies are modeled for the new teachers who then plan, microteach, and analyze their lessons with the help of their local school groups and their mentors.

Weekly meetings are held at the school with the mentors and at times the administrators. Topics

The mentors of the Glendale New Teacher Induction Program.

address the needs of the new teachers. The mentors teach two classes each day and serve as facilitators the remainder of the day. Some of their tasks include the following:

- Observing all new teachers using clinical supervision, cognitive coaching models, and other informal observation techniques
- Facilitating all local inservice which includes follow up to all district workshops and other professional topics
- Participating in ongoing staff development to improve the induction program

Second-year teachers receive four days of summer staff development which builds on first-year instructional strategies. Third-year teachers receive three days of advanced staff development. The induction program has served more than one-half of the district's professional staff since its inception.

Margaret Garcia-Dugan
Glendale Union High School District
7650 North 43rd Avenue
Glendale, AZ 85301

Arizona
Mesa Public Schools
Induction Program

The Mesa program is a six-year professional development process with a minimum of four days of classroom management training in **Year 1** prior to the beginning of school, as well as on-site support for classroom set-up and material preparation for the first days and weeks of school. **Years 1 and 2** also include one-on-one mentoring support, visits to demonstration classrooms, and release days for observation of best management and instructional practices. The content design is specific to regular

education, special education, and counseling assignments. New teachers receive a small stipend at the end of the third and sixth years for successful completion of the induction requirements. Professional teaching standards and state academic standards are an integral part of the program. Approximately 500 new teachers are hired each year and participate in this joint venture between the district's Career Ladder and Professional Development departments. The program has received national recognition and is featured in a *Video Journal*[5] and in *Assessing Impact: Evaluating Professional Development*[6] by Joellen Killion.

Nancy Fiandach
Mesa Public Schools
549 North Stapley Drive
Mesa, AZ 85203

Connecticut
Bridgeport Board of Education
New Teacher Induction Program

This induction program is a four-day event the week before school opens. The focus of the induction training is classroom management, curriculum, and instruction with emphasis on clear expectations and academic rigor. During this induction period, principals and district administration play an active role in welcoming the new staff and orienting them to their schools and to the climate within each building.

The induction process continues throughout the school year with monthly workshops offered in various areas of need as expressed by the new teachers through a survey. Members of the various departments and curriculum areas plan these monthly workshops. Continuous support in classroom management is also provided. Additionally, when each teacher is assigned to a building, he or she is assigned a mentor with at least 4 years of teaching experience. This veteran teacher has been trained as a mentor meeting the requirements of the state BEST (Beginning Educator Support Training) program. Mentors meet regularly (at least twice a month) with the new teachers to discuss issues and/or difficulties which the new teachers might be experiencing. A monthly *New Teacher Resource Guide* is produced with topics to be discussed with each new teacher by the mentor.

Kathleen Sochacki
Bridgeport Board of Education
Administrative Office Building
948 Main Street
Bridgeport, CT 06604

Georgia
Henry County Schools
Teacher Induction Program

TIP—Teacher Induction Program includes a five-day training session in early August for all teachers new to the district, the use of demonstration classrooms, and ongoing mentor support during the first year of teaching. In addition, follow-up training sessions are conducted throughout the year to address the needs of new teachers.

Wendy Hughes
Henry County Schools
396 Tomlinson Street
McDonough, GA 30253

California
Santa Cruz County
New Teacher Project

Helping new teachers with a structured, organized, and comprehensive approach is not a new phenomenon. Many of the school districts listed in Chapter 5 and 6 have been doing this for over ten years. The Santa Cruz New Teacher Project has been helping new teachers for over 14 years. The project is a collaborative effort among the University of California at Santa Cruz's Teacher Education Program, the Santa Cruz County Office of Education, and nearly thirty school districts in the greater Santa Cruz and Silicon Valley area.

The **Santa Cruz New Teacher Project (SCNTP)** is the local manifestation for the California **Beginning Teacher Support and Assessment (BTSA) program.** (See page 106.) The SCNTP claims a retention rate of 94 percent.

Because the success of their work is highly sought, they have formed the New Teacher Center (NTC), a national resource center dedicated to teacher development and the support of programs and practices that promote excellence and diversity in America's teaching force.

The induction process creates confident teachers.

They sponsor an outstanding annual national symposium on New Teacher Induction. Information can be found on www.newteachercenter.org.

Ellen Moir
Santa Cruz New Teacher Center
725 Front Street, Suite 400
Santa Cruz, CA 95060

Oregon
Medford School District
Induction Program

Medford's **Successful Beginnings: A Teacher Induction Program** has been in existence since 1989. It works with teachers new to the district for two consecutive years. First-year teachers attend a twenty-one hour course in Classroom Management. They attend three seven-hour sessions in August, for which two graduate credits are granted. They then are assigned to a peer coach, who works with them throughout the course of the ensuing school year on concepts presented in the classroom management course. Second-year teachers follow the same format, with the emphasis being on Essential Elements of Instruction.

The Classroom Management course content covers prevention, intervention, independence, rules, procedures, lesson plan format for procedures, motivation theory, reinforcement theory, the "law of least intervention," logical consequences, and critical attributes for the first days of school. The Essential Elements of Instruction targets active participation, Bloom's Taxonomy, formulating objectives, teaching to an objective, modeling, using an anticipatory set, providing closure, and using specific lesson design.

Kathy McCollum
Medford School District
500 Monroe Street
Medford, OR 97501

Illinois
Leyden High School
Induction Program

Everything You Ever Wanted to Know About Teaching . . . But Were Afraid to Ask is the program for all teachers new to the two public high schools in this suburban Chicago district. It involves a weeklong training seminar in early August, with a heavy emphasis on classroom management. New teachers meet on a monthly basis with their assigned mentors and building administrators. The induction program is part of Leyden University, an in-house staff development opportunity for all new and veteran teachers.

Kathryn Robbins
Leyden High School
3400 Rose Street
Franklin Park, IL 60131

Illinois
Homewood-Flossmoor Community
High School Induction Program

Two professional development coordinators and an administrator are the instructional leaders of the Homewood-Flossmoor induction program. Their role is to teach instructional skills and competencies necessary for the successful start of the school year while modeling effective instructional practices for participants. The new teachers begin their induction with a six-day program during early August and continue to meet regularly during the school year.

Homewood-Flossmoor's new teacher induction program is supported by a cadre of Model Teachers, veterans identified as exemplary professionals who serve as role models and mentors. Model Teachers receive two days of summer training and meet as a team frequently during the school year. Model Teachers and new teachers meet at least an hour weekly, observe one another's classes quarterly, and maintain learning journals.

Sandra Martin stands before a list of topics addressed during their induction program.

Both programs are part of the district's professional development program: **HF University.** This internal university is based on the design outlined in *Professional Development: Learning from the Best*[7] produced by NCREL (North Central Regional Educational Laboratory). All participants receive stipends or credit for advancement on the district's salary schedule.

Sandra Martin
Homewood-Flossmoor Community High School
999 Kedzie Avenue
Flossmoor, IL 60422

California
Stanislaus County Beginning Teacher Support and Assessment Program

The California **Beginning Teacher Support and Assessment (BTSA)** program was initiated in 1992 with California Senate Bill 1422, which endorses the gradual phase-in of support and assessment for all of the state's beginning teachers. As of 1999, approximately 75 percent of the state's first- and second-year teachers have participated in one of 130 BTSA programs. Participants receive two years of ongoing support from site support providers along with BTSA program activities and workshops. For Stanislaus County the overall retention rate of new teachers who have participated in its program is 95 percent! (See the References, page 216.)

Susan Rich
Stanislaus County Office of Education
1100 H Street
Modesto, CA 95354

California
New Haven Unified School District Induction Program

The New Haven Unified School District induction program begins with orientation and training through five days of pre–school year workshops, followed by monthly support meetings. Each new teacher receives support in four ways: a support team, professional development opportunities, release time, and financial support for supplies and materials. The support team consists of a partner teacher, the site mentor or the BTSA specialist (or both), and additional members as deemed necessary.

Donna Uyemoto
New Haven Unified School District
34200 Alvarado Niles Road
Union City, CA 94587

Teacher Quality Matters at New Haven

Careful! You don't want www.nctaf.com. But if you logon to it, it's quite amusing. What you want is www.nctaf.org, the website where you can find the document *What Matters Most: Teaching for America's Future*.[8] Also on that site is a report that features the New Haven Unified School District in California.[9] Whether you purchase the report or download all 132 pages, it is well worth your investment to read about a district that "has it all together." The bottom line, they say, is that **"teacher quality is the most important factor in student achievement."**

Perhaps this is why every school in the district has been recognized as a Distinguished School by the state of California and five of the schools in the district have received national Blue Ribbon awards.

This is a district that serves a low-wealth, ethnically diverse community and does not have a recruitment or attrition problem. They recruit the very best, get them, and keep them. One of the teachers aptly summarizes the overall atmosphere by saying,

> *Don't come to New Haven*
> *if you want to be*
> *a good teacher;*
> *come to New Haven*
> *if you want to be*
> *the best teacher you can possibly be.*
> *The atmosphere is creative, energetic,*
> *supportive, and challenging.*
> *Working here keeps me on the "high" road.*

— Chris Ryan
Language Arts Teacher, Logan High School

There is no recruitment problem in the New Haven Unified School District because retention is the key there. Read *What Matters Most* in its entirety at www.nctaf.org, or go to the New Haven Unified School District's website (www.nhusd.k12.ca.us), and you will understand why people do not leave this culture of creativity and success.

In a cooperative venture with the local university, California State University-Hayward, student teachers are treated as interns and their internship program is based within the district schools—ultimately providing a pool of trained, effective teachers who have been through their own district induction program.

See also "Daniel Goldfarb Elementary School Induction Program" on page 111 for information on Goldfarb Elementary School, where this same concept is practiced.

Most importantly, the New Haven Unified School District has developed a world-class recruitment program using the Internet, a program that has been recognized for exemplary use of technology in recruiting.

The district has a proactive culture. They will tell you that "New Haven does not have a 'gimme, gimme' attitude. They deliver. Every supervisor, every support provider, every cooperating teacher will be properly oriented and trained. You KNOW that."

New Haven succeeds because **its schools are organized around student AND teacher learning.**

California
Rio Linda Unified School District
Beginning Teacher Support and Assessment

Rio Linda is a district that participates in the California **Beginning Teacher Support and Assessment (BTSA)** program, too. They pay their teachers $185 per day for five days of pre–school year training. This is followed by monthly BTSA network meetings and quarterly new teacher meetings. There are also weekly meetings with the support provider, three Saturday meetings, and (available by prior arrangement) demonstration classrooms. They use the *California Standards for the Teaching Profession*[10] as an everyday model for effective teaching.

Frank Porter
Rio Linda Unified School District
6450 Twentieth Street
Rio Linda, CA 95673

California
Capistrano Unified School District
Beginning Teacher Support and Assessment

Using the California **Beginning Teacher Support and Assessment (BTSA)** program, the Capistrano Unified School District helps new teachers to focus on and internalize the *California Standards for the Teaching Profession.*[11] Each participating teacher receives over 10 hours of orientation and classroom management training before the school year, followed by workshops throughout the first two years. Other forms of assistance include one-on-one support provided by a qualified and trained veteran teacher, four release days to observe other teachers, attend conferences, or strategize and communicate with colleagues, $150 for the purchase of classroom materials, and up to $1,050 for district-

and site-specific professional development. The program has proved more than beneficial. No new teacher participating in their BTSA program has been referred for a professional improvement plan.

Jodee Brentlinger
Capistrano Unified School District
32972 Calle Perfecto
San Juan Capistrano, CA 92675

California
Dry Creek Joint Union Schools
New Teacher Induction Program

This suburban Sacramento school district has three components to its **New Teacher Induction Program. Component 1** includes two days of pre-school workshops with a focus on strategies to achieve success and effectiveness on the first days of school. Lunch is provided which helps to set a positive tone. Binders with ideas, district curriculum documents, and the book *The First Days of School*[12] are distributed.

Component 2 provides each teacher with at least one hour per week of support with a consulting teacher. Funding is through the California BTSA program, which provides every teacher with a small stipend plus $150 for classroom supplies and two days of release time to observe other teachers.

Component 3 is a series of monthly inservices with a multitude of topics helpful to new teachers. Components 2 and 3 run for two years.

Judy Rose
Dry Creek Joint Union School District
9707 Cook Riolo Road
Roseville, CA 95747

Florida
Orange County Public Schools
Great Beginnings

Each school in Orange County has an instructional coach as well as mentors assigned to each new teacher. The coach schedules training sessions throughout the year and mentors meet regularly with the new teachers. This entire process is structured before school begins, during a three-day training session that commences Orange County's new teacher induction program—**Great Beginnings**. The instructional coaches are trained in areas of verbal coaching skills, instructional strategies, and classroom management. They receive ongoing training on topics related to induction at the school site.

Nora Gledich
Orange County Public Schools
445 West Amelia Street
Orlando, FL 32801

Florida
Glades County School District
Quality Teachers Insure
Productive Students Program

A small rural district in Florida realized the need for an induction program. In the program's first year, 1997, the district invited all of its veteran teachers to the induction program for new teachers. Not only did over 90 percent of the veteran teachers attend, but they said it was one of the best in-service training programs in which they had ever participated.

The program, **Quality Teachers Insure Productive Students (QTIPS)**, provides the new teachers of Glades County with the opportunity to become familiar with the culture of the school system and the community. New teachers are introduced to the district in a family-type atmosphere. There are induction meetings for three days prior to the opening of school and monthly thereafter. Mentors are provided for each new teacher and novice teachers receive a second year of induction.

Mazie Ford
Glades County School District
P.O. Box 459
Moore Haven, FL 33471

South Carolina
Lexington County School District 3
Induction Program

Lexington's induction program has been developed to partner with South Carolina's Assisting, Developing, and Evaluating Professional Teaching (ADEPT) program. Their induction program begins with four to five days of pre–school year meetings and training. During the first year, beginning teachers must complete a professional growth plan that supports the district's strategic plan and must maintain an induction log. The induction training is designed by the district and is supplemented by a graduate course taken at a cooperating local university. Beginning teachers have the support of an assistance team consisting of a mentor, a building administrator, and a third observer, each receiving one and one-half days of release time. Time is also structured for beginning teachers to observe master teachers.

Frances K. Bouknight
Lexington County School District 3
338 West Columbia Avenue
Batesburg-Leesville, SC 29006

The Clark County Induction Program

An educational convention, Siegfried and Roy, or blackjack may draw you to Las Vegas. Regardless, as you pass through McCarran International Airport, you will see a sign that says, "Elvis has left the classroom and we have a vacancy."

Applicants come from over 40 states to teach in Clark County, Nevada—the sixth largest district in the United States—which hires over 1,500 new teachers each year. With 6,000 people moving to Las Vegas each month, Clark County opens six or more schools a year!

Karyn Wright is the director of the three-year new teacher induction program, and she has no intention of seeing her new teachers SURVIVE; they will **SUCCEED** and **STAY**. The Clark County attrition rate is well under 10 percent.

The induction program begins with the opening of the New Teacher Welcome Center. Karyn Wright says, "Moving from another state to Nevada can be overwhelming. Many come all by themselves." With that in mind, the welcome center is open for about six weeks, from mid-July to the end of August—providing everything from roommate referrals to information about utility services, banking services, child care, medical services, driver's licensing, and housing options. Local businesses provide an assortment of discounts and small gifts. Experienced teachers are on hand to answer questions about curriculum, school policies, the first paycheck, and a myriad of other new teacher concerns. (See "The Real Needs of New Teachers" on page 61.)

Then, like a high-powered Las Vegas show, the three-year induction program kicks into high gear, providing a whole range of activities and support materials for the new teachers:

- An orientation program prior to the beginning of the school year
- A Community Day at a mall, sponsored by local businesses
- A resource manual, *Great Beginnings*, with teaching strategies
- Monthly training sessions in everything from classroom management and student behavior to lesson delivery
- A teacher-training cadre available for training and assistance
- On-site mentor-facilitators
- Monthly newsletters
- New teacher socials
- A personal planner for weekly planning
- An intranet account number and an e-mail address, which allow new teachers to

  ❑ Access the new teacher training calendar
  ❑ Read classroom management tips
  ❑ Find curriculum resources
  ❑ View digital photographs of effective classrooms
  ❑ Exchange ideas
  ❑ Chat with new teachers
  ❑ Find friends

In 1996 Clark County began targeting its training toward helping new teachers who work in schools with high poverty and low student achievement. The effort has yielded results. One elementary school that hired 29 new teachers for 1996–97 needed to hire only 11 new teachers for 1998–99. Another school's new hires dropped from 33 to 7 in the same period. Induction more than pays for itself!

For information on this program contact

Karyn Wright
Clark County
School District
2832 East Flamingo Road
Las Vegas, NV 89121

Members of the Clark County Induction Program team include Heidi Olivé and Kari Bastin, teachers on special assignment to the program, and Karyn Wright, director.

Nevada
Daniel Goldfarb Elementary School
Induction Program

Daniel Goldfarb Elementary School is part of the Clark County School District in Las Vegas. Along with participation in Clark County's districtwide induction, new teachers at Goldfarb Elementary receive site-based induction training from their principal, Bridget Phillips. The principal provides ongoing after-school sessions during the first year of teaching, focusing on classroom management and instructional strategies. Similar training is also provided for student teachers in the school.

Bridget Phillips
Daniel Goldfarb Elementary School
1651 Orchard Valley Drive
Las Vegas, NV 89122

Texas
Killeen Independent School District
Excel Program

Killeen's **Excel** induction program begins with a four-day structured training session for all new teachers in early August, with ongoing follow-up training sessions throughout the year. Located next to the Fort Hood army base, one of the largest military installations in the world, both the teacher and student populations are highly mobile.

Susan Krals
Killeen Independent School District
200 North W.S. Young Drive
Killeen, TX 76543

Michigan
Waterford School District
Induction Program

This is a four-year program designed to fulfill the Michigan requirement of 15 days of professional development for new teachers. The program combines Charlotte Danielson's four domains of teaching from her book *Enhancing Professional Practice: A Framework for Teaching*[13] with the locally developed Waterford Instructional Model (WIM). Probationary teachers meet for three days before school begins and at additional times during the school year.

In **Year 1** teachers focus on the classroom environment. Each receives a new teacher notebook with local district information and a set of district curriculum guides and each is assigned a mentor.

In **Year 2** teachers focus on the domain of planning and preparation, receiving in-depth instruction on district expectations for curriculum, instruction, and assessment.

In **Year 3** teachers focus on success for all students through differentiated instruction using the elements of WIM.

In **Year 4** teachers focus on the development and use of standards-based thematic units for instruction. Working with the Michigan Education Association, mentor teachers are trained using the Pathwise System, which was developed by the Educational Testing Service, using Charlotte Danielson's domains of teaching.

Mike Kehoe
Waterford School District
1325 Crescent Lake Road
Waterford, MI 48237

Singapore Induction Program for Beginning Teachers

Singapore Airlines is consistently voted the best airline in the world by business travelers. Their success is based on a structured training program.[14] As part of the same national culture, Singapore's new teachers are trained in a similar exemplary manner.

The Singapore Ministry of Education is analogous to an American school district. With a population of 3.5 million people, this makes them similar to Philadelphia or Miami. With 246 square miles, this is like Dallas, Texas. But the similarities end there.

The professional development center occupies an entire former school campus and is staffed to support a culture of COLLABORATION and SELF-MASTERY. This teaching center is called the **Teachers' Network.** It has a vision of building a fraternity of reflective teachers dedicated to excellent practice through a network of support, professional exchange, and learning.

Collaboration. The need to work together as collaborative colleagues is critical. Teachers' Network helps schools form Learning Circles, small groups of teachers, engaged in collaborative research and ongoing learning.

Self-mastery. Self-mastery is an important pillar of a learning organization. Teachers will only be able to cope with and facilitate changes if they are able to master themselves and grow as persons and professionals. The Teachers' Network provides a variety of workshop activities to help teachers start and continue their journey toward self-mastery.

New teacher induction is a one-year program (the program is in its third year) and is organized by the Teachers' Network. The objectives of the new teacher induction program are as follows:

- Transmitting the culture of the educational system to beginning teachers
- Reinforcing positive attitudes toward the profession
- Improving teacher performance
- Increasing the retention of teachers
- Promoting the personal well being of beginning teachers

Intranet. The Teachers' Network continues to support the new teachers through its own intranet homepage. Some features include

- **ICARE (Individual Counseling and Advisory Resource for Educators).** Any individual who needs to correspond by phone, letter, or e-mail will find someone on site who can offer individual help and counseling. This service is not only provided on the intranet but through face-to-face contact as well as the telephone.
- **Teach and Share.** Teachers can share their successful practices and they can download an archive of best practices, lessons, activities, and strategies.
- **Teachers Forum.** Similar in concept to a chat room, this is a site where teachers can post their honest and unedited views without stating their names.
- **Teacher On-Line.** This is used to clarify employment questions where questions are forwarded to the right people for responses.

In addition to the Teachers' Network, other branches within the Ministry of Education provide additional services and programs. The personal development of a teacher does not stop with induction. Each teacher is encouraged to attend 100 hours of training each year. Most exceed the 100 hours!

The results of their culture are evident in the international test scores that appear periodically. Maslow would be happy to know that such a culture of collaboration and self-mastery produces self-actualized professionals.

Virginia
Rappahannock County High School
Induction Program

The Rappahannock County School District consists of two schools, an elementary school and a high school. Jack Raines, the principal at the high school, meets with all of his new teachers for one week before school starts and provides on-site training in classroom management and instructional practices. The induction training is ongoing throughout the first year.

Jack Raines[15]
Rappahannock County High School
12576 Lee Highway
Washington, VA 22747

Teacher Quality And Student Progress

A study of students and teachers in the Cincinnati Public Schools shows a connection between highly rated teachers and gains in student achievement. The district looked at grades 3 through 8 and examined each teacher's rating under the its detailed evaluation system. It also looked at individual student achievement on proficiency tests in 2000-01.

- Teachers rated "unsatisfactory" under the system had students who scored as much as 13 points under district expectations on science proficiency tests and 9 points under district expectations for math.
- Teachers rated "distinguished," however, had students whose scores in math and science were both 3 points above the expected averages.

"This study means teacher quality is a key component to determining student success and achievement. There is a correlation between excellence in teaching and raising student achievement," said Sue Taylor, president of the Cincinnati Federation of Teachers.[16]

See page 114 to read about Cincinnati's commitment to building effective teachers.

Oklahoma
Northeastern State University
Induction Course

An induction course has been developed at Northeastern State University to prepare students pragmatically for the experiences they will face during the first few days of teaching. The course was developed when returning students complained that school districts were offering no training or support. In this course students develop an individualized teacher induction notebook to assist with the transition to the reality of teaching. Information on this course is available at www.intellex.com/~eeac/4563.htm.

James Wilhite
Northeastern State University
College of Education
Tahlequah, OK 74464

California
California State Universities
CalStateTEACH

Just as Domino's delivers pizzas, the California State Universities can deliver a college instructor or mentor to your door. You say you live beyond commuting distance to a university, cannot access a university program due to personal circumstances, or have a full time teaching job? No problem. **CalStateTEACH** is an innovative 18-month program designed especially for non-credentialed elementary school teachers. The curriculum is delivered using a self-study format. Participants use online, print, and CD-ROM materials. They share ideas through web-based class discussions, share ideas via a special Internet website, and get professional feedback through on-site mentor teachers and a California State University faculty member. Information on this program is available at www.CalStateTEACH.com.

Professional Practice School

continuously improve and assume multiple professional roles as they move through career steps—from "intern" to "apprentice," "novice" to "career teacher," "advanced teacher," and ultimately "accomplished teacher." Each successive step requires higher-quality teaching performance.

"Apprentices" are first-year teachers, and they receive intensive induction (their description). Through a peer assistance program, new teachers are assigned to consulting teachers— "advanced" or "accomplished" teachers in the same subject area or grade level who are released from classroom duties to work with as many as 14 teachers.

The attrition rate for all Cincinnati teachers has been less than 10 percent over the past five years and only 3 percent of beginning teachers have resigned over the past five years.

The Cincinnati Public Schools have created the **Career-in-Teaching** program for developing continuous professional growth and teacher leadership. New teachers are recruited as interns in their second year of college to begin their teacher education and do their internship in Cincinnati's Professional Practice School, which works in cooperation with the University of Cincinnati and the Cincinnati Federation of Teachers.

No longer is there a traditional time-and-degree-model salary schedule. Rather, teachers can

Young teachers who demonstrate excellence in knowledge and skills at any point in their career can move up the salary scale and career ladder quickly, which gives them an incentive to stay with the city schools.

Even when teachers reach the "accomplished" level, the Career-in-Teaching program promotes professional development and expanded roles for them throughout their careers. The Cincinnati Public Schools have changed their thinking about recruitment and retention—they now have a systemwide commitment to teacher career development.[17]

Principals Need to Be Inducted Too!

I was given a set of keys and told to take over the school. There was no induction program for principals—not even a mentor.

— Name Withheld Upon Request

- **More than half of the nation's 92,000 principals are expected to retire or quit in the next five years.**[18]

- **The average age of principals in the United States is close to 50 and 40 percent of all principals will probably retire within the next decade.**

- **Among principals in Iowa who are eligible to retire by 2003, an astounding 93 percent plan to do so.**[19]

This is my first year in a new job. I am a principal of a building and I am the curriculum director of the corporation. I am finding that I am in need of an induction program for myself. I hired two new teachers this year. They need help, yet I am not able to help them as much as I would like because I am trying to figure out my own job. To further complicate the matter, we have a new superintendent. Guess what? He can't help me because he is trying to figure out his new role. The domino effect is endless and unnecessary (to a degree) in my opinion. If we had an induction program, it would solve a lot of problems.

— Doug Ballinger
Principal and Curriculum Director
LaFontaine Elementary School, Indiana

New Zealand Induction Course for Principals

New first time principals are taking part in the first principals' induction course being held in Auckland this year (2002).

Education Minister Trevor Mallard says,

"The principal is the critical factor in the success of a school. From an education standards perspective, if we can help principals do their job better, we will make a huge difference in the quality of education across all our schools. Many experienced principals think back and say, 'If I had known then what I know now, it would have been a lot easier.' I believe that if principals are better prepared, we will have better schools and better learning."

Other aspects of the initiative include these:

- Laptops for principals (starting with the new principals)
- A dedicated portal for principals and administrators providing essential information and services
- A private online network for principals

Trevor Mallard says that the four day residential course is designed to support new principals in understanding their role as educational leaders, clarify how they should monitor school culture, and build strong internal and external relationships.[20]

North Carolina
Leaders for a New Millennium

All companies have management training classes. Some school districts have seen the light and are now training their own principals to combat a shortage. It's **training**, not mentoring. If mentoring is the answer to all of education's teacher woes, then who will be the new principal's mentor and what and how will this person mentor when the district does not even have a plan for training administrators?

The National Association of Elementary School Principals estimates that 40 percent of the 93,000 principal positions in the U.S. could be vacant by 2006.[21] School systems nationwide have instituted training programs to groom aspiring principals. For example, North Carolina's Wake County reimburses teachers who participate in its **Leaders for a New Millennium** program for 50 percent of their costs to take required school leadership classes.

Louisiana
Principal Internship Program

Effective principals are not born—they are trained. Though successful classroom experiences and a thorough understanding of curriculum and instruction are vital to becoming an effective administrator, they are not enough. Being an administrator requires certain skills that are not acquired even from the most successful teaching experiences. This premise is the underlying thrust of the **Louisiana Principal Internship Program, an induction program for principals.** The mandatory program, which is a collaborative effort between the state's Department of Education and Southeastern Louisiana University's Colleges of Education and Business, provides new principals with two years of ongoing training and support in the areas of leadership and management.

The Louisiana Principal Internship Program is structured to align current state mandates and initiatives, research on leadership development, and the "Standards for School Principals in Louisiana." The major components of the program focus on school improvement processes and school accountability. The goal is to link leadership more closely to productive schools and enhanced student achievement. The program is designed to do this:

- Nurture, guide, and develop the leadership skills of beginning school administrators
- Lead the interns through best practices and research related to student and school improvement
- Assist in connecting networks and communities of administrators
- Understand the relationship between leadership and learning
- Assist administrators in the development of the school's improvement plan
- Assist new school leaders in the development of a personal administrative portfolio

During the two-year program for new principals and assistant principals, the main component is participation in a yearlong online professional development course powered by Blackboard, a national e Education software platform.[22]

The Year-1 course is seven modules based on the "Standards for Principals in Louisiana" and the "Interstate School Leaders Licensure Commission's Standards for School Leaders." A professor of Educational Leadership from a different state university facilitates each module. Their function is to monitor the Blackboard assignments and discussion board replies and monitor and provide insight to the participants. In addition, each intern is a member of a team, consisting of other new principals and mentored by a practicing experienced principal. The function of the mentor principal is one of support and encouragement and establishing a virtual network through Blackboard that will be useful long after the internship is over. Each of the modules is designed with guiding questions, readings from texts and web sites, and scenarios common to administrators.

Year-2 modules address issues of the principal as the instructional leader. **Through the Louisiana Principal Internship Program, a virtual network has been created for all principals in Louisiana that allows them direct contact with their peers throughout the state.** One of the strong points of this program is the number of contact hours between new principals and experienced principals, yet principals are not required to leave their schools as often due to the virtual component. As interns complete the online modules, they also begin preparing a professional portfolio, which is presented at the end of the program. The fact that all modules are based on state and national standards for principals has provided interns with core knowledge of the workings of the principalship and a better understanding of the day-to-day duties expected of them. Interns completing the program have given it a 93 percent excellence rating, citing it as a valuable and high quality professional development activity.

Kirk Guidry
Louisiana Department of Education
kguidry@doe.state.la.us

Helpful Web Sites[23]

Induction programs show new teachers that you care about their success. There is a shortage of teachers around the world. Wouldn't you want to provide some type of support to keep that new teacher?

Many organizations are addressing the national teacher supply crisis. The following websites provide information on this crisis:

Education Resource Information Clearinghouse (ERIC)
http://ericir.syr.edu/

National Association for Alternative Certification (NAAC)
www.alt-teachercert.org/index.asp

National Center for Alternative Teacher Certification Information (NCATCI)
www.altcert.org

National Center for Education Information (NCEI)
www.ncei.com

National Council on Teacher Quality (NCTQ)
www.nctq.org

Recruiting New Teachers, Inc. (RNT)
www.rnt.org

Teach for America (TFA)
www.tfanetwork.org

Troops to Teachers (TTT)
http://voled.doded.mil/dantes/ttt

New Leaders for New Schools

New Leaders for New Schools (NLNS) is a national nonprofit organization devoted to improving education for all children by attracting and preparing the next generation of outstanding leaders for urban public schools. NLNS aggressively recruits and provides rigorous hands-on training (including course work and a yearlong internship with an exceptional mentor principal) for extremely talented people to become urban school principals.

NLNS has three central goals:

1   To recruit and develop talented, dedicated individuals who will become successful principals in urban public schools and who will provide a strong commitment to the success of each graduate.

2   To create a pathway for principal recruitment, preparation, and ongoing support that will serve as a model for school districts, universities, and nonprofit organizations.

3   To provide school districts and charter schools with the effective school leaders they urgently need, to accomplish the mission of educating all students at high levels.

The components of the induction process include the following:

- **Recruitment:** NLNS rigorously screens and selects extremely talented individuals with diverse, proven skills and successes to become New Leaders Fellows. Each fellow receives a fully funded fellowship and living stipend to participate in the program.

- **Training:** Drawing on the best practices from the country's finest education and business schools, NLNS training begins with intensive preparatory summer course work in the foundations of leadership. These courses are taught and developed by leading practitioners and academics. Fellows then use these skills during a yearlong residency, under the guidance of an experienced mentor principal, during which they participate in the daily leadership responsibilities of a school.

- **Support:** NLNS graduates receive intensive support and professional development for two years after graduation. Graduates become lifelong members of an active support network of peers, mentors, academics, and other educational and business leaders.

NLNS (www.nlns.org) is devoted to making the American dream possible for every child. It is dedicated to providing leaders with the necessary skills to create and lead schools that will prepare all students for the challenges of the future.

New Leaders for New Schools
18 West Twenty-Seventh Street, Suite 7C
New York, NY 10001

Do You Have a Success Story to Share?

The districts and the people represented in this section embrace the philosophy of Somerset Maugham's quote that began this chapter. To paraphrase this quote on behalf of these educators:

It's a funny thing about education; if you refuse to accept anything but the best from your administrators, teachers, and students, you very often get it.

And, how do they get it? By using their best people to train all members of the organization to be their best.

The primary purpose of this book is to share information so that school districts can help their new teachers succeed by becoming effective teachers who will impact the lives of every student they teach. Thus we have shared a variety of exemplary new teacher induction programs used by various schools and school districts.

Please share your induction program with us. If you have a comprehensive induction program and would like to have it added to future editions of this book, please send information to either of the authors. (See "About the Authors" on page 221.)

We ask that you send information about your induction program only if it meets the following three simple criteria:

1. There must be a minimum of two days of workshops held before the beginning of school with emphasis on effective teacher training and an introduction to the school or school district's culture.

2. There must be regularly scheduled meetings held during the first year and a structured program of learning that continues into the second year of new teachers' employment.

3. There must be some form of structured, personal support provided for each new teacher, at least during the first year.

Thank you for sharing. We look forward to hearing from you.

More Induction Programs

Summary and Implementation

Planting the Seeds
Information We've Shared

- Rural, urban, and suburban schools and districts across the country and beyond have increased the retention of more qualified, capable, competent new teachers by offering induction training.
- Louisiana has an induction program for principals.
- A school district in Illinois prepares its new teachers for national board certification.
- North Carolina offers high school seniors generous scholarships to become teachers.
- School districts are teaming with local universities to induct prospective teachers.

Nurturing Growth
What You Can Do to Make a Difference

- Make contact with schools and districts just like yours that are successfully inducting prospective teachers, new teachers, and even principals.
- Share your successes with us so that we can share them with others.

Reaping the Harvest
Benefits to Your School System

- Induction is one of the best investments any school district can make.
- Collaboration between school districts and universities is invaluable.
- New teachers stay and succeed with districts that train and support them.

chapter seven

*We make a living by what we get,
but we make a life by what
we give.*

— Norman MacEwan

Collecting the fruits.

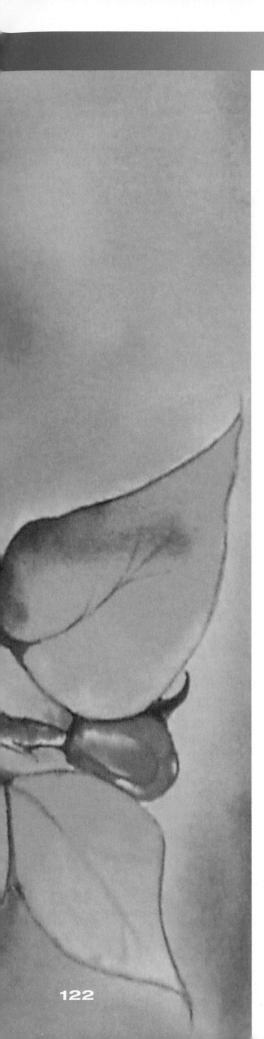

Sources and Notes for Chapter 7

[1]Wong, Harry K. (September 2002). "Play for Keeps." *Principal Leadership*, p. 55.
Available: www.principals.org/news/pl_playkeeps_0902.html.

[2]Resta, Virginia and Leslie Huling. (1998). "Implementing a Campus-Level Support Program for Novice Teachers." Southwest Texas State University. Unpublished.

Too Many Questions . . .

You say I ask too many questions

But you just don't seem to see

That I wonder about so many things

For which answers there surely

    must be

But once I know an answer

A new question grows in my mind

Because what I learn uncovers

New problems with answers to find

So be patient with my questioning

There still is so much I don't know

But I do know that learning

    more answers

Will certainly help me to grow.

— Annette L. Breaux

Though most of the questions that follow are answered in detail throughout the book, this chapter serves as a quick guide to some of the questions most frequently asked by people who are setting up induction programs.

1.

What is "induction"?

Induction is actually more a PROCESS than a PROGRAM, but induction programs are created in order to structure the process. The process entails systematic training and ongoing support for all new teachers, commencing BEFORE the first day of school and continuing for several years.

2.

Who should attend induction?

Though some districts offer induction for first-time teachers only, the ideal is to induct **all teachers new to the district,**

whether or not they have prior teaching experience. Experienced teachers entering the district should not require as much support as first-time teachers, but they still must be inducted into the district. They need to know what will be expected of them and where to turn when they have questions. They need to be orientated to both their school's and their new district's policies, procedures, philosophies, and overall culture.

Because each school district is unique, both experienced and inexperienced teachers new to any district require support, guidance, and training.

3.

What is the difference between "orientation" and "induction"?

Orientation is just one component of a well-planned, successful induction program. It involves becoming familiar with the policies and procedures of the school and school district. Induction is the entire process of systematically training and supporting new teachers during their first few years of teaching. Orientation can be done in one day, whereas induction can take several years.

> *A strong induction program helps teachers acclimate and continue to learn and it helps principals keep the teachers they hire. All in all, it's an investment that pays off for everyone—especially students.*[1]

A Tragic Attitude

Because of the financial instability of 2002 and the escalating unemployment rates, human resources personnel are reporting that there is no teacher shortage because out-of-work people are flocking to become teachers.

Sadly, many school districts have reverted to the same old tragic attitude—doing what they have always done—replenishing the troops.

Effective school districts, with enlightened administrators and school boards, institute or continue to refine structured, sustained, multiyear induction programs to ensure even more effective teachers.

They are leaving no teacher behind.

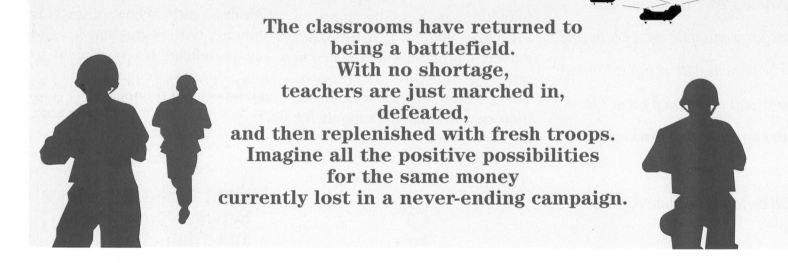

The classrooms have returned to
being a battlefield.
With no shortage,
teachers are just marched in,
defeated,
and then replenished with fresh troops.
Imagine all the positive possibilities
for the same money
currently lost in a never-ending campaign.

4.

What is the difference between "mentoring" and "induction"?

Mentoring is only one component of the induction process. It involves pairing new teachers with experienced teachers, or "mentor teachers." These mentor teachers work with the new teachers in their classrooms for a period of at least one year. Induction encompasses orientation, mentoring, ongoing structured training, and other components.

5.

When should induction begin and how long should it last?

Induction should begin BEFORE the first day of school. The initial induction should last a minimum of four days. Further training sessions, support group meetings, observations, and so on, should be ongoing for the next two or three years.

6.

Who should be included on the induction team? Who should do the actual presenting and modeling for new teachers?

The induction team should consist of successful classroom teachers. Though some of these people may currently serve as coordinators, administrators, or supervisors, it is imperative that all team members share knowledge of effective teaching, knowledge of classroom management techniques, and a love of children. These people should also be the ones who will continue to work very closely with the inductees throughout the entire induction process. Classroom teachers currently teaching should also be included on the team.

These demonstration classrooms may also be used throughout the year to provide opportunities for new teachers to observe successful veteran teachers in action.

Homewood-Flossmoor's John Schmidt opens his classroom for new teachers to see. As a second year teacher, he is concrete proof that Homewood-Flossmoor creates exceptional teachers.

7.

What is a "demonstration classroom"?

Demonstration classrooms are classrooms of the district's most successful veteran teachers. These classrooms are opened to the new teachers during the initial induction week. The veteran teachers walk them through the preparation stage by doing the following:

- Showing how the room is set up
- Explaining pre-school year preparation procedures
- Explaining first-day and first-week procedures
- Offering expert advice and instruction on effective classroom management
- Entertaining questions from the new teachers

8.

What topics should be covered during the initial induction week?

Though there is definitely no shortage of topics relevant to the needs of new teachers, we caution you not to try to cover EVERYTHING in the initial induction week. The main focus should be on **classroom management** because without it, teaching and learning cannot take place. Along with a heavy emphasis on basic classroom management skills, the following topics are frequently included:

- Lesson planning
- Instructional strategies
- Discipline
- First-day classroom procedures
- Local policies and procedures

- Time management
- Assessment
- Parental involvement
- Learning styles
- Critical thinking
- Needs of special students

But remember, the focus throughout should remain on how to effectively MANAGE a classroom.

9.

Where can I find information to help me get started with my own induction program?

Chapters 5 and 6 provide information on many successful induction programs, along with contact information. Any of these districts will be happy to share information with you on their programs.

10.

Can an individual school have its own induction program even if there is no districtwide program for all new teachers?

Absolutely! Many schools have their own induction programs. Actually, this is ideal, as each school is unique. A school that develops its own program has the luxury of tailoring all of its training to the specific needs of its teachers. Daniel Goldfarb Elementary School in Las Vegas has its own induction program in addition to being a part of the Clark County induction process. (See page 111.) Rappahannock County High School in Virginia has its own induction program because the county has no induction process for its new teachers. (See page 113.)

It matters not where the induction process is initiated. What's important is to provide instruction and support for all new teachers.

11.

Should participation in induction be mandatory?

Unless induction is mandated by the state, whether participation is to be voluntary or mandatory must be determined by the group implementing the program. Some school districts add extra days to new teachers' contracts for induction participation. Others pay stipends to participants. Interestingly, successful induction programs, whether voluntary or mandatory, tend to have about the same rate of participation.

12.

How do schools or school districts typically fund induction programs?

Induction programs are funded through a variety of means. Some districts receive state funding. Other districts allocate local funding in their yearly budgets for teacher induction. Some use a combination of funding sources, which might include general education funds, special education funds, Title 1 funds, or staff development funds. Induction programs at the school level are usually self-funded.

13.

How much does an induction program cost?

The operating budget for the Lafourche FIRST induction program is $50,000 a year. (See page 79.) At Leyden University the pre-school year induction training costs about $100 a day, and most of that is for food! (See page 105.)

The bottom line is that induction saves money! As one study points out, "If a bad hire costs a company nearly 2 1/2 times the employee's initial salary in recruitment and personnel costs, as well as lost productivity, then <u>each teacher</u> (emphasis added) who leaves the profession during the induction years likely costs taxpayers in excess of $50,000."[2] Considering this research, if Lafourche retains only one new teacher a year, it recoups its entire investment.

Karyn Wright of Clark County, Nevada, says, **"Induction more than pays for itself!"**

14.

How do we induct a teacher who is hired after the first day of school?

Many school districts host two initial induction training sessions per year—one in August and one in January. New teachers hired during the school year do not have to wait until the following year to begin the induction process.

$50,000
What Will It Buy You?
How Far Does It Go?

1
Lexus LS 430

4
First class airline tickets to Europe

10
Nights in the Presidential Suite
Fairmont Hotel in San Francisco

500
Tickets to *The Lion King* on Broadway

1,004
Shares of Microsoft stock (valued on 8-16-02)

15,873
Happy Meals® at McDonald's®

50,000
California State Lottery Tickets
(Your odds of winning are 40 million to 1.)

135,135
First class U.S. postage stamps

Number of children's lives affected with
just ONE
knowledgeable, skillful, effective teacher

Frequently Asked Questions

Summary and Implementation

Planting the Seeds
Information We've Shared

- Induction is more a process than a program, beginning before the first day of school and continuing for two or more years.
- Orientation and mentoring are merely components of the overall induction process.
- Though a variety of topics are addressed during the initial induction, the focus should remain on classroom management.
- Demonstration classrooms afford new teachers the opportunity to learn from the "experts."
- Induction does not pose a financial burden for a school or district. It actually saves money.

Nurturing Growth
What You Can Do to Make a Difference

- If you are a staff developer and in a system without an induction program, it's time to get the ball rolling and implement an induction program for your district.
- If you are a principal and there is no district induction, it's time to implement an induction program in your school.

Reaping the Harvest
Benefits to Your School System

- It typically costs a district $50,000 to recoup the financial losses of one new teacher leaving the district.
- Unless you have NO problem with teacher retention, then you simply cannot afford NOT having an induction program.
  (By the way, if you have no problem with teacher retention, call us—collect!)

chapter eight

An Investment in Our Future

The greatest thing is, at any moment, to be willing to give up who we are in order to become all that we can become.

— Max De Pree

Treasuring the harvest.

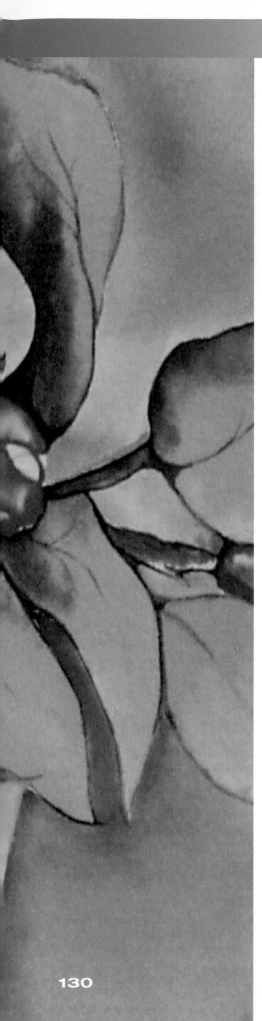

Sources and Notes for Chapter 8

[1]Wise, Arthur E. (February/March 1997). "Teachers Are the Key." *Reading Today*, p.8.

[2]National Commission on Teaching and America's Future. (1996). *What Matters Most: Teaching for America's Future.* New York.

[3]National Commission on Teaching and America's Future. (1996).

[4]Fideler, E. and D. Haselkorn. (1999). *Learning the Ropes: Urban Teacher Induction Programs and Practices in the United States.* Executive Summary. Belmont, MA: Recruiting New Teachers, Inc.
Available: http://www.rnt.org/publications/publications4.html.

[5]National Commission on Teaching and America's Future. (1996). p. 5.

[6]Further information on this legislation is available at the following website: www.ed.gov/legislation/ESEA02/pg20.html.

[7]Breaux, Annette L. (2003). *101 "Answers" for New Teachers & Their Mentors: Effective Teaching Tips for Daily Classroom Use.* Larchmont, NY: Eye on Education.

I feel confident that there is no other place in the world for me than to be a teacher. My convictions have been validated because of the outpours of love and support I felt in this induction program.

I was guided, directed, and shown that what truly makes a person a teacher is dedication, compassion, and love. I know that now more than ever. I have direction and a framework now to strive forward to be the most effective teacher that I can be.

— Christy Day
Raceland Upper Elementary School
Raceland, Louisiana

> If we are going to ask teachers to make a difference in every child's life—and we must— then we have a responsibility to build a teacher development system that guarantees every teacher has the skills and knowledge to make that difference.

This we know. We know what truly effective teaching looks like. What we lack is a comprehensive teacher development system—from the college, to the school, to the classroom—that puts this knowledge into practice. Recognizing this fact, knowledgeable leaders in schools and school districts have organized comprehensive induction programs. Some of these programs are so comprehensive that after several years in the induction program, the teachers are qualified to apply for National Board Certification or are deemed expert teachers.

Induction—not mentoring —is a comprehensive process through which many schools and school districts ensure a supportive culture, effective teaching, and student success. When teachers are trained and supported, they succeed and stay. When teachers succeed, students achieve!

This Matters Most

Arthur E. Wise, president of the National Council for Accreditation of Teacher Education (NCATE), says, "The report of the National Commission on Teaching and America's Future represents an unprecedented vision and opportunity to advance teaching as a profession. For the first time in American education history, a comprehensive vision for the creation of a profession of teaching—from recruitment and preparation to induction and continuing professional development—has been advanced by a commission of political, business, and education leaders."[1]

The report Wise refers to is *What Matters Most: Teaching for America's Future.*[2] Information in this document is profound.

We have selected some **critical findings of this study** to share with you. According to *What Matters Most: Teaching for America's Future*, there are several major flaws plaguing American schools:

1. Low expectations for student performance
2. **Inadequate induction for beginning teachers**
3. Schools structured for failure rather than success

Begin With a Firm Foundation

Kyle Taylor

When **Kyle Taylor** graduated from California State University at Northridge with a degree in finance and accounting, he considered and entertained offers from such renowned companies as Pricewaterhouse Coopers, Ernst & Young, Deloitte & Touche, and Sobul, Primes & Schenkel. His final decision was not based on pay, location, or position. **He picked the company he felt had the best training program.**

In education we provide insufficient training, if any, for our teachers. And many new teachers do not realize—until it's too late—just how lacking they are in basic teaching skills. In the business world, college graduates look to the company that offers them the best training as they begin their life's career, for they know their future successes and rewards are contingent on their initial training. Companies also know they can retain workers who are well trained and in return will stay and be a benefit to the company. New teachers should expect no less!

Nicole Tripi

Nicole Tripi will graduate from the University of New Orleans next year. She has already asked us, her godparents, where she should go to teach. We know where there are openings, which are not difficult to find in today's marketplace. We know where the good salaries are—starting at over $40,000 a year. We know where she can find supportive administrators. We know where she can find affordable housing. We know where she can raise her child in a good community.

Nonetheless, we know of a school district where the salary will be average. Some students will be challenging. The heat and humidity along the bayous can be unforgiving. But we can't think of a better way for her to receive her initial training and get started correctly than to be trained by the four people who run the Lafourche Parish induction program in Louisiana. Her future is dependent on starting successfully, under the tutelage of caring and supportive people. And because their attrition rate is less than 8 percent, she will succeed in the Lafourche Parish schools. What a wonderful way to begin a career!

— Harry K. Wong and Rosemary T. Wong

What Matters Most is built on three simple premises:

1. What teachers know and can do is the most important influence on what students learn.
2. **Recruiting, preparing, and retaining good teachers is the central strategy for improving our schools.**
3. School reform cannot succeed unless it focuses on creating the conditions in which teachers can teach and teach well.

It's no surprise that this is a major finding of the report:

Studies have shown that *teacher expertise* **is the single most important factor in determining student achievement** and fully trained teachers are far more effective with students than those who are not prepared.[3]

If the United States is to address the burgeoning teacher shortage and distribution crisis with more than just "warm bodies," **induction must become a top priority** for school districts, state education agencies, and the nation as a whole.[4]

The United States government legislation **No Child Left Behind Act** holds firm to the belief that it is the teacher that makes a difference in the classroom. Over **3 billion dollars** have been targeted for increasing student academic achievement through strategies such as these:

1. Improving teacher and principal quality
2. **Increasing the number of highly qualified teachers**
3. Increasing the number of highly qualified principals and assistant principals in schools

This $3,000,000,000 is a large (35 percent) increase in Federal funds to help states and local schools train, recruit, and retain highly qualified teachers.[6]

What are you waiting for?

According to the National Commission on Teaching and America's Future,

"On the whole, the school reform movement has ignored the obvious. What teachers know and can do makes the crucial difference in what children learn. And the ways school systems organize their work makes a big difference in what teachers can accomplish. New courses, tests, and curriculum reforms can be important starting points, but they are meaningless if teachers cannot use them well.

"Policies can improve schools only if the people in them are armed with the knowledge, skills, and supports they need. **Student learning in this country will improve only when we focus our efforts on improving teaching.**"[5]

> "I know of no adults who owe their successes to the efficacy of a textbook, but of many who owe their successes to the influence of a teacher."[7]

The time has come to do just that—to focus our efforts on improving teaching. And where better to begin than with investing in structured induction programs for the 2 million new teachers who will be entering our schools over the next few years and who will be influencing the lives of countless children?

Our future lies in the hands of these children. And their education lies in the hands of their teachers. Let us do our utmost to ensure that all of these teachers are capable, caring, qualified individuals.

Our children deserve no less.

An Investment in Our Future

Summary and Implementation

Planting the Seeds
Information We've Shared

- Inadequate induction for beginning teachers is a major flaw plaguing our public schools.
- What teachers know and can do is the most important influence on what students learn.
- The only way to improve our schools is by training, supporting, and retaining effective teachers for our classrooms.

Nurturing Growth
What You Can Do to Make a Difference

- If you are serious about improving teaching and learning in your schools or district, make induction a top priority.
- If you are already realizing the benefits of an induction program, read on. The Epilogue will take you "beyond induction."

Reaping the Harvest
Benefits to Your School System

- When teachers are trained and supported, they succeed and stay.
- When teachers succeed and stay, students achieve.

epilogue

Beyond Induction

Only those who risk going too far can possibly find out how far one can go.

— T. S. Eliot

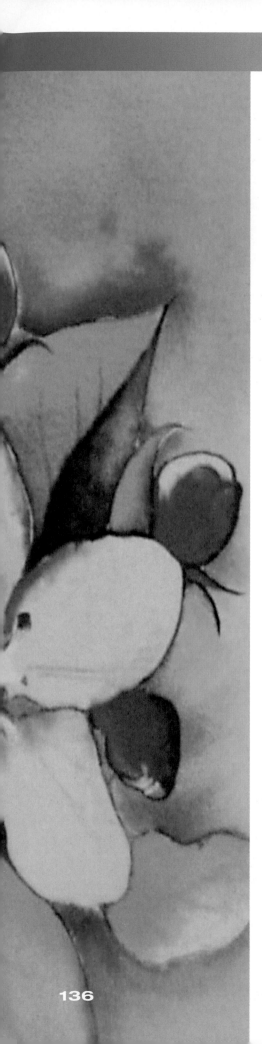

Sources and Notes for the Epilogue

[1]Saphier, Jon, S. Freedman, and B. Aschheim. (2001). *Beyond Mentoring: How to Nurture, Support, and Retain New Teachers.* Newton, MA: Teachers 21.

[2]Portner, Hal. (2001). *Training Mentors Is Not Enough.* Thousand Oaks, CA: Corwin Press.

[3]Garet, Michael, Andrew Porter, Laura Desmoine, Beatrice Birman, and Kwang Suk Yoon. (Winter 2002). "What Makes Professional Development Effective?" *American Educational Research Journal,* pp. 915-946.

[4]Hiebert, James, Ronald Gallimore, and James W. Stigler. (June/July 2002). "A Knowledge Base for the Teaching Profession: What Would It Look Like and How Can We Get One?" *Educational Researcher,* pp. 3-15.

[5]Stigler, James W. and James Hiebert. (1999). *The Teaching Gap.* New York, NY: The Free Press.

[6]Wong, Harry K. (2002). "Induction: The Best Form of Professional Development." *Educational Leadership,* pp. 52-54.

Our Responsibility to the Next Generation of Teachers

This book has been about those educators who have gone beyond mentoring. Books by Jon Saphier[1] and Hal Portner[2] suggest in their titles that mentoring is not enough to ensure effective teachers for our children. We now have a new group of cutting edge educational leaders who are going **beyond** new teacher induction!

❏ Steve Zickafoose, director of Florida's **Manatee County Public Schools** New Teacher Induction Program, is planning a complete Professional Development Framework that will encompass substitute teachers, teacher aides, induction teachers, and all teachers, continuing up to and beyond instructional leadership with the site principal.

❏ **The Medford Public Schools** in Oregon supplements its new teacher induction program with a 95 page "Staff Development Handbook" listing over 80 class offerings for all teachers who want to grow professionally. They have very few teacher openings each year.

❏ **The Flowing Wells Schools** in Arizona organizes its staff development process under the banner, "The Institute for New Teacher Induction and Veteran Teacher Renewal." The new teacher induction program is a highly organized five-year process that takes new teachers through five stages: novice, advanced beginner, competent teacher, proficient teacher, and expert. Like Medford, they have an extensive array of professional development classes for veteran teacher renewal listed in a booklet "The Science and Art of Teaching."

❏ **The Lafourche Parish Schools** in Louisiana have a three-year induction process for brand new teachers, an induction process for teachers new to the district, on-site curriculum facilitators to provide ongoing, systematic staff development for all teachers, and an upcoming induction process for aspiring administrators. The district also has a program, in conjunction with the local university, for certifying non-certified teachers. Teachers at all levels of development have access to a variety of professional development opportunities. The district's new teacher induction program has been so successful in supporting, training, and retaining new teachers that it has been adopted by the Louisiana Department of Education as a model for every school district in Louisiana.

❏ **The Community Consolidated Schools** in Illinois have a mandatory four-year induction program with a strong mentoring component that helps prepare new teachers for national board certification.

❏ **The Islip Public Schools** in New York recognize that induction is the best form of professional development. This is where new teachers acquire the habits of lifelong learning and leadership. The Islip induction program aligns itself with the six features of effective professional development, sometimes referred to as the Eisenhower Features, as reported by the American Educational Research Association. (See page 100.) To implement these features, the induction program provides essential skills at monthly meetings through study group workshops, collegial circles, teacher networks, and focus groups to foster a sense of community among the staff. The best opportunity for personal and professional growth is through collective participation.

Thus, the goal of the induction program is to promote an atmosphere where continued lifelong learning is the norm.

❏ **The Louisiana Principal Internship Program**, a mandatory two-year induction program, has expanded so that much of the program exists as a virtual network where principals can work on online modules and stay in direct contact with their peers throughout the state.

Although each of the above induction programs is different, they all have one obvious, fundamental goal: **Student achievement!** The hallmark of a successful induction program is

Student Success and Achievement.

Successful induction programs are driven by the knowledge that **it is the teacher who holds the key to student achievement**—much more so than time, creative scheduling, class sizes, technology, the parents, vouchers, or any of the other myriad of reform philosophies, programs, or faddish agendas.

To attract and retain effective teachers, a district must fund and support a comprehensive, sustained, and organized new teacher induction program.

Successful induction programs base their organization on significant research. A study in the *American Educational Research Journal* reported the six features of how teachers learn best. Three of them are presented here:

Form: Teachers learn best in teacher networks or study groups, not in traditional classes, workshops or through mentoring.

Duration: Longer, sustained, and intensive professional development programs are more likely to make an impact than shorter ones.

Active learning: Teachers learn through observing, being observed, teaching, planning for classroom implementation, reviewing student work, and presenting, leading, and writing.[3]

What the teacher knows and can do is the most significant factor influencing student achievement.

Implications of the Research

The research presented in this book substantiates what many staff developers know. One-shot workshops, one-day inservice meetings, and indiscriminate mentoring are not effective. So, what's effective?

**Structured, sustained, intensive
professional development programs
that allow new teachers
to observe others, to be observed by others,
and to be part of networks or study groups
where all teachers
share with each other and
learn to respect each other's work.**

Research consistently supports the need for systematic induction of new teachers and the ongoing professional development of all teachers. James Hiebert, Ronald Gallimore, and James Stigler, who write about building and sustaining a professional knowledge base for teaching in *Educational Researcher*, state the following:

"There is a growing consensus that professional development yields the best result when it is long-term, school-based, collaborative, focused on students' learning, and linked to curricula."[4]

For this to happen, it is imperative that ALL new teachers participate in a structured and sustained induction process. The benefits to our new teachers, their school districts, and their students will be immeasurable.

James W. Stigler and James Hiebert write in *The Teaching Gap* that teaching is the one process in the educational system that is designed specifically to facilitate students' learning. Yet, this is the staggering reality:

The most alarming aspect of classroom
teaching in the United States
is not how we are teaching now, but that we have
no mechanism for getting better.[5]

But, we do have a mechanism for improving the quality of teachers—Organized, Sustained Professional Development.[6] The roles and decision making capabilities of the staff developers, the administrators, and the school boards are of paramount importance in controlling the quality of the teachers produced by the system.

If your desired outcome is student achievement and if your desired outcome is a quality teaching force—as the two go hand-in-hand—then the conditions and structures that provide for an intensive and sustained induction process must become a priority in the budgets and policies of school board members, policy makers, and school leaders for one singular reason:

**The student's success and achievement
are first and foremost,
now and always.**

References

So often the last section of a book is called the "appendix." Although this is the correct term to use, it is also the term used to describe a part of the human anatomy that is a vestigial organ, an organ that is degenerate and has no useful known function!

The items in this section are not degenerate; rather they are true references and a very important, integral part of this book. We urge you to study them either independently or in conjunction with the chapters and page numbers referenced.

Listing of Reference Items

Reference Location	Item and Description	Correlation
one **Page 142**	**"Beginning Teacher Induction"** Eileen Mary Weiss and Stephen Gary Weiss. (1999). ERIC Clearinghouse on Teaching and Teacher Education. Washington, DC. (ED436487) This document contains everything you want to know about just how little support schools and schools districts typically provide for the beginning teacher.	**Chapter 1** **Page 11**
two **Page 146**	**"Induction: The Best Form of Professional Development"** Harry K. Wong. (March 2002). *Educational Leadership*, pp. 52-54. The theme of the issue was "Redefining Professional Development." This article contends that to redefine professional development, a structured induction process, not mentoring, is the best form of sustained, professional development.	**Chapter 3** **Page 33**
three **Page 150**	**"Teacher Mentoring: A Critical Review"** Sharon Feiman-Nemser. (July 1996). ERIC Clearinghouse on Teaching and Teacher Education. Washington, DC. (ED397060) This article documents why giving a teacher only a mentor does not work.	**Chapter 4** **Page 57**
four **Page 154**	**Lafourche Parish Schools Three-Year Induction Structure** Induction is an organized, structured, comprehensive process of preparing and retaining effective new teachers. The structure of the three-year process may be found here. The Lafourche Parish induction model has proven so successful that Louisiana has adopted it for the entire state. The state model can be accessed at www.doe.state.la.us/DOE/OQE/certification/La_First_r1.pdf or www.doe.state.la.us and click on Louisiana First under Mentor.	**Chapter 5** **Page 79**

Reference Location	Item and Description	Correlation
five Page 169	**Flowing Wells School District Information Packet** The new teacher induction program of the Flowing Wells Schools has been in existence since the early 80s. Theirs is a five-year to lifelong plan designed to produce expert teachers. Their results have been nothing short of phenomenal. Flowing Wells has received so many requests for information that they have prepared a packet. Their packet, *Induction: The Engine That Drives Effective Staff Development and Mentoring*, is shared with you in this Reference section.	**Chapter 5** **Page 85**
six Page 200	**Homewood-Flossmoor New Teacher Induction Program** Homewood-Flossmoor High School is a three-time recipient of the *National Blue Ribbon School of Excellence Award*. To insure that their culture of excellence is nourished and disseminated, they utilize an outstanding new teacher induction program to acculturate their newly hired teachers. Patterned after a technique of using "Aha Notes," teachers are presented information and they are encouraged to reflect and crystallize moments of "Ahas," which can then be implemented. Anyone walking through this Flossmoor, Illinois, high school will immediately know that there is a learning community and a culture in existence.	**Chapter 6** **Page 105**
seven Page 216	**Stanislaus County Retention Data Table** Stanislaus County, two hours west of San Francisco, is one of the many units of the California Beginning Teacher Support and Assessment (BTSA) program. Their retention rate has been 95 percent with 409 of 431 teachers still teaching. The data can be seen in this graphic.	**Chapter 6** **Page 106**
eight Page 217	**"Play for Keeps"** Harry K. Wong. (September 2002). *Principal Leadership*, pp. 55-58. The theme for the journal of the National Association of Secondary Principals was "Hiring and Keeping Quality Teachers." This article provides evidence that a strong induction program helps teachers acclimate and continue to learn and helps principals keep the teachers they hire.	**Chapter 7** **Page 123**

ERIC 📖 Digests

ERIC Identifier: ED436487
Publication Date: 1999-11-00
Author: Weiss, Eileen Mary - Weiss, Stephen Gary
Source: ERIC Clearinghouse on Teaching and Teacher Education Washington DC.

Beginning Teacher Induction. ERIC Digest.

THIS DIGEST WAS CREATED BY ERIC, THE EDUCATIONAL RESOURCES INFORMATION CENTER. FOR MORE INFORMATION ABOUT ERIC, CONTACT ACCESS ERIC 1-800-LET-ERIC

Over two million new K-12 teachers will be employed in the U.S. over the next decade due to increased student enrollments, reductions in class size, and accelerating retirements among an aging teacher population (Darling-Hammond, 1997). More than one- third of these new teachers will be hired in low wealth urban and rural school districts, and the majority of these in center city public schools with minority student enrollments of at least 20% (Recruiting New Teachers, Inc., 1999). This large population of new teachers will be challenged to educate diverse learners in an increasingly complex knowledge-based, technology-oriented society.

Unfortunately, first-year teachers are frequently left in a "sink or swim" position with little support from colleagues and few opportunities for professional development (Darling-Hammond & Sclan, 1996). Well-organized induction programs are the exception rather than the rule, and informal, haphazard induction experiences have been associated with higher levels of attrition as well as lower levels of teacher effectiveness (National Commission on Teaching and America's Future, 1996). Current estimates are that more than 20% of public school teachers leave their positions within three years and 9.3% quit before finishing their first year (Recruiting New Teachers, Inc., 1999).

Recruiting New Teachers, Inc. (1999) reports that a growing number of low wealth urban districts with acute shortages are turning toward induction programs to keep new teachers from leaving. Urban districts reported a 93% retention rate for teachers who participated in such programs. Despite the positive impact of induction programs on retention rates, there has been little sustained commitment in recent years to permanently institute teacher induction programs as part of a formal entry process into the field (National Commission on Teaching & America's Future, 1996).

TEACHER INDUCTION PROGRAMS: CURRENT DESIGN

Numerous studies document the value of teacher induction programs and describe multiple prototypes for implementation. The benefits of the programs include not only reduced attrition rates among new teachers, but also improved teaching capabilities. The availability of formal induction programs and their structures vary among states and local school districts.

The number of state and local school districts that have created programs for beginning teachers has grown substantially since the early 1980s, but the nature of those programs vary by state and district (Sclan and Darling-Hammond, 1992). According to NASDTEC data, in 1984 only eight states reported initiating, approving or implementing teacher induction programs; that number rose to 31 states in 1991 (Gold, 1996) but currently stands at 26 states and the District of Columbia (Andrews & Andrews, 1998). Many states eliminated programs due to reduced or restricted funding.

Within the states that have created programs for beginning teachers, local school districts are not always required to offer the programs, nor are all teachers required to participate. In 1998-99, local district participation was discretionary in eight states and beginning teacher attendance was voluntary in five states. In New Jersey participation was discretionary for districts, but all beginning teachers were required to participate in the districts where programs were offered. In Washington, participation is voluntary for districts, and those districts offering programs can decide if all teachers are required to participate. New Hampshire and California induction programs currently reach only 30% of their beginning teachers. However, California reports plans to phase in beginning teacher support for all new teachers (Andrews & Andrews, 1998). Nationally, 55% of public school teachers with less than five years of teaching recently reported having participated in some kind of formal induction program (Darling-Hammond, 1997).

Funding levels also vary strikingly among states, from $17.5 million in California to $20,000 in Mississippi and New Hampshire. Washington state's funding pattern is subject to change with each legislative session (Andrews & Andrews, 1998). In states where induction program design was left to the localities, little support was given to the programs and fewer teachers had access to them (Hirsch, et al., 1998).

The structure of teacher induction programs and their underlying conceptualization of teaching differ among districts. Some induction programs are based upon "effective teaching" criteria relating to direct instruction for mastering skills and academic content as measured by students' achievement on standardized tests. Other programs underscore the complexities of teaching and the need for dynamic, regenerative school environments that rely on a broad base of knowledge to inform teachers' behavior (Weiss & Weiss, 1998). States such as Connecticut, California, Massachusetts, Minnesota, and Vermont as well as National Education Association and American Federation of Teacher local chapters in districts such as Toledo, Cincinnati, Columbus, Rochester, and Seattle (National Commission on Teaching and America's Future, 1996) have adopted "constructivist" approaches that expect teachers to practice reflective and collaborative action, which engender a wide repertoire of techniques to respond to student needs (Sclan & Darling-Hammond, 1992).

Since the mid-1980s, induction programs have increasingly provided assistance to new teachers by assigning them to mentors: veteran teachers help beginners learn the philosophy, cultural values and established sets of behaviors expected by the schools where they are employed (Little, 1990; Recruiting New Teachers, Inc., 1999). Some new teachers receive regular coaching and opportunities for collaboration, while others see their mentors sporadically. In the California New Teacher Project, the "intensity of the support and instruction...did differ across projects and had an impact on new teachers' perceptions of teaching and their performance in the classroom" (Gold, 1996). Not only the frequency, but the quality of support is important for beginning teacher success; less than one-quarter of the programs (6 of the 27) reported some kind of training for the support team in 1998. North Carolina is the only state that requires mentor teachers to hold a mentor license (Andrews & Andrews, 1998).

Successful mentor programs are dependent upon the quality of training afforded the mentors (Feiman-Nemser, 1996; Ganser, 1996; Ganser & Koskela, 1997). Research indicates that beginning teachers who are mentored are more effective teachers in their early years, since they learn from guided practice rather than depending upon trial-and-error alone. Mentored novice teachers tend to focus on student learning sooner and leave teaching at a lower rate (National Commission on Teaching and America's Future, 1996).

TEACHER INDUCTION PROGRAMS: FUTURE DEVELOPMENT

There has been limited agreement in the profession about what new teachers should know and be able to do and what constitutes the best learning environments; it is no wonder that induction programs are divergent. A consensus slowly is emerging about beginning teachers needing to meet standards for practice that will attest to their grasp of essential skills, knowledge and dispositions (INTASC, 1992; National Commission on Teaching & America's Future, 1996). Performance-based licensing standards for new teachers, informed by research and tested in practice, have been developed by the Interstate New Teacher Assessment and Consortium (INTASC, 1992). The INTASC standards provide an overall framework for documenting accomplishments across the domains of teaching and may be useful for communicating expectations for new teachers' behavior, structuring induction experiences, and evaluating professional development.

A growing number of school systems are working with colleges to create learner-centered environments, such as Professional Development Schools (PDSs), in which reflective practice and teacher decision-making are part of a school culture where new teachers are naturally expected to collaborate with more experienced university- and school-based colleagues (Levine & Trachtman, 1997). The PDS movement has led to an attitudinal shift away from the concept of mentor as veteran whose unidirectional role is to impart basic knowledge to an unknowing novice, towards that of an experienced co-worker who, in a relationship of mutuality with new colleagues, offers assistance and also learns from the experience. The former concept implicitly stresses the differences and distances between trainer and trainee; the latter concept accentuates the connectedness among teachers even at different career stages. In a collaborative culture, new and experienced teachers who communicate ideas and work together on real problems put their collective knowledge base into action and experience the reciprocal relationship between theory and practice. This model of teacher induction has the potential to influence both members of the mentoring relationship: the veteran also may learn from the novice. New teachers who spend their first year in collaborative school environments are likely to have higher morale, be more committed to teaching, and plan to remain in the profession (Weiss, in press).

CONCLUSIONS

New teachers, who have an inordinate rate of attrition and are assigned to the neediest students in schools with the least resources, will comprise the large majority of the teaching force within the next decade. Although shown to be valuable, induction programs that include sustained feedback in collaborative environments remain a rare experience for most beginning teachers. Thus far, teacher induction has been a variegated landscape of policies and programs.

REFERENCES

Andrews, T. E., & Andrews, L. (Eds.) (1998). The NASDTEC Manual 1998-1999. Manual on the Preparation and Certification of Educational Personnel. Dubuque, IA: Kendall/Hunt.

Darling-Hammond, L. (1997). Doing what matters most: Investing in quality teaching. New York: National Commission on Teaching & America's Future.

Darling-Hammond, L., & Sclan, E. M. (1996). Who teaches and why. Dilemmas of building a profession for twenty-first century schools. In Handbook of Research on Teacher Education, second edition, J. Sikula, T. J. Buttery, & E. Guyton (Eds.), pp. 67- 101. New York: Macmillan.

Feiman-Nemser, S. (1996). Teacher mentoring: A critical review. Washington, DC: ERIC DIGEST, ERIC Clearinghouse on Teaching and Teacher Education, AACTE.

Ganser, T. (1996). Mentor roles: Views of participants in a state-mandated program. Mid-Western Educational Researcher, 9, (2), pp. 15-20.

Ganser, T., & Koskela, R. (1997). A comparison of six Wisconsin mentoring programs for beginning teachers. NASSP Bulletin, (81), 591, pp. 71-80.

Gold, Y. (1996). Beginning teacher support. Attrition, mentoring, and induction. In C. B. Courtney (Ed.) Review of Research in Education, 16, pp. 548-594. Washington, DC: American Educational Research Association.

http://www.ed.gov/databases/ERIC_Digests/ed436487.html

Heck, R., & Wolcott, L. P. (1997). Beginning teachers: A statewide study of factors explaining successful completion of the probationary period. Educational Policy, (11), 1, p. 111-133.

Hirsch, E., Koppich, J. E., & Knapp, M. S. (1998). What states are doing to improve the quality of teaching. A brief review of current patterns and trends. A CTP Working Paper. Seattle, WA: Center for the Study of Teaching and Policy.

Interstate New Teacher Assessment and Support Consortium (INTASC) (1992). Model standards for beginning teacher licensing and development: A resource for state dialogue. Washington, DC: Council for Chief State School Officers.

Levine, M. & Trachtman, R., eds. (1997). Making Professional Development Schools Work: Politics, Practice, and Policy. New York: Teachers College Press.

Little, J. W. (1990). The mentor phenomenon and the social organization of teaching. In C. B. Courtney (Ed.) Review of Research in Education, 16, pp. 297-35. Washington, DC: American Educational Research Association.

National Commission on Teaching and America's Future (1996). What matters most: Teaching for America's Future. New York: Author, Teachers College Columbia University.

Perez, K., Swain, C. , & Hartsough, C. S. (1997). An analysis of practices used to support new teachers. Teacher Education Quarterly, Spring, pp. 41-52.

Recruiting New Teachers, Inc. (1999). Learning the ropes: Urban teacher induction programs and practices in the United States. Belmont, MA.

Robinson, G. W. (1998). New teacher induction: A study of selected new teacher induction models and common practices. Paper presented at the Annual Meeting of the Midwestern Educational Research Association, Chicago.

Sclan, E. M., & Darling-Hammond, L. (1992). Beginning teacher performance evaluation: An overview of state policies. Trends and Issues Paper No. 7. Washington, DC: ERIC Clearinghouse on Teacher Education. American Association of Colleges for Teacher Education.

Weiss, E. M. (in press) Perceived workplace conditions and first-year teachers' morale, commitment, and planned retention: A Secondary Analysis. Journal of Teaching and Teacher Education.

Weiss, E.M., & Weiss, S.G. (1998). New directions in teacher evaluation. Washington, DC: ERIC DIGEST, ERIC Clearinghouse on Teaching and Teacher Education, AACTE.

Wise, A., Darling-Hammond, L., and Berry, B. (1987). Effective Teacher Selection: From Recruitment to Retention. Santa Monica CA: RAND.

This project has been funded at least in part with Federal funds from the U.S. Department of Education, Office of Educational Research and Improvement, under contract number ED-99-CO-0007. The content of this publication does not necessarily reflect the views of or policies of the U.S. Department of Education nor does mention of trade names, commercial products, or organizations imply endorsement by the U.S. Government.

EDUCATIONAL LEADERSHIP

Volume **59** Number **6**
March 2002
Pages 52-55

Redesigning Professional Development

Induction: The Best Form of Professional Development

Harry K. Wong

New teachers need more than mentors; they need induction programs that acculturate them to the school and equip them for the classroom.

You don't wait until after school begins and new teachers are in trouble to start a professional development program. Instead, you create a culture of professional growth and lifelong learning before beginning teachers ever see their first class. The best way to support, develop, and cultivate an attitude of lifelong learning in beginning teachers is through a new teacher induction program focused on teacher training, support, and retention.

What makes a successful induction program? The best programs kick off with four or five days of workshops before school begins. They offer new teachers systematic training over two or three years. They have administrative support. They integrate a mentoring component and a structure for modeling effective teaching during inservice and mentoring experiences. They also include opportunities for inductees to visit demonstration classrooms.

Although induction programs differ from school district to school district, they share certain characteristics. For example, all successful induction programs help new teachers establish effective classroom management procedures, routines, and instructional practices. They help develop teachers' sensitivity to and understanding of the community, as well as their passion for lifelong learning and professional growth. Successful programs also promote unity and teamwork among the entire learning community.

If we hope to redesign professional development, we must go beyond mentoring to comprehensive induction programs. You don't prepare lifelong learners—much less leaders—simply by giving them a mentor to call when they are in trouble. Induction includes all the activities that train and support new teachers, and it acculturates them to the mission and philosophy of their school and district. And the good news is that teachers stay where they feel successful, supported, and part of a team working toward the achievement of common goals.

Exemplary Induction Programs

Flowing Wells School District Tucson, Arizona

More than 6,000 students attend the Flowing Wells School District's six elementary schools, junior high school, and high school on the northwest side of Tucson, Arizona. Despite the community's lower-middle-income status, the district has produced 12 Arizona teachers of the year. Since the early 1980s, the five-year Flowing Wells induction program, directed by Susie Heintz, has taken teachers through five stages: novice, advanced beginner, competent teacher, proficient teacher, and expert.

http://www.ascd.org/author/el/2002/03march/wong.html

The induction program kicks off with several days of activities for novice teachers before the beginning of the school year. Induction activities include

- A bus tour—The district superintendent acts as a tour guide on a chartered bus trip through the school district. A trivia contest introduces new teachers to the district's culture. For example, one question asks, How did the Flowing Wells School District get its name? (In 1881, the Allison brothers discovered water at the base of Sentinel Park.)

- Demonstration classrooms—Master teachers set up their rooms to model the first day of school in an effective classroom. Afterward, observers can discuss with the master teacher the strategies that the new teachers found useful.

- A SPA (Special Professional Assistance) Day with a mentor—New teachers and their mentors observe each other teach. After observations, mentors and protégés have lunch together.

- A graduation luncheon—At the end of several days of new teacher induction activities, Flowing Wells honors new teachers with a graduation celebration in a beautifully decorated boardroom. Induction graduates sit with their principals and district administrators and enjoy a formal, candlelit luncheon. The superintendent presents framed certificates to the graduates.

Toby Gregory, who teaches at Flowing Wells High School, says that after induction he was

> so excited to be an English teacher that I went in [to the classroom], started with a few procedures, and then went right into teaching English, which is what I had been waiting to do.

The Flowing Wells induction process is so successful that educators from around the country come to the district to attend an annual workshop to learn how to implement such a program in their own districts.

Lafourche Parish Public Schools Thibodaux, Louisiana

If you dare to teach, you must never cease to learn. Lafourche Parish, located southwest of New Orleans along the banks of the Bayou Lafourche, educates 15,200 students—72 percent white and 28 percent nonwhite—in 30 schools. Trainers for the Lafourche Parish Public Schools induction program strive to immerse new teachers in the district's lifelong learning culture and help them become part of a cohesive, supportive instructional team. The program has become an important teacher recruitment tool for the district.

The Lafourche Parish program begins with a highly structured four-day training session for all new teachers before school begins and includes three years of ongoing training and support. Three district-level curriculum coordinators oversee the entire program and provide all the training to the new teachers, principals, curriculum facilitators, and mentors. Lafourche Parish also offers demonstration classrooms and a graduation ceremony at which new teachers receive certificates of achievement along with hugs and words of encouragement from master teachers. Additional induction offerings include

- Monthly support group meetings—At district and school-site meetings, new teachers can discuss their concerns, challenges, and successes and receive ongoing guidance and support.

- Curriculum facilitators—In addition to mentors, both new and veteran teachers have daily access to on-site curriculum facilitators. These master teachers provide ongoing support, teach demonstration lessons, conduct informal teacher observations, and offer constructive suggestions for improvement.

One result of the district's emphasis on new teacher induction is the overwhelming enthusiasm of new teachers, mentors, school and district administrators, school board members, and the community. New teachers use a variety of effective teaching techniques that they learn in the district's induction program, which is very different from the old lecture-and-endless-worksheets approach. Principals say that induction-trained teachers are much more classroom-ready from day one. A telling statistic: More than 99 percent of new teachers who have participated in the district's induction program have successfully completed the performance-based Louisiana Teacher Assistance and Assessment Program, required for teacher certification in the state.

Another outgrowth of the induction program is a drop in the teacher attrition rate. Before implementing the program in 1996, Lafourche Parish had a 51 percent annual teacher attrition rate. That rate decreased to 15 percent almost immediately upon implementting the program. Today, the district's teacher attrition hovers around 7 percent—a decrease of approximately 80 percent since the inception of the induction program. In fact, the Lafourche Parish induction program is so successful that Louisiana has adopted it as the statewide model for all school districts.[1]

Port Huron Area Schools Port Huron, Michigan

The Port Huron Area School District serves 11,850 students in 13 elementary schools, 4 middle schools, and 2 high schools. Port Huron personnel developed the district's induction program in conjunction with the Port Huron Education Association, the area teachers' union. The joint work of the education association and school district administrators models teamwork as a way of achieving mutually desired goals.

Cathy Lozen, director of Port Huron's new teacher induction program for 10 years, says,

> One-shot staff development meetings do not work. We wanted a sustained training program, one where we could keep new teachers close to us for a year, nurture them, and take them step-by-step through the year—and beyond. Then they'd have a really solid foundation about the district, about teaching, and about our expectations. We're kind of a "no excuses" district; the job of the teacher is to help all students succeed.

The program begins with a four-day orientation before the beginning of the school year that includes workshops introducing new teachers to district departments and programs, principles of classroom management, professional standards and expectations, and effective preparation for the first day and week of school. The induction program continues with monthly seminars during the teachers' first year. In addition, the Port Huron Education Association appoints support or mentor teachers for every newly hired teacher.

Describing the results of the induction workshops, Lozen said, "We became a cohesive and caring group in four days. We all bonded, and our district is truly better for it. What a feeling!"

The district's induction program has reaped additional unforeseen benefits. William Kimball, responsible for initiating the program, became the superintendent of Port Huron in 1998. Commenting on the induction program, he said,

> After seven years, there were more induction-bred teachers than veteran teachers in our system, and you can see it today by the change in our culture.

http://www.ascd.org/author/el/2002/03march/wong.html

Treating New Teachers with Dignity

Annette L. Breaux, director of the Lafourche Parish new teacher induction program, writes

- Every child—and every new teacher—should be treated with dignity and respect.

- Every child—and every new teacher—can learn and succeed.

- Every new teacher is a human resource, a person who has invested years in preparing for a life dedicated to helping young people; we have a responsibility to ensure that these new teachers will learn and succeed, just as we have a responsibility to ensure that every child will learn and succeed.

- New teachers must be trained if we want them to succeed; it is much better to train new teachers and risk losing them than not to train them and risk keeping them.

- An induction process is the best way to send a message to your teachers that you value them and want them to succeed and stay.[2]

If we want quality teachers in our classrooms, we must make new teacher training, support, and retention top priorities. School districts that develop and implement new teacher induction programs send a message to teachers that the district values them, wants them to excel, and hopes they will stay.

Endnotes

[1] Information on Louisiana's induction program is available at www.doe.state.la.us/DOE/OQE/ certification/LaFirst_r1.pdf.

[2] Breaux, A. L., & Wong, H. K. (2002). *New teacher induction: How to train, support, and retain new teachers* (p. i). Mountain View, CA: Harry K. Wong.

Copyright © 2002 Harry K. Wong.

Harry K. Wong is a former high school science teacher. He is an education consultant and author of *The First Days of School: How to Be an Effective Teacher* (Harry K. Wong, 1998); harrykrose@aol.com .

ERIC **Digests**

ERIC Identifier: ED397060
Publication Date: 1996-07-00
Author: Feiman-Nemser, Sharon
Source: ERIC Clearinghouse on Teaching and Teacher Education Washington DC.

Teacher Mentoring: A Critical Review. ERIC Digest.

THIS DIGEST WAS CREATED BY ERIC, THE EDUCATIONAL RESOURCES INFORMATION CENTER. FOR MORE INFORMATION ABOUT ERIC, CONTACT ACCESS ERIC 1-800-LET-ERIC

Mentoring is a critical topic in education today and a favored strategy in U.S. policy initiatives focused on teacher induction. Besides creating new career opportunities for veteran teachers, assigning mentors to work with beginning teachers represents an improvement over the abrupt and unassisted entry into teaching that characterizes the experience of many novices. Still, the promise of mentoring goes beyond helping novices survive their first year of teaching. If mentoring is to function as a strategy of reform, it must be linked to a vision of good teaching, guided by an understanding of teacher learning, and supported by a professional culture that favors collaboration and inquiry. This Digest examines the spread of mentoring in the United States, obstacles to realizing the potential of mentoring as a vehicle of reform, needed research, and selected issues of policy and practice.

THE SPREAD OF MENTORING

Since the early 1980s, when mentoring burst onto the educational scene as part of a broad movement aimed at improving education, policymakers and educational leaders have pinned high hopes on mentoring as a vehicle for reforming teaching and teacher education. Concerned about the rate of attrition during the first 3 years of teaching and aware of the problems faced by beginning teachers, policymakers saw the logic of providing on-site support and assistance to novices during their first year of teaching (Little, 1990). The scale of mentoring has increased rapidly, with over 30 states mandating some form of mentored support for beginning teachers.

The mentoring idea has also been extended to the preservice level. Proposals for the redesign of teacher preparation (e.g., Holmes Group, 1990) call for teacher candidates to work closely with experienced teachers in internship sites and restructured school settings such as professional development schools. The hope is that experienced teachers will serve as mentors and models, helping novices learn new pedagogies and socializing them to new professional norms. This vision of mentoring depends on school-university partnerships that support professional development for both mentors and teacher candidates.

A CAUTIONARY NOTE

Enthusiasm for mentoring has not been matched by clarity about the purposes of mentoring. Nor have claims about mentoring been subjected to rigorous empirical scrutiny. The education community understands that mentors have a positive affect on teacher retention, but that leaves open the question of what mentors should do, what they actually do, and what novices learn as a result. Just as research on student teaching highlights the conservative influence of cooperating teachers and school cultures on novices practice, so some studies show that mentors promote conventional norms and practices, thus limiting reform (e.g., Feiman-Nemser, Parker, & Zeichner, 1993).

http://www.ed.gov/databases/ERIC_Digests/ed397060.html

These findings should not surprise us. Mentor teachers have little experience with the core activities of mentoring--observing and discussing teaching with colleagues. Most teachers work alone, in the privacy of their classroom, protected by norms of autonomy and noninterference. Nor does the culture of teaching encourage distinctions among teachers based on expertise. The persistence of privacy, the lack of opportunities to observe and discuss each other's practice, and the tendency to treat all teachers as equal limits what mentors can do, even when working with novices (Little, 1990).

In addition, few mentor teachers practice the kind of conceptually oriented, learner-centered teaching advocated by reformers (Cohen, McLaughlin, & Talbert, 1993). If we want mentors to help novices learn the ways of thinking and acting associated with new kinds of teaching, then we have to place them with mentors who are already reformers in their schools and classrooms (Cochran-Smith, 1991), or develop collaborative contexts where mentors and novices can explore new approaches together.

NEEDED RESEARCH

Before 1990, the literature on mentoring consisted mainly of program descriptions, survey-based evaluations, definitions of mentoring, and general discussions of mentors roles and responsibilities. Researchers did not conceptualize mentors work in relation to novices learning or study the practice of mentoring directly. Reviewing the literature, Little (1990) found few comprehensive studies well-informed by theory and designed to examine in depth the context, content and consequences of mentoring (p. 297).

Since 1990, some researchers have begun to fill in those gaps. In one comparison of two beginning teacher programs, researchers documented striking differences in the way mentor teachers conceived of and carried out their work with novices. They linked these differences in mentors perspectives and practices to differences in role expectations, working conditions, program orientations, and mentor preparation (Feiman-Nemser & Parker, 1993). In a reform-oriented preservice program, Cochran-Smith (1991) studied the conversations of student teachers and experienced teachers in weekly, school-site meetings at four urban schools. She shows how these conversations, occasions for group mentoring, expose novices to broad themes of reform through discussions of highly contextualized problems of practice. Between 1991-95, researchers at the National Center for Research on Teacher Learning at Michigan State carried out a comparative, cross-cultural study of mentoring in selected sites in the United States, England, and China. The study sought insights about learning to teach, mentoring practices, and the conditions that enable novices and mentors to work together in productive ways. Preliminary findings underscore the influence of mentors beliefs about learning to teach, the challenges of learning to teach for understanding, and the impact of different contextual factors (e.g., school culture, national policies) on mentors practice and novices learning.

To inform mentoring policy and practice, we need more direct studies of mentoring and its affects on teaching and teacher retention, especially in urban settings where turnover is high. We also need to know more about how mentors learn to work with novices in productive ways, what structures and resources enable that work, and how mentoring fits into broader frameworks of professional development and accountability.

THORNY ISSUES OF POLICY AND PRACTICE

According to conventional wisdom, mentors should assist not assess on the grounds that novices are more likely to share problems and ask for help if mentors do not evaluate them. The issue is not so straightforward. Some state-level programs use a team approach in which mentor teachers fulfill the support function while others (e.g., a principal or professor) judge the novice's performance for purposes of employment or certification. Other programs give mentor teachers a prominent role in these gatekeeping decisions on the grounds of professionalism and accountability. Clearly different ways of resolving the assistance vs. assessment issue involve different costs and benefits for mentors and novices, for states and districts, and for the profession of teaching.

http://www.ed.gov/databases/ERIC_Digests/ed397060.html

A second issue is whether something as personal as a mentoring relationship can be formalized in a program. Should mentors be chosen or assigned? Skeptics might consider the possibility that what a novice learns from a mentor depends as much on what they do together as it does on the affective quality of their relationship (Tharp & Gallimore, l988). Still, mentoring relationships are bound to be unpredictable. Program developers may be wise to focus on creating optimal conditions rather than trying to make optimal matches (Tauer, l995).

A third issue is time--time to mentor and time to learn to mentor. Some programs hire retired teachers. Others release mentor teachers from some or all of their classroom responsibilities. Still others expect mentors to combine mentoring with full-time teaching. Besides sending different messages about the purposes of mentoring, these arrangements create different situations in which mentors can learn and apply their skills. Most mentoring programs provide some orientation or training. Common topics include clinical supervision, research on effective teaching, beginning teacher concerns, and theories of adult learning. Less common but no less important are opportunities for mentors to analyze their own beliefs about learning to teach and to articulate their practical knowledge of teaching. While training usually occurs before mentors take up their new responsibilities, mentors are more likely to develop their practice as mentors if they also have opportunities to discuss questions and problems that arise in the course of their work with novices.

SUMMARY

By promoting observation and conversation about teaching, mentoring can help teachers develop tools for continuous improvement. If learning to teach in reform-minded ways is the focus of this joint work, mentoring will also fulfill its promise as an instrument of reform. Unfortunately budget shortfalls in the l990s may be leading districts and states to eliminate mentoring programs before this possibility is realized.

REFERENCES

Cochran-Smith, M. (1991). Learning to teach against the grain. Harvard Educational Review, 61(3), 279-310. EJ432149

Cohen, D., McLaughlin, M., & Talbert, J. (1993). Teaching for understanding: Challenges for policy and practice. San Francisco: Jossey Bass.

Darling-Hammond, L., & Cobb, V. (1996). The changing context of teacher education. In F. Murray (Ed.), The teacher educator's handbook (pp. 14-64). San Francisco: Jossey Bass.

Feiman-Nemser, S., & Parker, M. B. (1993). Mentoring in context: A comparison of two U.S. programs for beginning teachers. International Journal of Educational Research, 19(8), 699-718.

Feiman-Nemser, S., Parker, M. B., & Zeichner, K. (1993). Are mentor teachers teacher educators? In D. McIntyre, H. Hagger, & M. Wilkin (Eds), Mentoring: Perspectives on school-based teacher education (pp. 147-165). London: Kogan Page (see ED 353 251).

Holmes Group. (1990). Tomorrow's schools: Principles for the design of professional development schools. East Lansing, MI: Author. (see ED 328 533).

Little, J. W. (1990). The mentor phenomenon and the social organization of teaching. In C. Cazden (Ed.), Review of research in education. Vol. 16 (pp. 297-351). Washington: DC: American Educational Research Association.

Tauer, S. (1995). The mentor-protege relationship and its impact on the experienced teacher. Unpublished doctoral dissertation, Boston University.

http://www.ed.gov/databases/ERIC_Digests/ed397060.html

Tharp, R. & Gallimore, R. (1988). Rousing minds to life. Cambridge: Cambridge University Press.

This publication was prepared with funding from the Office of Educational Research and Improvement, U.S. Department of Education, under contract number RR93002015. The opinions expressed in this report do not necessarily reflect the positions or policies of OERI or the Department.

Title: Teacher Mentoring: A Critical Review. ERIC Digest.
Document Type: Information Analyses---ERIC Information Analysis Products (IAPs) (071); Information Analyses---ERIC Digests (Selected) in Full Text (073);
Target Audience: Administrators, Teachers, Practitioners, Policymakers
Descriptors: Beginning Teachers, Educational Practices, Elementary Secondary Education, Inservice Teacher Education, Mentors, Policy Formation, Preservice Teacher Education, Professional Development Schools, Research Needs, Teacher Persistence
Identifiers: ERIC Digests, Preservice Teachers, Protege Mentor Relationship, Reform Efforts

Lafourche Parish Public Schools'

FIRST Program

Framework for Inducting, Retaining, and Supporting Teachers

Lafourche Parish Schools
Thibodaux, Louisiana

Elmo Broussard, Superintendent

Components of the FIRST Program

- An initial four days of induction before school begins
- Monthly support group meetings
- A one-day "Induction Review" in April of the first year
- A continuum of professional development through systematic training over a period of three years
- Support of school-based curriculum facilitators
- Support of district-level curriculum coordinators
- A 2-year mentoring component to the induction process
- A structure for modeling effective teaching during in-services and mentoring
- Opportunities for inductees to visit demonstration classrooms

Lafourche Parish's FIRST Program
(Framework for Inducting, Retaining, and Supporting Teachers)

Overview

The **Lafourche Parish FIRST Program** provides three years of ongoing training and support for new teachers. Participants are paid stipends to attend. *Year One* begins with four highly structured days of training in areas such as *classroom management, discipline, the first days of school, local policies/procedures, planning,* and *effective teaching.* The focus, however, remains on **classroom management.** On the fourth day, there is an awards ceremony and a luncheon where new teachers meet their mentors, principals, school board members, and supervisory staff. Then all of the participants visit actual demonstration classrooms and receive instruction from veteran teachers. This takes place before school begins. In April, there is a one-day *"Induction Review"* where additional training is provided.

Years Two and *Three* are structured to provide further training and support.

Since the inception of the program in 1996, the average attrition rate of new teachers has dropped from fifty one percent (51%) to eleven percent (11%). The bottom line is that **INDUCTION WORKS!**

Managing the Program

The district's three curriculum coordinators oversee the program. They identify participants, handle all correspondence, structure and schedule all induction activities, and provide the majority of the training. These same people also provide the district's Mentor Training and New Teacher Orientation Training to ensure a consistent message throughout all new teacher activities.

Contact Information

Superintendent, Lafourche Parish School System: Elmo Broussard

For additional information about the Lafourche Parish FIRST Program, contact:
> FIRST Coordinator: Annette Breaux
> Lafourche Parish School System
> 110 Bowie Road
> Thibodaux, LA 70301
> Phone: 985 446 1559
> Fax: 985 435 3110
> E-mail: abreaux.pac@lafourche.k12.la.us

Lafourche Parish FIRST Program

Induction Materials for Participants

During the initial induction week in August, each new teacher receives the following materials:

- A copy of *The First Days of School* by Harry and Rosemary Wong
- Classroom Supplies
- A *New Teacher Binder* which includes:
  - A letter of welcome from the superintendent
  - The district's philosophy and mission statements
  - Staff and faculty rosters for each school
  - A place for posting the school's daily schedule
  - A place for posting duty schedules
  - A guide for developing a classroom management plan
  - A place for posting classroom and/or school-wide discipline plans
  - Checklists of things that must be in place before school begins
  - Sheets for recording individual student data
  - Interest inventories for students
  - Tips for parent communication and teacher-parent relations
  - Classroom management tips
  - A success journal for teachers' daily classroom experiences

Note: The book, *The First Days of School,* is used as the training text throughout the induction years. The New Teacher Binder is used as an organizational tool for new teachers.

Lessons Taught and Modeled During Induction

- How to set up a classroom management plan
- How to structure the first day of school
- How to communicate effectively with students
- How to defuse potential discipline problems
- How to deal with negative co-workers
- How to instruct effectively
- How to treat all students with dignity
- How to relate lessons to real life
- How to use cooperative learning
- How to be proactive
- How to encourage active student participation
- How to communicate with parents effectively
- How to structure bellwork
- How to maintain a positive attitude

FIRST

(Framework for Inducting, Retaining, and Supporting Teachers)

Day 1

8:00 AM to 3:30 PM
Multi-Purpose Room
Nicholls State University

Agenda topics

8:00-8:30 AM	Welcome	Elmo Broussard
8:30-9:30 AM	Overview of Teacher Induction Program	Annette Breaux
9:30-10:00 AM	Classroom Management	Annette Breaux
10:00-10:10 AM	BREAK	
10:10-11:30 AM	Classroom Management (continued)	
11:30-12:30 PM	LUNCH	
12:30-1:30 PM	Local Policies and Procedures	Noelee Brooks
1:30-1:45 PM	BREAK	
1:45-3:15 PM	Planning	Elizabeth Yates
3:15-3:30 PM	Questions and Answers	

FIRST

(Framework for Inducting, Retaining, and Supporting Teachers)

Day 2

8:00 AM to 3:30 PM
Multi-Purpose Room
Nicholls State University

Agenda topics

8:00-9:45 AM	Bellwork/Discipline	Annette Breaux
9:45-10:00 AM	BREAK	
10:00-11:00 AM	The First Days of School	Noelee Brooks
11:00-11:30 AM	The Typical New Teacher	Annette Breaux
11:30-12:30 PM	LUNCH	
12:30-1:15 PM	Children with Special Needs	Annette Breaux
1:15-1:45 PM	Content Standards	Debbie Toups
1:45-2:00 PM	BREAK	
2:00-2:30 PM	Time Management	Annette Breaux
2:30-3:15 PM	Instructional Strategies	Elizabeth Yates
3:15-3:30 PM	Questions and Answers	

FIRST

(Framework for Inducting, Retaining, and Supporting Teachers)

Day 3

8:00 AM to 3:30 PM
Multi-Purpose Room
Nicholls State University

Agenda topics

8:00-10:00 AM	Bellwork/Individual Differences	Annette Breaux
10:00-10:15 AM	BREAK	
10:15-10:45 AM	Systematic Assessment	Debbie Toups
10:45-11:30 AM	Critical Thinking	Elizabeth Yates
11:30-12:30 PM	Lunch	
12:30-1:15 PM	Critical Thinking	Elizabeth Yates
1:15-1:45 PM	A Former New Teacher's Experiences	Second-Year Teacher
1:45-2:00 PM	BREAK	
2:00-2:30 PM	Parental Involvement	Annette Breaux
2:30-3:15 PM	Effective Teaching	Annette Breaux
3:15-3:30 PM	Questions and Answers	

Agenda

FIRST
(Framework for Inducting, Retaining, and Supporting Teachers)

Day 4

8:00 AM to 3:30 PM
Multi-Purpose Room
Nicholls State University

Agenda topics

Time	Topic	Presenter
8:00-9:00 AM	Bellwork Activity	Annette Breaux
9:00-9:30 AM	Group Activity (All We've Learned)	Annette Breaux
9:30-9:45 AM	BREAK	
9:45-10:30 AM	Authentic Assessment	Debbie Toups
10:30-11:15 AM	Awards Ceremony/Evaluation	Annette, Liz, and Debbie
11:30-1:00 PM	LUNCH WITH STAFF	
1:00-3:30 PM	Demonstration Classroom Visits	

On the afternoon of the fourth day, new teachers will visit demonstration classrooms at their respective grade levels and will meet with the teachers of those particular classrooms to receive instruction and advice about room preparation and first-day activities.

AGENDA
(New Teacher Induction Review Day in April)

Welcome	Annette Breaux	8:30 a.m.
Activity (Race to Effective Teaching)	Debbie Toups	8:45 a.m.
Group Activity (Teacher Effectiveness)	Debbie Toups Liz Yates	8:55 a.m.
BREAK		10:00 a.m.
Results of "Race"	Liz	10:15 a.m.
Coordinator Observations	Annette, Liz, and Debbie	10:20 a.m.
LUNCH		11:30 a.m.
Total Lesson Design	Liz	12:30 p.m.
Discipline	Annette	1:30 p.m.
BREAK		2:20 p.m.
Unanswered Questions	Annette, Liz, and Debbie	2:30 p.m.
Closing/Evaluations	Annette	3:00 p.m.

Agenda

F.I.R.S.T.
(Framework for Inducting, Retaining, and Supporting Teachers)
YEAR TWO
First Meeting

8:30 AM to 11:30 AM

September

Agenda topics

Time	Topic	Presenter
8:30-8:40 AM	Introduction	Annette Breaux
8:40-9:25 AM	Classroom Management	Annette Breaux
9:25-9:55 AM	Case Studies	Liz Yates
9:55-10:05 AM	BREAK	
10:05-10:35 AM	Effective Teaching	Liz Yates
10:35-11:05 AM	New Teacher Concerns	Annette and Liz
11:05-11:15 AM	Closing Activity	Annette Breaux
11:15-11:30 AM	Evaluations	

Agenda

F.I.R.S.T.
(Framework for Inducting, Retaining, and Supporting Teachers)
YEAR TWO
Second Meeting

4:30 PM to 7:30 PM

November

Agenda topics

4:30-4:40 PM	Introduction	Annette Breaux
4:40-5:25 PM	Phases of Teaching Authentic Assessment	Annette Breaux
5:25-5:55 PM	Case Studies	Liz Yates
5:55-6:05 PM	BREAK	
6:05-6:35 PM	Preparing for High Stakes Testing	Liz Yates
6:35-7:05 PM	New Teacher Concerns/Classroom Experiences	Annette and Liz
7:05-7:15 PM	Closing Activity	Annette and Liz
7:15-7:30 PM	Evaluations	

Agenda

F.I.R.S.T.
(Framework for Inducting, Retaining, and Supporting Teachers)
YEAR TWO
Third Meeting

4:30 PM to 7:30 PM

February

Agenda topics

Time	Topic	Presenter
4:30-5:25 PM	Introduction / Stages of Teaching / Professional Behaviors of Beginning Teachers	Annette Breaux
5:25-5:55 PM	Case Studies	Liz Yates
5:55-6:05 PM	BREAK	
6:05 -6:35 PM	Update on High-Stakes Testing	Liz Yates
6:35-7:05 PM	New Teacher Concerns/Classroom Experiences	Annette and Liz
7:05-7:15 PM	Closing Activity	Annette and Liz
7:15-7:30 PM	Evaluations	

Agenda

F.I.R.S.T.
(Framework for Inducting, Retaining, and Supporting Teachers)
YEAR TWO
Fourth Meeting

4:30 PM to 7:30 PM

April

Agenda topics

4:30-5:25 PM	Introduction	Annette Breaux
	Teaching - What's Effective and What's Not	
5:25-5:55 PM	Case Studies	Liz Yates
5:55-6:05 PM	BREAK	
6:05-6:35 PM	Homework Solutions	Liz Yates
6:35-7:05 PM	New Teacher Concerns/Classroom Experiences	Annette and Liz
7:05-7:15 PM	Closing Activity	Annette and Liz
7:15-7:30 PM	Evaluations	

What do new teachers and others in Lafourche Parish have to say about induction?

"I feel fortunate to have had the opportunity to attend the FIRST program. I believe that I am a more effective teacher because experienced educators took the time to prepare me for the first days of my teaching career."

—2nd grade teacher

"The program was wonderful. It helped me to know exactly what to expect and what to do on my very first day of teaching. Maybe programs like this will lower the number of teachers leaving the profession after their first year of teaching. Thank you."

—4th grade teacher

"This program taught me more about teaching than my entire education thus far. I now feel prepared to teach."

—high school teacher

"New Teacher Induction is one of the best things that ever happened to this school system."

— Gary Babin,
Assistant Superintendent

"I don't know if you realize what an impact induction has had on our new teachers. They are coming to us so much more ready to teach."

— junior high school principal

"Your FIRST Program not only saved my wife as a classroom teacher, but it also saved our marriage. My wife had been teaching for a few months before she went through induction, and she was miserable. Whatever you did in that induction program made her so much more successful as a teacher and a much happier person in general. Thank you."

—husband of a new teacher

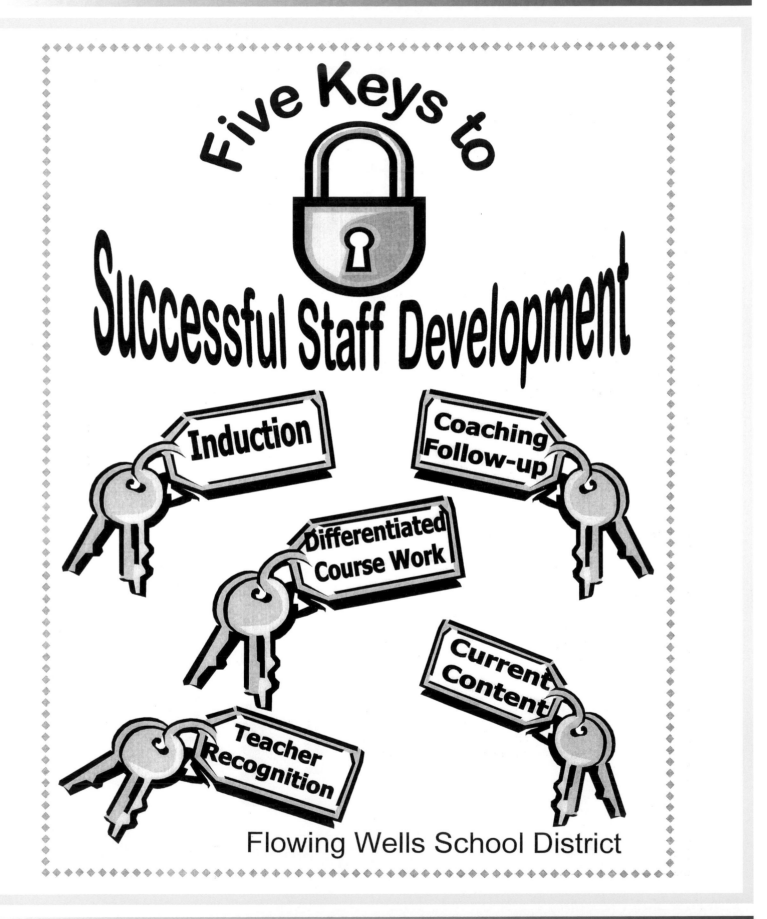

Five Keys to Successful Staff Development

Induction

Coaching Follow-up

Differentiated Course Work

Current Content

Teacher Recognition

Flowing Wells School District

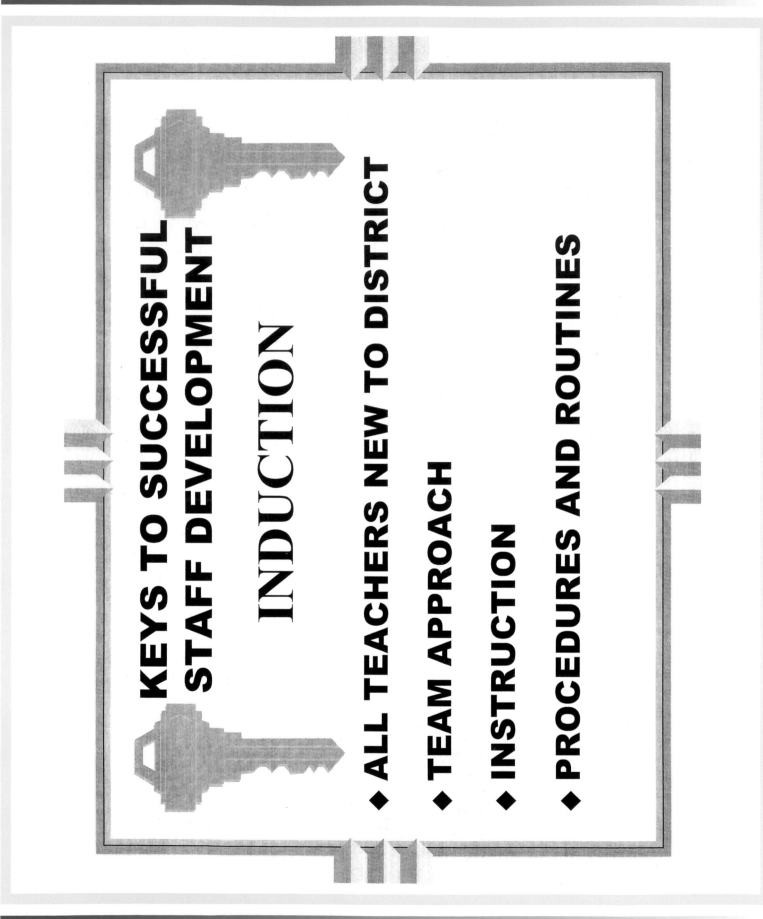

KEYS TO SUCCESSSFUL STAFF DEVELOPMENT

INDUCTION

◆ ALL TEACHERS NEW TO DISTRICT

◆ TEAM APPROACH

◆ INSTRUCTION

◆ PROCEDURES AND ROUTINES

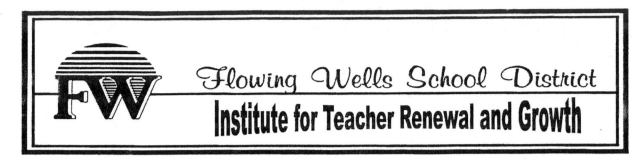

Staff Development Program Description

The Flowing Wells School District recognizes at a time when the needs of our students and community are great, the need for teachers with multiple skills and understanding is of utmost importance. During the 1983-84 school year, the district decided to implement a staff development program which addressed the renewal and improvement of instructional delivery in the classroom.

Over the last eleven years, the program has developed into a model which offers differentiated staff development matched to the level of teaching expertise. This concept was originally developed by Dr. David Berliner from Arizona State University, and Dr. Thomas McGreal from the University of Illinois. the Flowing Wells Staff Development Program provides workshops for Novice (first year), Advanced Beginners (second year), Competent (third-fifth years), and Proficient and Expert Level teachers.

The content of the workshops is based upon the different needs of teachers as they progress in their professional careers. The key concepts in each workshop relfect a "building block" framework from simple to more complex decision making. Additionally, the INDUCTION PROGRAM and the beginning workshops emphasize classroom performance while the advanced workshops include training that impacts the school, district, and community (refer to attached graph).

The American Association of School Administrators recognized the Flowing Wells Institute for Teacher Renewal and Growth as the 1986 Exemplary Staff Development Program.

If we don't model what we teach, we're teaching something else.

The Flowing Wells Staff Development Program:

> ➤ **INDUCTION**
>
> ➤ **DIFFERENTIATED AND DEVELOPMENTALLY APPROPRIATE WORK-SHOP TRAINING FOR CONTINUING TEACHERS**
>
> ➤ **COACHING FOLLOW-UP IN THE FORM OF MENTOR-ING AND FORMATIVE SUPERVISION**

INDUCTION

The Flowing Wells Induction Program is the transmission of the district and community culture. The major goals of this program are to build a sense of culture and to articulate the district's mission and philosophy. INDUCTION is a structured training program for all teachers new to the district which instructs and models "the way it is done" in the Flowing Wells School District. This program is not merely an orientation to the district's organizational pattern, but a framework of the district's vision for student learning and success.

The Flowing Wells Staff Development Program (Continued)

The Flowing Wells Induction Program emphasizes five critical attributes that are the cornerstones of the vision:

♦ effective instructional practices

♦ effective classroom management procedures and routines

♦ a sensitivity and understanding of the unique community we serve

♦ teaching is a reflection of life-long learning and professional growth

♦ unity of teamwork among administration, teachers, support staff and community members is essential (refer to attached handouts regarding **INDUCTION OVERVIEW** and **EIGHT-DAY INDUCTION SCHEDULE**).

DIFFERENTIATED AND **D**EVELOPMENTALLY APPROPRIATE WORKSHOP TRAINING FOR CONTINUING TEACHERS (refer to Staff Development Brochure).

COACHING FOLLOW-UP IN THE FORM OF MENTORING AND FORMATIVE SUPERVISION

Based upon the research of Dr. Bruce Joyce and Dr. Beverly Showers regarding the need for follow-up coaching as an essential aspect of teacher training, the Flowing Wells District has designed an extensive system of intense, formative supervision. The coaching component incorporates pre-conferences, classroom observations, and post-conferences. These observations are not used for summative evaluations; the intent is to give teachers specific, immediate, and non-threatening feedback on their teaching performance. A cadre of "expert" level teachers serve as building level Mentors/Instructional Coordinators in addition to their regular teaching assignments. The District Staff Development Coordinator facilitates the mentoring and coaching efforts.

To conclude, the Mentoring and the Coaching Follow-up are fundamental to the success of the new teacher **INDUCTION PROGRAM.**

Staff Development Program Outcomes

♦ 100% of all new teachers to Flowing Wells attend the **INDUCTION PROGRAM** during their first year in the district.

♦ Approximately 85% - 90% of all Flowing Wells teachers attend staff development training each year on a voluntary basis.

♦ Based on feedback from school principals, the quality of teaching performance has increased significantly over the last eleven years.

♦ "Proficient" and "Expert" teachers design individual growth plans based on increased awareness of teaching research and methodology. These teachers are the Mentor/Instructional Coordinators that provide the new teacher support.

♦ An increased ability for teachers to reflect on their instructional practices has promoted professional dialogue among teachers, support staff, and community.

♦ An attitude that "professional growth" is the norm for a Flowing Wells educator is evidenced by participation in after school and summer workshops.

FLOWING WELLS SCHOOL DISTRICT
INSTITUTE FOR TEACHER RENEWAL AND GROWTH

STAFF DEVELOPMENT

Teacher Induction ------→ Teacher Leadership

	Novices (1st year teachers)	Advanced Beginners (2nd year teachers)	Competent (3rd year teachers)	Proficient (4th year +)	Expert (8th year +)
Workshops	Induction • Procedures/Routines • Instruction • Community Culture	• Refresher Course • Class Mgmt. • Task Analysis	• Advanced Instruction • Cooperative Learning • Teaching Fundamentals Revisited	• Teaching Higher Level Thinking and Creativity • Integrated Thematic Instruction • Portfolio Assessment • Multiple Intelligences	• Cognitive Coaching • Clinical Supervision • Alignment of Curriculum with State Standards • Current Research Topics
Key Concepts	• Classroom Mgmt. • Planning Skills • Lesson Sequence • Special Education Modifications	• Basic Learning Theory • Climate/Student Teacher Control • Curriculum Sequence	• Transfer Theory • Teaching of Concepts and Processes • Teaching Group Dynamics • Self-Esteem	• Alternative Instructional Strategies • Question/Response Patterns • Critical and Creative Thinking • Integration • Authentic Assessment	• Mentoring • Articulation • Study Team Leaders
Follow-Up Coaching **Mentors** **Instructional Coordinators**	Formative • 4 Classroom Observations and Conferences with Staff Development Coord. • 1 Video Analysis • 2 "SPA" Days with Mentor • Ongoing Contacts with Mentor Summative • 2 Observations (Principal)	Formative • 4 Classroom Observations (Instructional Coordinator) • 2 Observation by Mentor Summative • 2 Observations (Principal)	Formative • 2 Announced Classroom Observations – (I.C.) • One Additional Pre/Post Conference • 2 I.A. Meetings Summative • 1-2 Observations (Principal) or Alternative Evaluation Designed by Teacher & Principal	Formative • Study Teams • Peer Coaching • One Unannounced I.C. Observation • SAP Proposal Review Conference Summative • Alternative Evaluation Designed by Teacher & Principal	Formative • Study Teams • Peer Coaching • One I.C. Scheduled Contact Summative • Alternative Evaluation Designed by Teacher & Principal

Classroom ------→ District/Community

FLOWING WELLS SCHOOL DISTRICT

NEW TEACHER INDUCTION - FORMAL TRAINING
"New Teacher" includes all teachers (new or experienced) to the FW District.

CATEGORIES OF SUPPORT (Odell)

	New Teachers # of hours	Experienced Teachers # of hours	Before School # of hours	Ongoing Training # of hours
Organizational Culture: Giving information to transmit the culture of the system and organization. Guidelines, expectations, policies, procedures, customs, beliefs, core values.	7 hours	7 hours	5 hours	2 hours
Systems Information: Giving information related to procedures, guidelines, and expectations of the school district and the school.	7 hours	7 hours	7 hours	Every two weeks or once a month at sites - "Rookie" mtgs.
Mustering of Resources: Collecting, disseminating, or locating materials or other resources.	3 hours	3 hours	3 hours	Every two weeks or once a month at sites - "Rookie" mtgs.
Instructional Information: Giving information about teaching strategies or the instructional process.	21 hours	21 hours	21 hours	14 hours
Emotional Support: Offering support by listening empathetically and sharing experiences.	2 hours	2 hours	2 hours	Ongoing at follow-up sessions and Rookie mtgs.
Advice on Student Management: Giving guidance and ideas related to discipline and managing students. *All new teachers required to read First Days of School by Harry Wong.	4 hours	4 hours	4 hours	Ongoing at follow-up sessions and "Rookie" mtgs.
Advice on Scheduling and Planning: Offering information about organizing and planning the school day. *See Mustering of Resources section.	3 hours	3 hours	3 hours	Ongoing at sites and "Rookie" mtgs.
Help with Classroom Environment: Helping arrange, organize, or analyze the physical setting of the classroom. *See advice in Student Mgmt. section.	4 hours	4 hours	4 hours	Ongoing at sites and "Rookie" mtgs.
Demonstration Teaching: Teaching while new teacher observes, preceded and followed with conferencing to focus and analyze instructional strategies.	7 hours	7 hours	7 hours	5 hours
Coaching: Critiquing and providing feedback on the teacher's performance.	14 hours	14 hours	1 hour	13 hours

Advice on Working with Parents: Giving help or ideas related to conferencing or working with parents.				Informal at sites.
Special Education Issues:	2 hours	2 hours		Two hours and ongoing at sites.
Other topics or activities: * See attached brochure for ongoing staff development program for second year teachers and above. * New teacher contract includes four before school induction days - no extra money. * Substitutes are hired for teachers who attend workshops during school hours. * Technology Training available after first year in district * Methods used to evaluate success: - Participant feedback - Teacher retention - Teachers' voluntary participation beginning in 2nd year - Recruitment numbers - Student test scores used to provide areas for staff development focus				

New Teacher Induction Program
Seminar Schedule/Topics

ESSENTIAL ELEMENTS OF INSTRUCTION/CLASSROOM MANAGEMENT
August 5 – 8, 2002

August 5, 2002 – Monday

8:00	-	8:15	Coffee and Donuts
8:15	-	8:30	Welcome – Dr. Pedicone, Superintendent
8:30	-	12:15	Essential Elements of Instruction Workshop
12:15	-	1:30	Lunch
1:30	-	3:30	Essential Elements of Instruction Workshop

August 6, 2002 – Tuesday

8:00	-	8:15	Coffee and Donuts
8:15	-	12:15	Essential Elements of Instruction Workshop
12:15	-	1:30	Lunch
1:30	-	3:30	Essential Elements Workshop

August 7, 2002 – Wednesday

7:45	-	8:30	FWEA Hosted Breakfast – High School Cafeteria
8:30	-	11:00	Essential Elements of Instruction Workshop
11:00	-	12:30	Bus Tour of District – Dr. Pedicone, Superintendent
12:30	-	1:45	Lunch
1:45	-	3:30	Return to Buildings for Classroom Preparation

August 8, 2002 – Thursday

8:00	-	8:15	Coffee and Donuts
8:15	-	10:30	Demonstration Classrooms
10:30	-	12:15	Classroom Management Workshop
12:15	-	1:30	Lunch
1:30	-	3:30	Return to Buildings for Classroom Preparation

August 5, 2002 – Monday   ****HIGH SCHOOL TEACHERS ONLY****
Rookies Meeting in the High School Faculty Cafeteria

FLOWING WELLS SCHOOL DISTRICT
1556 W. Prince Rd.
Tucson, Arizona 85705

FLOWING WELLS INSTITUTE
FOR TEACHER RENEWAL AND GROWTH

INDUCTION OVERVIEW (8 DAYS)
(refer to attached daily schedules for specific times and topics)

All teachers new to the district are required to attend four days of inservice prior to the return of the continuing teachers. A first year teacher's contract includes four additional days to meet this expectation. Each new teacher is required to read The First Days of School, by Dr. Harry Wong, prior to the start of the **INDUCTION** training.

DAY 1 – Focus: **Team Building and Instruction**

A. Welcome by Superintendent and the Governing Board President
    Introduction of all Central Administration, Principals, Directors of Maintenance, Food Services, Transportation
    Welcome by the Educational Association
    The feeling of "family" or "team" is stressed

B. Introduction of all new teachers
    Pictures are taken and displayed
    Organization of cooperative, new teacher groups (K-12)
    Team building and collegial support are stressed

C. Day 1 Content – Instructional Practices

D. Instructors – Staff Development Coordinator, Principals, and "Expert" Level Classroom Teachers

DAY 2 - Focus: **Instruction**

A. Classroom Instructional Practices

B. Teaching Practicums in small, cooperative groups

DAY 3 – Focus: **Flowing Wells Community and Culture**

A. Professional Needs (insurance, health care, etc.)

B. Inspirational Video – Flowing Wells Community in Action

C.	Bus Tour of District and Flowing Wells Cultural Literacy "Quiz" – conducted by Superintendent

D.	New Teacher Luncheon – sponsored by Flowing Wells Education Association

E.	New teachers return to respective buildings for planning time with principals. Curriculum, texts, and building specific procedures are discussed.

DAY 4 – Focus: Classroom Management Procedures and Routines

A.	Bell Work, Signal, Dismissal, Homework, etc.

B.	Harry Wong Tapes – Discipline Plan, Rules, and Consequences

C.	"Expert" level elementary, junior high, and high school teachers share with the new teachers their current, successful classroom strategies.

D.	Demonstration classrooms are visited by all new staff. The demonstration teachers model the First Day Procedures and Routines used at the beginning of the year.

E.	Slates and markers distributed to all new teachers to encourage the use of student Active Participation.

F.	Follow-up Mentoring explained and organized for the school year (five visits per teacher by mentors).

G.	During the afternoon, new teachers return to their individual classrooms for preparation.

DAYS 5, 6, 7, and 8 – Focus: Instruction and Classroom Management

A.	The days are scheduled throughout the year (October, November, January, and March).

B.	Follow-up days include on-site Demonstration Classrooms in Instruction. Also, one-half day is spent on the new Special Education requirements.

C.	Day 8 includes:

- Celebration of Learning (Candlelight Luncheon) with Governing Board Members, Central Administration, Principals, and Assistant Principals

- Teacher Awards (framed certificates) presented by Superintendent

New Teacher Induction Program

Seminar Schedule/Topics

FOCUS: ESSENTIAL ELEMENTS OF INSTRUCTION

Staff Development Training Team:

Susie Heintz
Carol Gowler
J. J. Johnson
Alberto Urquidez
Kevin Stoltzfus
Denise Reilly

Monday, August 5, 2002

8:00 - 8:15	Coffee and Donuts
8:15 - 8:30	Welcome - Dr. John Pedicone, Superintendent
8:30 - 9:30	Business/Class Building/Form Base Groups Team Building
9:30 - 10:30	Overview of Classroom Responsibilities
10:30 - 10:40	Break
10:40 - 11:20	Overview of Essential Elements
11:20 - 11:25	Stretch
11:25 - 12:15	Teach to the Objective
12:15 - 1:30	Lunch
1:30 - 2:30	Active Participation
2:30 - 2:45	Break
2:45 - 3:30	Active Participation (cont.) Homework

Flowing Wells School District

New Teacher Induction Program
Seminar Schedule/Topics

FOCUS: ESSENTIAL ELEMENTS OF INSTRUCTION

Staff Development Team

> **Susie Heintz**
> **Carol Gowler**
> **J.J. Johnson**
> **Alberto Urquidez**
> **Kevin Stoltzfus**
> **Denise Reilly**

Tuesday, August 6, 2002

8:00 - 8:15	Coffee and Donuts
8:15 - 9:15	NAU Registration New Teacher Induction Book (T.I.P.S.) Class Building/Team Building - "What's My Bag?" Review of Previous Day
9:15 - 9:45	Active Participation (cont.)/Video
9:45 - 10:15	Formulating Instructional Objectives
10:15 - 10:30	Break
10:30 - 11:00	Anticipatory Set
11:00 - 12:15	Sample Lesson/Planning and Set-Up for Teaching Practicum
12:15 - 1:30	Lunch
1:30 - 2:45	Motivation
2:45 - 3:00	Break
3:00 - 3:30	Motivation (contd.) Homework - Reading

Flowing Wells School District

New Teacher Induction Program
Seminar Schedule/Topics

FOCUS: FLOWING WELLS' CULTURE

Staff Development Team:

> **Susie Heintz**
> **Carol Gowler**
> **Kevin Stoltzfus**

Wednesday, August 7, 2002

7:45 – 8:30	FWEA Breakfast – High School Cafeteria
8:30 – 9:15	Team Builder - "Summer of '02" Review - "Find Someone Who…"
9:15 – 10:15	Teaching Practicums
10:15 – 10:45	Business/Insurance Information -- Mr. Stuart Meinke, Assistant Superintendent, Business Services
10:45 – 11:00	Break
11:00 – 12:30	Bus Tour – Dr. John Pedicone, Superintendent
12:30 – 1:45	Lunch
1:45 – 3:30	Return to Buildings for Classroom Preparation

Flowing Wells School District

New Teacher Induction Program
Seminar Schedule/Topics

FOCUS: CLASSROOM MANAGEMENT AND COACHING

Staff Development Team:

Susie Heintz
J.J. Johnson
Kevin Stoltzfus

Thursday, August 8, 2002

8:00 - 8:15	Coffee and Donuts
8:15 - 8:30	Welcome/Review
8:30 - 10:30	Demonstration Classrooms - First Day of School Procedures and Routines

- Kdg - 2nd Gr. Teachers – Brenda Powell, Hendricks Elem., Rm. 12
- 3rd – 6th Gr. Teachers – Jaime Diaz, Douglas Elem., Rm. 25
- Jr. High/High School Teachers – Phyllis Fassio, FWHS, Rm M-3
- Special Ed., Instructional Assts., Speech – Mary Beth Scheller, Richardson Elem., Rm. 18

10:30 - 10:45	Break
10:45 - 11:15	Mentor Program – Phyllis Fassio Next Steps/Implementation – Dr. John Pedicone and Susie Sign Up for Observations
11:15 - 11:45	Classroom Management/Professional Dress - Harry Wong Video Tapes
11:45 - 12:15	Flowing Wells Video – Dr. John Pedicone, Superintendent
12:15 - 1:30	Lunch
1:30 - 3:30	Return to Buildings for Classroom Preparation

Flowing Wells School District

New Teacher Induction Program

Seminar Schedule/Topics

FOCUS: ESSENTIAL ELEMENTS OF INSTRUCTION

Staff Development Team:
  Susie Heintz
  J. J. Johnson
  Kevin Stoltzfus
  Denise Reilly
  Carol Gowler
  Alberto Urquidez
  Jean Baxter

Wednesday, October 9, 2002

7:30 - 7:45	Refreshments
7:45 - 8:45	Teambuilder/Agenda Rotating Review/Sharing Explain Peer Observations Anticipatory Set Video
8:45 - 9:15	Closure
9:15 - 10:30	Motivation
10:30 - 10:45	Break
10:45 - 12:00	4-Part Objective/Bloom
12:00 - 1:15	Lunch
1:15 - 2:15	Retention
2:15 - 2:30	Break
2:30 - 3:00	Retention

Flowing Wells School District

New Teacher Induction Program

Seminar Schedule/Topics

FOCUS: ESSENTIAL ELEMENTS OF INSTRUCTION

Instructors:	Susie Heintz	Carolyn Jacobsen
	Jean Baxter	Diane Swan
	Kevin Stoltzfus	

Tuesday, November 26, 2002

7:30 - 7:45	Refreshments
7:45 - 8:00	Discuss Peer Observations
8:00 - 9:00	Bloom's Taxonomy/4-part Objective
9:00 – 11:00	Motivation Monitor and Adjust (Break Included)
11:00 - 11:45	Procedures and Routines – Harry Wong Video
11:45 - 1:00	Lunch
1:00 - 2:15	Modifications for Special Needs Students – *Pupil Services Team*
2:15 - 2:30	Break
2:30 - 3:00	Modifications (Cont.)

Flowing Wells School District

New Teacher Induction Program

Seminar Schedule/Topics

FOCUS: ESSENTIAL ELEMENTS OF INSTRUCTION

Instructor: Susie Heintz
Kevin Stoltzfus

<u>**Wednesday, January 15, 2003**</u>

7:30 - 7:45	Refreshments
7:45 - 8:45	"Personal Preferences" Teambuilder Explain Visitations/Lesson Design Civil War Lesson – "Putting It All Together"
8:45 - 10:30	Task Analysis
10:30 - 10:45	Break
10:45 - 11:15	Task Analysis (Cont.)
11:15 - 2:00	Lunch and Classroom Visitations
2:00 - 2:15	Break
2:15 - 3:00	Videotapes – "Active Participation and Anticipatory Set" / "Flowing Wells Induction, Staff Development, and Mentoring"

Flowing Wells School District

New Teacher Induction Program

Seminar Schedule/Topics

FOCUS: ESSENTIAL ELEMENTS OF INSTRUCTION

Instructors: **Susie Heintz**
Jean Baxter
Kevin Stolzfus

Tuesday, March 4, 2003

7:30 - 7:45	Refreshments
7:45 - 8:30	Review Discovery Lesson
8:30 - 9:10	Task Analysis
9:10 - 9:15	Stretch
9:15 - 10:35	Diagnostic Prescriptive Process *Dr. Renate Krompasky*
10:35 -10:45	Break
10:45 - 12:00	Gregorc Learning Styles
12:00 - 1:00	Graduation Luncheon - Board Room Certificates - *Dr. John Pedicone*
1:00 - 1:30	Characteristics of Flowing Wells Teachers - "Why You Were Hired!" *Dr. John Pedicone*
1:30 - 2:00	Final Exam Self-Analysis
2:00 - 3:00	Procedures and Routines (Harry Wong tape) (Break Included)

Flowing Wells School District

STAFF DEVELOPMENT

A Picture = 1,000 Words

- ☑ Welcome signs for location of workshop
- ☑ Greet at door/administration present
- ☑ Refreshments
- ☑ Favors on tables
- ☑ Take pictures
- ☑ Sign-in/agenda/nameplates
- ☑ Materials ready
- ☑ Professional dress
- ☑ Bellwork
- ☑ Procedures – physical and psychological comfort
- ☑ Signal
- ☑ Learning names
- ☑ Room decorated
- ☑ Technology modeled
- ☑ Monitoring group/available for questions
- ☑ Introductions – "class builder"
- ☑ Team builder
- ☑ Team approach – staff development

Induction Topics

Susie School

- ☒ Classroom discipline
- ☒ Motivating students
- ☒ Individual differences
- ☒ Assessing student work
- ☒ Relations with parents
- ☒ Organization of classroom
- ☒ Lack of familiarity with existing resources (people and materials)
- ☒ Problems of individual students
- ☒ District/school procedure/policy
- ☒ Terminology
- ☒ Professional growth

**Checklist
Preparing for the First Day**

1. Curriculum

    ____ Guides

    ____ Procedures

2. ____ Attendance/Tardy Policies

3. ____ Discipline Policy & Procedures

4. ____ Teacher Supplies

5. Beginning Class

    ____ Roll Call, Absent, Tardy

    ____ Bellwork

    ____ Distributing Materials

    ____ Class Opening

6. Room/School Areas

    ____ Shared Materials

    ____ Teacher's Desk

    ____ Drinks, Bathroom, Pencil Sharpener

    ____ Student Storage/Lockers

    ____ Student Desks

    ____ Learning Centers, Stations

    ____ Playground, Schoolgrounds

    ____ Lunchroom

    ____ Halls

7. Setting Up Independent Work

    ____ Defining "Working Alone"

    ____ Identifying Problems

    ____ Identifying Resources

    ____ Identifying Solutions

    ____ Scheduling

    ____ Interim Checkpoints

8. Procedures

    ____ Teacher, Student Contacts

    ____ Student Movement in the Room

    ____ Signals for Students' Attention

    ____ Signals for Teacher's Attention

    ____ Student Talk During Seatwork

    ____ Activities to Do When Work is Done

    ____ Student Participation

    ____ Laboratory Procedures

    ____ Movement In and Out of Small Groups

    ____ Expected Behavior in Group

    ____ Behavior of Students Not in Group

9. Ending Class

    ____ Putting Away Supplies and Equipment

    ____ Cleaning Up

    ____ Organizing Class Materials

    ____ Dismissing Class

10. Procedures for Movement

    ____ Rules

    ____ Talk Among Students

    ____ Conduct

    ____ Passing Out Books, Supplies

    ____ Turning in Work

    ____ Handing Back Assignments

    ____ Getting Back Assignments

    ____ Out-of-Seat Policies

    ____ Consequences for Misbehavior

11.	Other Procedures
___	Fire Drills
___	Lunch Procedures
___	Student Helpers
___	Safety Procedures
12.	Work Requirements
___	Heading of Papers
___	Use of Pen or Pencil
___	Writing on Back of Paper
___	Neatness, Legibility
___	Incomplete Work
___	Late Work
___	Missed Work
___	Due Dates
___	Make-up Work
___	Supplies
___	Coloring or Drawing on Paper
___	Use of Manuscript or Cursive
13.	Communicating Assignments
___	Posting Assignments
___	Orally Giving Assignments
___	Provision for Absences
___	Long-term Assignments
___	Term Schedule
___	Homework Assignments
14.	Student Work
___	In-class Participation
___	In-class Assignments
___	Homework
___	Stages of Long-term Assignments

15.	Checking Assignments in Class
___	Students Exchanging Papers
___	Marking and Grading Assignments
___	Turning in Assignments
___	Students Correcting Errors
16.	Grading Procedures
___	Determining Grades
___	Recording Grades
___	Grading Long Assignments
___	Extra Credit Work
___	Keeping Papers, Grades, Assignments
___	Grading Criteria
___	Contracting for Grades
17.	Academic Feedback
___	Rewards and Incentives
___	Posting Student Work
___	Communicating with Parents
___	Students' Record of Grades
___	Written Comments on Assignments
18.	Testing
___	Timelines
___	State Mandated
___	District Mandated

FLOWING WELLS FORMATIVE COACHING

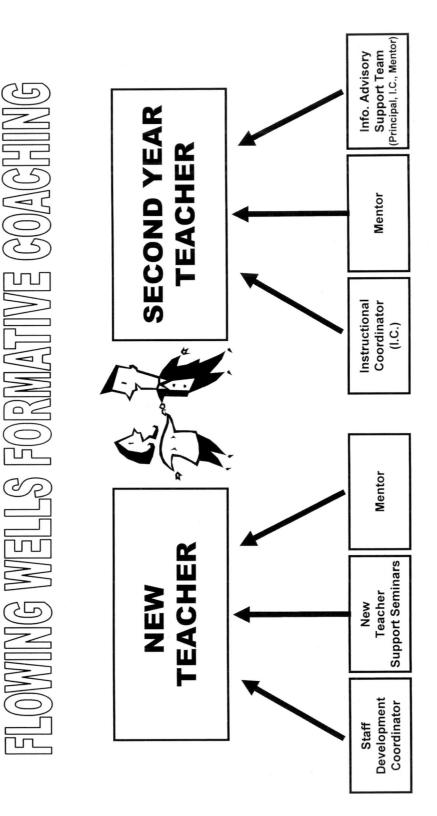

New Teacher Meetings
Elementary

2002-2003

Davis Elementary School Conference Room

Thursday, August 8	School Tour/District Culture, Bell Work, Door Greeting, Classroom Environment, Lunch Procedures & ½ Day Procedure
Monday, August 12	Introduce Mentors, Attendance Procedures, Supplies, Nurse Information, Subfinder Information, Dismissal Procedures, DAP/Assessment Collection Phase I
Tuesday, August 20	DAP/Assessment Collection Phase II, Dragon of Character, Peace Builder Program/Counseling Services, Discipline Procedures/Sub Folder, Welcome Back Night, Homework Expectations, Fire Drill/Emergency Plan
Tuesday, September 3	Progress Report/Report Cards/Midterms, Parent/Teacher Conferences, Field Trips, Personal Leave, and Sick Days, Student Confidentiality
Tuesday, October 8	Special Education In-Service, School Assemblies/School Performance
Tuesday, November 5	TAT Process, Classroom Management, DAP/Assessment Collection Phase III
Tuesday, December 3	Report Cards, Student Project for Parents Night, Holiday Luncheon, You made it through the 1st Semester! Whew! I need a break. Holiday/Winter Break Schedule

Tuesday, January 14   Stanford 9 Exams, AIMS Testing

Tuesday, February 4   Parent/Teacher Conferences, Capital/Instructional Ordering

Tuesday, March 4   Career Ladder, Staffing Update, DAP/Assessment Collection Phase IV

Tuesday, April 29   Purple Pre-Registration Forms, Perm Cards, Pink/Blue Cards, Report Cards, Classroom Check-out, End-of-the-Year Luncheon

You made it!

New Teacher Meetings
Junior High School

2002-2003

Monday, August 12	Attendance Procedure, IMC Information, Bellwork, Door Greeting, Voice Level, Duties Discipline Referral Process
Tuesday, August 27	Athletic Eligibility, Science Trips Textbook Accountability
Tuesday, September 10	Progress, Report Cards, Special Education
Tuesday, September 24	Personal Leave, Sick Days, Recourse Work and Suspensions
Tuesday, October 8	Report Cards, Conferences, 2nd Quarter -- Fresh Start!
Tuesday, November 5	Classroom Parties, Breaks, Movies, School Performances
Tuesday, December 10	Semester Grading, New Teacher Debriefing
Tuesday, January 21	Capital Items, Science Trips, Rating Sheets, 8th grade Awards Assembly
Tuesday, February 11	Scheduling, AIMS Testing, Stanford-9
Tuesday, March 11	Parent Conferences, Field Day, Staffing, Career Ladder
Tuesday, April 29	Year-End Reminders You made it ☺

*Mentors will join the discussion at these two meetings.

New Teacher Meetings
High School

2002-2003

Friday, August 2	Luncheon, Orientation, and Tour
Thursday, August 22	Processing the First Week/Meet the Counselors/Sub-finder
Thursday, August 29*	Film: Blood Borne Pathogens
Thursday, September 5	Preparing Progress Reports/Meet "Dear John"
Thursday, October 3	Issuing First Quarter Grades/Meet Probation Officer
Thursday, November 14	Understanding the Re-certification Process with Dr. Clement
Thursday, December 5	Closing the First Semester
Thursday, January 23	Ordering Supplies with Dr. Blair
Friday, March 7	Lunch and a Movie with Dr. Blair: "Fat City" at 11:30 a.m.
Thursday, April 10	Making a Million Through the 403b7 Plan
Thursday, May 1	Closing the School Year

*Only those teachers who have not seen "Blood Borne Pathogens" need to attend.

A Dozen
GUIDELINES
For Effective Mentors

1) **Establish rapport.**

2) **Be friendly and positive.**

3) **Acknowledge the mentee's skills.**

4) **Emphasize the importance of the teacher's role.**

5) **Be tactfully honest.**

6) **Be empathetic.**

7) **Provide articles, pamphlets, or techniques in order to demonstrate helpfulness.**

8) **Be a good listener.**

9) **Ask objective rather than personal questions.**

10) **Set realistic mentor-role expectations.**

11) **Demonstrate the benefits of experience and change by building your own knowledge.**

12) **Share ideas and solutions.**

Maggie Westhoff

FLOWING WELLS
COGNITIVE COACHING PROGRAM

Size of District = Approximately 6,200 students
Number of Teachers = 350

1 High School (2,000 students)
1 Junior High School (900 students)
6 Elementary Schools (500-650 students each)

The primary goal of the Coaching Follow-Up Program is to impact student success by increasing new teacher effectiveness. The staff development coordinator is responsible for <u>new teacher</u> coaching. The mentors are "expert" level educators who provide support to:

    ✓   Teachers new to teaching (1-2 years experience)

    ✓   Teachers who are new to Flowing Wells School District (1-2 years experience)

The new teachers are informed of the coaching follow-up during the New Teacher Induction Program in August.

The initial focus is to support and assist the new teacher in becoming accustomed to the Flowing Wells School District responsibilities and to model classroom management skills. Professional skills, instructional and student assessment strategies, curriculum implementation, and orientation to Flowing Wells School District policies and procedures are also emphasized. Coaches individualize the program to meet the needs of the new teachers and to enhance their present skills. Evaluation of new teachers is NOT a part of this process.

<u>**Personnel:**</u>

1.   **1 Staff Development Coordinator** – full-time

2.   **21 Instructional Coordinators*** - full-time classroom teachers with approximately nine release days per year for coaching and a stipend of approximately $2,000.00.

    *The I.C. is the "linchpin" of our coaching.

    6 I.C.'s – High School
    4 I.C.'s – Junior High School
    1 or 2 – Each Elementary School

    Training: *Essential Elements of Instruction*, *Classroom Management*, 4 days of *Clinical Supervision* and/or *Cognitive Coaching*. Also, each I.C. has two days of field training with the staff development coordinator to receive feedback on actual conferencing skills.

    I.C.'s are required to attend bi-monthly meetings after school for district articulation. These are facilitated by the staff development coordinator.

Formative Coaching Program
Page Two

3. **Mentors** – full-time teachers who agree to serve as mentors for teachers on beginning levels of Career Ladder.

    Reimbursement:

    a. 2001-2002 Mentor Grant - $500.00 (all first year teachers and selected second year teachers)

    b. 4-7 points for Career Ladder portfolio, depending on teacher's level
        Stipend: Approximately $100.00 per point

    Training: *Essential Elements of Instruction, Classroom Management,* and a one-day mentor training are required. *Cognitive Coaching* and scripting skills are highly recommended. Mentors are responsible for keeping a log, observing, and answering questions.

4. **Support Seminars** – There are monthly meetings (study teams for new teachers). A mentor coordinator arranges the meetings.

    Training: None is required.

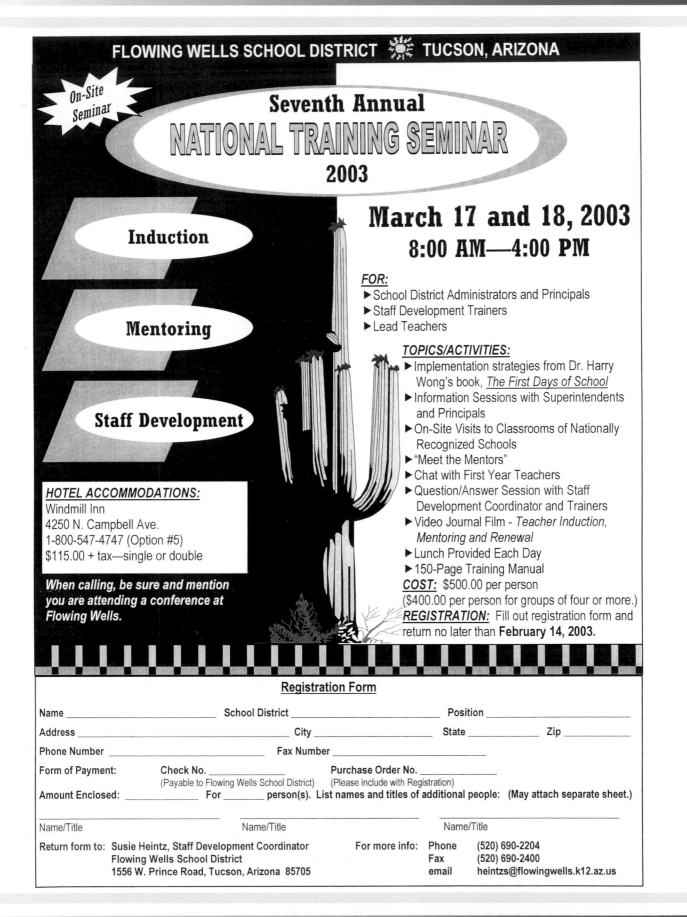

FLOWING WELLS SCHOOL DISTRICT ☀ TUCSON, ARIZONA

On-Site Seminar

Seventh Annual
NATIONAL TRAINING SEMINAR
2003

Induction

Mentoring

Staff Development

March 17 and 18, 2003
8:00 AM—4:00 PM

FOR:
▶ School District Administrators and Principals
▶ Staff Development Trainers
▶ Lead Teachers

TOPICS/ACTIVITIES:
▶ Implementation strategies from Dr. Harry Wong's book, *The First Days of School*
▶ Information Sessions with Superintendents and Principals
▶ On-Site Visits to Classrooms of Nationally Recognized Schools
▶ "Meet the Mentors"
▶ Chat with First Year Teachers
▶ Question/Answer Session with Staff Development Coordinator and Trainers
▶ Video Journal Film - *Teacher Induction, Mentoring and Renewal*
▶ Lunch Provided Each Day
▶ 150-Page Training Manual
COST: $500.00 per person
($400.00 per person for groups of four or more.)
REGISTRATION: Fill out registration form and return no later than **February 14, 2003.**

HOTEL ACCOMMODATIONS:
Windmill Inn
4250 N. Campbell Ave.
1-800-547-4747 (Option #5)
$115.00 + tax—single or double

When calling, be sure and mention you are attending a conference at Flowing Wells.

Registration Form

Name _____ School District _____ Position _____

Address _____ City _____ State _____ Zip _____

Phone Number _____ Fax Number _____

Form of Payment: Check No. _____ Purchase Order No. _____
(Payable to Flowing Wells School District) (Please include with Registration)
Amount Enclosed: _____ For _____ person(s). List names and titles of additional people: (May attach separate sheet.)

_____ _____ _____
Name/Title   Name/Title   Name/Title

Return form to: Susie Heintz, Staff Development Coordinator   For more info: Phone (520) 690-2204
Flowing Wells School District   Fax   (520) 690-2400
1556 W. Prince Road, Tucson, Arizona 85705   email   heintzs@flowingwells.k12.az.us

Homewood~Flossmoor High School

Voyage to Excellence
A New Teacher Induction Program

Achieving Student Success
Through Teacher Success

A NATIONAL SCHOOL
of
EXCELLENCE

July/August 2002

New Teacher Induction Schedule--Summer 2002

Wednesday, July 31, 2002
District Vision, Mission and Culture
Welcome Aboard the Viking Ship

North Building—Professional Development Room (101 North)

7:40   Refreshments and Bellwork – Assignment #1   (Overhead 1)
What are your concerns about your first year teaching at H-F? What worries you? What do you need to know? What do you hope to learn during the New Teacher Induction course?

8:00   Welcome!

Introduction of Instructors – Dr. Sandy Martin, Dr. Von Mansfield, Dean Auriemma & Terry McHugh

Ice Breaker/Participant Introductions (Overhead 2)
Introduce yourself and share four goals you have for the next several days. Each table to come up with 4 goals.

8:20   Process Responses from Assignment #1

8:30   Goals of Induction Program (Dr. Martin leads; Dean and Terry assist)
Culture   (Overhead 3)
Model Effective Instruction
Fill Gap Between University & Actual Teaching
Review Schedule

8:45   Welcome from Laura Murray, Administration, Board Members
District Vision and Mission – Shared Presentation
   • Background
   Best Teachers in America
   Continuing Tradition of Excellence
   • Translate into practice
   Here to help you make a successful transition to H-F.
   • We hired you to carry on the H-F tradition of excellence. You are the best of the best!

New Teacher Induction Schedule--Summer 2002

- Board of Education Expectations   (Overhead 4 "Vision Statement"/Binder)
  What we are looking for… Needs of the school…
- Board of Education Goals   (Overhead 5/Binder)

9:15   Preparation Activity for Video--Team Questions (Binder Section 2)

9:30   Explain "Aha Notes" (Binder Section 3)

          Video #1 "The Effective Teacher"
          Teaching vs. a Job
          Four stages of teaching: Fantasy, Survival, Mastery, Impact
          Three characteristics of the Effective Teachers:
              Management, Lesson Design, Expectations

9:40   Discussion—"Aha Moments" (Binder Section 3)

          Individual Questions—(Journaling Activity) (Binder Section 3)

10:00   Break

10:15   "Viking Pursuit" ("Who am I?") & Introductions (45 min.) (Handout)

10:50   Begin walk to South   (New Teachers divided into two groups)

11:00   Building Tour(s)

          Group 1   Group 2
          Dave Thieman   Dr. Von Mansfield
          "E" Building   "G Building"
          "B" Building   "Dean's/Guidance"
          "Tech & AV" Building   "H, D, N Buildings"
          "A" Building   (Athletics/Campus Store)
                                           "J & M Buildings"

          Tours end at Faculty Cafeteria for Lunch

New Teacher Induction Schedule--Summer 2002

11:45   Lunch with Administrators and Department Chairs

12:45   "The Basics"   New Teacher Meetings with Department Chairpersons &
                           Dr. Mansfield

- Room Keys
- Individual Teacher Schedules
- Class Lists
- Building Schedule
- The Block Schedule
- Lunch Duty/Prep Periods/Official School Day

Make Blank School ID Schedules

New Teachers are to reconvene in 101 North Building at 2:00 PM

2:00   Assignment #2
       Picture your Ideal Classroom ("group brainstorm") (Overhead—Use Notes pages in binder)

2:10   Process in Small Groups then Share in Large Group (assign task by Birthday)
- Spokesperson (1st Birth Date)
- Timekeeper (2nd Birth Date)
- Recorder (3rd Birth Date)
- Encourager (4th Birth Date)   Groups will Report Out

3:00   Distribute Books, Assign Reading – Unit C, Preview Thursday

       Exit Activity: "Head, Heart, Hand" (Handout)

Thursday, August 1, 2002
Positive Expectation and Classroom Management
Preparing for the Journey

North Building—Professional Development Room (101 North)

7:40   Refreshments and Assignment #3   (Overhead)
        Think about the first day of school. What will you wear? How will
        you welcome students? Organize your classroom? Be
        "intentionally inviting?" Learn student's names?

        Review Unit C

8:00   Share Assignment #3, Bellwork, Discuss Unit C
        Hog Call—Matching Pairs

8:30-   Human Resources Department
9:30   Dave Thieman, Director of Human Resources
        Sandy Sullivan (Personnel) and Pat Johnson (Payroll and Benefits) work with new
        teachers.

9:30   Break

9:45   Team Questions—Video 2 (Question 4 only—Binder Section 2)

        Video #2 "The First Days of School"   ("Aha Notes" Binder Section 3)
            Classroom Management   (Video = 35 minutes)
            Learning Processes
            Home and Parent Relationship
            Teacher and Student Relationship
            Seven Things Kids Want to Know on the First Day of School

        Discuss "Aha Notes" (Overhead—Binder Section 3)

        Following video Journal/Reflection/"Memories of the Future"
        [1st Individual Question]

New Teacher Induction Schedule--Summer 2002

11:30   Load vans for Trip to OFCC

11:45   Lunch at Olympia Fields Country Club with Intergovernmental Group, New Teachers District 153 and New Teachers District 161

12:45   Intergovernmental Group Presentation

1:30   Return to H-F (Drop off at South Building)

1:45   Building Tour II   (Alternate tours from Monday)

Group 1	Group 2
Dr. Von Mansfield	Dave Theiman
"G" Building	"E" Building
Dean's/Guidance	"B" Building
"H, D, N" Buildings	"Tech/AV"
(Athletics/Campus Store)	"A" Building

Following South Building Tour—Part II, New Teachers move to 101 North

2:00   Team Questions   (Binder Section 2)
[Divide teams: 3 work on Set 1 questions; 4 on Set 2 questions]
[Team questions on reserve should they be needed]

Video #3 "Discipline & Routines"("Aha Notes" Binder Section 3)
Rules Consequences Rewards   (Video = 35 minutes)

Discussion—"Aha Notes"   (Binder Section 3)
Reflection—Individual Questions (Binder section 3)

3:00   Distribute Faculty Handbooks and Closing Activities (Handout)

Review Faculty Handbook—Develop Questions for Tomorrow
Homework:
Quadrant Evaluation   (Handout)
Work on Discipline Plan   (Binder Section 2)

New Teacher Induction Schedule--Summer 2002

Friday, August 2, 2002
Classroom Management, Procedures & Routines
Helping the Sailors Succeed

North Building—Professional Development Room (101 North)

7:40   Refreshments / Bellwork

         Share Homework in Small Groups (Review Discipline Plans)
         *Incorporations: Find someone in the group who has the same
         department, pet, etc.*

7:55   Answer questions regarding Faculty Handbook/Questions from
         Comments/Suggestions/Questions

8:30   "HFEO and you", Scott Nemecek, President Homewood-Flossmoor
         Educational Organization

9:00   Video 4 "Procedure & Routines" (55 minutes)
         ("Aha Notes" Binder Section 3)
         #1 Getting Attention (Brainstorm 2-3 ways)
         #2 Dealing with Absent Students
         #3 Collecting Papers
         (Collect Ideas from Veteran Teachers)

9:50   Discuss "Aha Moments"   (Binder Section 3)

         Individual questions "1-2-4 Strategy"
         (1) Answer questions individually, (2) pair up share with (3) foursome

10:10   Break...Move South for Demonstration Classroom

10:30   Demonstration Classroom—John Schmidt
         Model--First Day of School/Back-to-School Night

11:30   Lunch--South Building Faculty Cafeteria

         Following Lunch Teachers move to North Building

Sandra Martin, Terry McHugh, Dean Auriemma   Page 6 of 12   *Revised 7/22/02*

New Teacher Induction Schedule--Summer 2002

12:30   Group A—North Building Tour, Barb Luoma

Group B—Credit Union Presentation

12:45   Group B—North Building Tour

Group A—Credit Union Presentation

1:00   Observations & Evaluations, Dr. Martin

- Forms & processes
- Form of professional development
- Dialogue
- Artifact file/professional portfolio

1:30   Team Questions   (Binder Section 2) (Video = 21 minutes)

Video 7 "The Professional Educator"
Journaling Activity; Discuss nature of goal-stetting activities

"Life-Long, Reflective Learning"

- Keeping A Journal
- Setting Goals
- Reflections
- What am I working on?
- What I achieved in relation to goals…?
- Questions I still have?

2:20   Break

2:30   "Preparing for a Substitute Teacher", Terry McHugh

3:00   Closure Activities & Homework

Evaluation "Today..."
Homework:
Review/Read First Days of School, Sections A and E
Complete Critical Attributes (Binder Section 2)

New Teacher Induction Schedule--Summer 2002

Wednesday, August 7, 2000
Classroom Management, Procedures & Routines
Smooth Sailing through Stormy Seas

North Building—Professional Development Room (101 North)

7:40   Bellwork/Opening Activity

             (Select 2-3 articles related to school culture, Teachers as Leaders, etc.
             Model CRISS strategies, have new teachers process the articles and report out)

8:40   Group reports begin

9:10   Quick Break

9:20   Discipline Overview—Pam-Allen Tucker & Sue Tantillo

- Code of Conduct—Levels of Discipline
- Referable Offence
- Student Dress Code, Language
- Have a Plan!
- The H-F Student
- Due Process & Documentation
- Forms & Phone Calls
- Calling Parents

11:00   "Get on the Bus"

11:10   Bus Tour of District

12:10   Lunch at Aurellios

New Teacher Induction Schedule--Summer 2002

1:15   Return to H-F (continue last portion of Bus tour)

1:30   "Verbal Judo"—Von Mansfield/Tom Fleming

2:00   H-F Dean's & Acting Students
           Classroom Management
           Role Playing
           Rehearsing Opening Speeches to Class

3:00   Closure Activities

New Teacher Induction Schedule--Summer 2002

Thursday, August 8, 2002
Lesson Design & Assessment
Charting the Journey

North Building—Professional Development Room (101 North)

7:40   Bellwork (Graffiti)

8:00   Planning for the Block Schedule, Terry McHugh

           Michael Rettig material/ideas
           Harvey Silver unit planning…i.e. R.O.S.E

           Reading Strategies for Beginning Teachers, Terry McHugh

10:00   Break

10:15   Curriculum/Instruction/Assessment, Dr. Martin
- The H-F Curriculum
- Understanding the H-F Grading System
- Sharing your System with Students and Parents
- ACT, SAT, AP, PSAE
- Test Prep
- Illinois Learning Standards
- VIP/Teacher Course Profile
- Academic Honesty

11:00   Video #8 "Positive Expectations"

11:20   Professional expectations—Dr. Laura Murray & Dr. Sandra Martin

- Evening Obligation
- Professional Development/Certification
- Coaching & Sponsoring Activities—Ken Schultz
- Weekly Grade Checks

Sandra Martin, Terry McHugh, Dean Auriemma   *Page 10 of 12*   *Revised 7/22/02*

New Teacher Induction Schedule--Summer 2002

- Selecting Role Models
- Professional Development Room/Library
- Taking Graduate Classes & Earning Advanced Degrees
- Homewood-Flossmoor University
- Computer Literacy Requirement

11:50   Move to South Building

12:00   Lunch with Model Teachers

1:00   Joint Time—New Teachers and Model Teachers

         Activities to Be Determined

2:30   H-F Students & Parents (VIP Program)

3:15   Closure Activity/Homework

New Teacher Induction Schedule--Summer 2002

***

Friday, August 9, 2002
The Professional Educator
Setting Sail

***

South Building—Various locations (101 North)

Breakfast will not be provided; suggestion that New Teacher/Model Teacher make arrangements on their own

7:40-9:40	**Model Teachers and New Teacher Divided into two groups**	
	Group A	Tech Center--Computer Services Orientation *"Email, Course Profile, Web Pages"*
	Group B	Model Teachers/New Teacher work in classrooms

9:50-11:50	**Model Teachers and New Teacher Divided into two groups**	
	Group B	Tech Center--Computer Services Orientation *"Email, Course Profile, Web Pages"*
	Group A	Model Teachers/New Teacher work in classrooms

12:00   Lunch (with School Board)

1:00   Blue Ribbon Presentation (Denny Schillings)

1:30   Model Teacher Panel

> *What did you learn your first year?*
> *What would you have done differently?*
> *What gives you joy in teaching?*
> *What keeps you going?*
> *What are the best aspects of teaching at H-F?*
> *How can these teachers, new to H-F, carry on the tradition?*

2:30   Graduation from HFU

H-F Model Teacher Program 2002-2003
A Professional Development Mentoring Program

DESCRIPTION

H-F's New Teacher Induction Program is supported by Model Teachers, veterans who are identified as exemplary professionals who serve as role models and mentors to a specific new teacher. Model Teachers, depending on their "partners," meet at least weekly to discuss a wide-range of topics from "How to handle a disruptive student," to "Where do I find a form for taking a field trip?" Model teachers, who in most instances, teach in the same department, provide support for teachers new to H-F during their first year in the district. In many instances, Model Teachers are the first source of immediate information. Perhaps the most compelling aspect of this relationship is the capacity to plan lessons and related activities together, implement these plans, and analyze the work's impact on student achievement. This professional development activity has great potential to impact student achievement and build teacher confidence and expertise.

MODEL TEACHER SELECTION

Teachers may apply to be part of this program through the assistant superintendent and their department chairs. Teachers will be selected based on the following criteria:
- Excellent or Superior Performance Rating
- Experienced Faculty
- Co-curricular Involvement (preferred, but not required)
- Match to Course Preparation of New Teacher (preferred, but not required)
- Match to Planning Period of New Teacher (preferred, but not required)

Model teachers will apply to a committee comprised of the Department Chair, Assistant Superintendent, Superintendent, Professional Development Coordinator and HFEO representative.

TIMELINE

Teachers interested in serving as a model teacher should notify the assistant superintendent and their department chair beginning March 1st of the spring preceding the employment of the new teacher. Interested teachers will complete an application (see attached) indicating their qualifications, goals for working with new teachers, and their capacity to fulfill the expectations of the position. Applications should be submitted to the assistant superintendent and the department chair by **April 22**. In most instances, model teachers will be notified of their selection prior to the end of the school year preceding the employment of the new teacher.

POSITION EXPECTATIONS
Training
Model Teachers must participate in the summer training program to acquaint them with the goals, expectations, and specific instructional strategies used with new teachers in the district's new teacher induction program. Model Teachers are expected to take a leadership role, reinforcing these aspects of the program throughout the school year. Model Teachers will also participate in the new teacher induction program and help acclimate their partner to the school, department and curriculum. (Total: minimum 2 days) *Summer 2002: August 8 & 9, 7:40-3:20.*

Weekly Contact
Model Teachers and their partners are expected to meet at least once a week, minimally a half hour, to discuss lesson planning, student achievement, classroom management, and other topics as they arise. Model Teachers will maintain a log/journal of their contacts with new teachers to be turned in to the Professional Development Coordinator (Semester I & Semester II).

Classroom Visitations
Model Teachers and their partners are to observe one another and reflect on their observations at least once during quarters one, two and three. The goal of these classroom visitations is supportive coaching and sharing of strategies and resources. The specific data collected from these visits are to be shared between the Model Teacher and his or her partner. Only general recommendations for professional development/program improvement will be shared beyond the partnership.

Task List
Model Teachers are expected to complete at minimum the tasks outlined on the following page. This list may change as recommendations are received.

Goal Setting
Model Teachers and their partners are expected to establish goals for the year related to improving student achievement. Together they develop plans for achieving these goals and a means of evaluating that achievement. Periodically, they review their plans and make adjustments as needed. Prior to May 1st, they should conduct their evaluations and analyze their results. Together, new goals are established for the following year.

Program Improvement
Model Teachers will participate in a series of meetings to evaluate the program, participate in continued professional development related to their role as mentors and make recommendations for continued improvement. They may also discuss professional development and policy needs of the district. Model Teachers will work directly with the Professional Development Coordinator. (Anticipated schedule for 2002-2003: 3 ½ hours on a Saturday—1st Quarter, 1 hour meeting—1st Quarter, 2 one-hour meetings—2nd Quarter, 2 one-hour meetings—3rd Quarter, and 1 hour meeting—4th Quarter.

Attitudes, Competencies, and General Expectations
- Express positive feelings about teaching at HF and help the new teacher attain those same feelings. Address the new teacher's thoughts about being a teacher.
- Listen to daily concerns, progress, and questions.
- Serve as a source of ideas.
- Be easily accessible, trustworthy, and understanding.
- Offer assistance on classroom management.
- Demonstrate professional competence.
- Schedule time willingly with the new teacher.

Update 9/5/02

H-F Model Teacher Program 2002-2003
Task List

Model Teacher_____

Partner Teacher_____

We have discussed/reviewed the following:
- ❑ Department Grading Policy
- ❑ Deadlines for IPR, Quarter Grades, Semester Grades, Getting Finals Copied
- ❑ Teacher Policies
- ❑ Course of Study Outline
- ❑ Unit Planning
- ❑ Weekly Planning
- ❑ Department Outcome Statements/Curriculum Guide
- ❑ Daily Planning for 50 & 80 Minutes (See handouts.)
- ❑ Professional Development Opportunities (Workshops, Conferences, University Coursework)
- ❑ Discipline (Philosophy of Dean's Office & Professional Expectations for Student Behavior)
- ❑ Hallway Supervision & Interaction
- ❑ Grade (XYZ)
- ❑ Final Exam Policy
- ❑ Academic Dishonesty
- ❑ Attendance
- ❑ Tardy/Absent Policy
- ❑ Referrals
- ❑ School Business Forms
- ❑ Budget & Supplies
- ❑ Athletic/Co-Curricular Eligibility Form
- ❑ Assigning & Checking Homework
- ❑ E-mail
- ❑ Voice Mail
- ❑ Security/Safety
- ❑ Fire Drill, Tornado Drill, Emergency/Crisis Plan
- ❑ Substitute Procedures & Lesson Plans & Substitute Folder
- ❑ Emergency Lesson Plans
- ❑ Parent Contact Logs
- ❑ Textbook Use, Policies & Procedures
- ❑ Back to School Night
- ❑ Voyage to Excellence/AP Showcase
- ❑ School Board Meetings
- ❑ Red & White Day
- ❑ Observation of New Teacher_____ (dates) X 3 Quarters 1, 2, 3
- ❑ New Teacher Observes Model Teacher _____ (dates) X 3 Quarters 1, 2, 3

Signature of Model Teacher_____

Signature of Partner_____

Date Completed:

Update 9/5/02

Stanislaus County BTSA Consortium
Beginning Teacher Retention Study

	BTSA Participants 1998-1999	BTSA Participants All Other Years	TOTALS
Retained Teachers			
Retained at the school	183	160	343
Retained within the district	8	9	17
Moved to another district within BTSA area	6	10	16
Moved out of BTSA area and still teaching		13	13
Moved with the intent to keep teaching (marrying, etc.)	13		13
Temporary leave with intent to return to teaching (maternity, etc.)	1	1	2
Released due to declining enrollment; intent to rehire if possible	5		5
Sub-Total	216[1]	193[2]	409
Teachers Not Retained			
Teachers not rehired	4	4	8
Teachers who have resigned		11	11
Teachers who have disappeared or passed away	2	1	3
Sub-Total	6	16	21
Grand Totals	222	209	431

[1] The BTSA candidates from 1998-99 who were retained number 216 out of a possible 222 or 98%.

[2] In previous years,193 out of 209 BTSA candidates or 92% of the BTSA candidates were retained.

Overall, the retention rate for the program is 409 out of 431 or 95%.

Play Keeps for

A strong induction program helps teachers acclimate and continue to learn and helps principals keep the teachers they hire. All in all, it's an investment that pays off for everyone—especially students.

By Harry K. Wong

If you want to win the game of education, you need to play for keeps. But current estimates show that between 40% and 50% of new teachers will leave the profession during the first seven years of their career, and more than two-thirds of those will leave in the first four years of teaching. In urban schools, up to 17% will leave within their first year of teaching (Hare & Heap, 2001).

In contrast, Leyden High School District in Franklin Park, IL, has an attrition rate of only 4.4%—in the past three years, 86 of the 90 new teachers hired stayed in the district. Lafourche Parish Public Schools, in Thibodaux, LA, lost 1 teacher out of the 46 new teachers hired for the 2001—2002 school year. Even more remarkable, of the 279 teachers the district has hired in the past four years, only 11 have left teaching. Those are attrition rates of 2.2% and 3.9%, respectively.

The Leyden and Lafourche districts have something in common that explains their low attrition rates: new-teacher induction programs.

Kathryn Robbins, superintendent of Leyden, who runs the induction program, says, "Our induction program has proved to be one of our best investments. Every district should absolutely be doing it." In the Leyden High School

District, all the teachers attend Leyden University, an in-house, lifelong learning community. This program capitalizes on the fact that successful teachers stay in districts where administrators are visible, academic leaders.

The Lafourche induction program—Framework of Inducting, Retaining, and Supporting Teachers (FIRST)—is so successful that Louisiana has adopted it as the statewide model for all school districts.

More important, more than 99% of the new teachers who have participated in the Lafourche induction program have successfully completed the performance-based Louisiana Teacher Assistance and Assessment Program, which is required for teacher certification in the state.

When a new teacher is hired, an administrator can do three things:

Nothing but give the teacher an assignment. Ineffective teaching and lack of student achievement will bounce right back to the principal. Teachers quickly leave situations where their principal does not have a coherent vision.

Provide a mentor and hope that the mentor gives adequate support. Mentoring has been in vogue for 20 years, and it alone does not guarantee a successful induction period for new teachers (Feiman-Nemser, 1996).

Provide an induction program that will train, support, and retain new teachers. The goal of a structured, comprehensive, sustained induction program is to produce effective teachers. Effective teachers are successful; students of effective teachers are successful; and, most important, successful teachers stay.

What Is Induction?

Induction is the process of training, supporting, and retaining new teachers by:

- Providing instruction in classroom management and effective teaching techniques
- Reducing the difficulty of the transition into teaching
- Maximizing the retention rate of highly qualified teachers.

A good induction process begins before the first day of school and typically runs for two or three years. The new-teacher induction program of the Community Consolidated School District 15, Palatine, IL, is a mandatory four-year program, at the end of which the teachers are prepared to apply for national board certification.

And the quintessential induction program, which has been in existence for 17 years, is the five-year program at the Flowing Wells School District in Tucson, AZ, which aims to turn novice teachers into experts. Flowing Wells' model is so widely copied that its administrators hold an annual workshop to answer all the inquiries they receive.

Teachers Stay When They Are Trained

In every aspect of the real world, people are trained. Wal-Mart, Home Depot, and American Airlines train their employees. Even local small businesses—real estate offices, dentists, and grocery stores—train their new workers. Compare this with many schools where training is nonexistent. It's little wonder that many teachers don't succeed—and neither do their students—and quickly leave the profession. Then, administrators hire more unsupported teachers. As a result, many promising new teachers leave the profession after only a few years. The classroom becomes a battlefield, and the strategy is to keep sending in fresh troops. The military spends considerably more time training, supporting, and retaining its troops than we do for our teachers. All too commonly, new teachers are hired, handed a key, given an assignment, and told to go forth and teach. Many are never introduced to their colleagues nor even walked to their room.

As one teacher said, "I walked to the other building in a daze. Wasn't somebody going to walk over with me and tell me a little bit about what to expect? Wasn't anyone going to show me where the bathroom was or tell me what the other teachers do for lunch? Wasn't I going to get a few words of encouragement, or, for heaven's sake, an idea of what time the first period started? I felt very alone. I started to really understand that I was totally on my own."

Mentoring Itself Is Not Induction

It is important to understand that one day of orientation or simply assigning a teacher to a mentor is not induction. Orientation and mentoring are components of a comprehensive, sustained induction program.

The North Carolina Teaching Fellows Commission says, "Giving a teacher a mentor 'only' is a convenient and unconsciously foolish way for an administrator to divorce himself or herself from the leadership required to bring a beginning teacher up to professional maturity level" (North Carolina Teaching Fellows Commission, 1995). The commission has found that principals and new teachers rated mentoring as the least effective way to help new teachers. One out of four new teachers claimed that they received either "poor support" or "no support" from their mentors (North Carolina Teaching Fellows Commission, 1995). Simply assigning a mentor does little to remedy the likelihood that new teachers will become discouraged and leave the profession. Even worse, by only assigning a mentor, principals relinquish their responsibilities as educational and instructional leaders and cast their problem teachers on mentors, who are expected to solve their inadequacies.

Inherent in the title of *Beyond Mentoring* (Saphier, Freedman, & Aschheim, 2001) is the direction leaders and well-informed administrators are moving. If we are to train, support, and retain new teachers, we must recognize that mentoring is only one component of a successful induction program. If this is not taken into account, there is the danger that mentors will be viewed incorrectly as substitutes for the school community of teachers, teacher leaders, administrators, staff developers, and others who have the professional responsibility to help new teachers become successful.

Components of Successful Induction Programs

All new teaching employees should be formally welcomed and introduced to the district's mission, philosophies, procedures, and culture. New teachers need initial training in classroom management to ensure their success from the very first day of school, an understanding of exactly what will be expected of them, and the necessary ongoing training and support to carry out those duties and responsibilities. They need the guiding hands of mentors as well as the understanding and support of administrators, faculty members, and staff members. They need to feel accepted as vital contributors to the overall effectiveness of their schools. When they have all these things *and* receive affirmation of their success, they will stay.

No two induction programs are exactly alike; each caters to the individual culture and specific needs of its school or district. However, there are several common components that underlie the most successful induction programs. The following are all components of more than 30 replicable induction programs (Breaux & Wong, 2002):

- Four or five days of induction workshops before school begins

In every aspect of the real world, people are trained. Even local small businesses...train their new workers. Compare this with many schools where training is nonexistent. It's little wonder that many teachers don't succeed...and quickly leave the profession.

- Professional development through systematic training over two or three years
- Strong administrative support
- Mentoring
- Modeling effective teaching during inservice training and mentoring
- Opportunities to visit demonstration classrooms.

Islip Public Schools New Teacher Induction Program

The Islip (NY) School District has a comprehensive, three-year induction program that begins with an orientation program before the first year begins and continues as ongoing professional development throughout the initial tenure school years.

Year 1: Teachers attend a three-day orientation that is facilitated by the director of human resources. The orientation combines basic procedural information; introductions; a bus tour through the community; team-building activities; food; first-day advice; icebreakers; organizational strategies; and meetings with central office administrators, the payroll account clerk, building principals, and the union president. The new teachers proceed through the three-year tenure-track program, building relationships in support groups. They meet monthly with the director of human resources and focus on *The Effective Teacher* video series as a catalyst for conversation and discussion. Collegial circles are held between formal monthly meetings.

Year 2: Teachers have a one-day orientation that includes an introduction to Linda Albert's Cooperative Discipline program, which becomes the focus of monthly meetings. The program addresses classroom management techniques and interventions for encouraging appropriate behavior and understanding that discipline means "to teach." Team-building activities are also included to promote a sense of cohesion and belonging.

Year 3: Teachers attend a one-day orientation that is facilitated by the director of human resources that focuses on reviewing the intervention strategies espoused by Cooperative Discipline. Third-year teachers also meet monthly, but each meeting is shaped by a needs assessment, and has appropriate workshop presenters.

A newsletter called TIPS (Teacher Induction Program Stuff) is distributed three times throughout the school year to new staff members and includes information about teaching strategies, cooperative learning, and district information.

At the end of the year, after the board of education has approved tenure for eligible teachers, a celebration is held. The theme one year was "I Believe," based on Nancy Sifford Alana's poem from *The Effective Teacher* series. Each teacher was asked to create an "I Believe" statement that, with their picture, was presented to the community as they received their "diploma" of "That Noble Title, Teacher" by Trish Marcuzzo.

New Haven Unified School District, CA

Another example of a school district able to keep many of its new teachers is New Haven, a district that has a total grasp of its system. Perhaps this is why every school in the district has been recognized as a Distinguished School by the state of California and 5 of the 12 schools in the district have received national Blue Ribbon awards. Chris Ryan, a language arts teacher at Logan High School, in Union City, CA, summarizes the overall atmosphere by saying, "Don't come to New Haven if you want to be a good teacher; come to New Haven if you want to be the best teacher you can possibly be. The atmosphere is creative, energetic, supportive, and challenging. Working here keeps me on the 'high' road."

The school district has used the Internet to develop a world-class recruitment program that has received an award for exemplary use of technology in recruiting. There is no recruitment problem in the New Haven Unified School District because retention is so high.

Principals Need Induction, Too

In December 2001, Steve Zickafoose, director of the new-teacher induction program for Manatee County, FL, received the New Staff Developer award from the National Staff Development Council. Zickafoose is one of many who have already started to think way beyond mentoring. He calls his program a complete professional development framework that encompasses induction for professionals—from teacher's aides to principals and beyond.

A study from Harvard University's Principals' Center reports that more than half of the nation's 92,000 principals are expected to retire or quit in the next five years (Portner, 2001). With many principals retiring, one new principal said, "I was given a set of keys and told to take over the school. There was no induction program for principals—not even a mentor." But many associations and schools are building their own programs:

- Wake County (NC) Public School System has teamed with North Carolina State University to create a training program, Leaders for a New Millennium, to groom new principals.
- The Louisiana Principal Internship Program is a mandatory induction program for principals. It provides new principals with two years of ongoing training and support in the areas of leadership and management. Much of the program exists as a virtual network that principals can use to work on online modules and stay in direct contact with their peers through the state.
- New Leaders for New Schools (NLNS) is a national non-profit organization devoted to attracting and preparing the next generation of outstanding leaders for urban public schools. NLNS, which has offices in Boston and New York, aggressively recruits educators and provides rigorous hands-on training for them to become principals of urban schools. Its induction process includes three components: recruitment, training, and support.

How an Induction Program Can Keep Teachers

> As a central office staff developer, I truly believe in the induction process. If you do not transmit a district's culture, mission, and beliefs as employees join the family, then when do you?
> —*Joan Hearne, Wichita (KS) Public Schools*

The bottom line is that there is no way to create good schools without good teachers and active administrators. The best way to have effective teachers is to create a culture of effective teaching and to train your new teachers with an induction program. You know you've succeeded with your teachers when they say, as Carla Holzer of Thibodaux (LA)

High School did, "On the last day of our induction program, I felt that I had definitely made the right choice of a career. I have seen the joy that teaching can bring to both teachers and students, and I can't wait to begin what I know will be a very rewarding career."

An induction program will foster a culture of effective teaching. Without effective teachers, we cannot and will not have effective schools. And with an effective school, your teachers are there for keeps. **PL**

References

❑ Breaux, A. L., & Wong, H. K. (2002). *New teacher induction: How to train, support, and retain new teachers.* Mountain View, CA: Harry K. Wong Publications.

❑ Feiman-Nemser, S. (1996). *Teacher mentoring: A critical review.* Washington, DC: Office of Educational Research and Improvement. (ERIC Digest No. ED397060)

❑ Hare, D., & Heap, J. (2001, May). *Effective teacher recruitment and retention strategies in the Midwest.* Naperville, IL: North Central Regional Laboratory. Retrieved June 26, 2002, from www.ncrel.org/policy/pubs/html/strategy/index.html

❑ North Carolina Teaching Fellows Commission. (1995). *Keeping talented teachers.* Raleigh, NC: Public School Forum of North Carolina.

❑ Portner, J. (2001, May 26). "Bay Area Faces Shortage of Principals; Schools Struggling to Find Qualified, Willing Candidates." *San Jose Mercury News,* p. 1A.

❑ Saphier, J., Freedman, S., & Aschheim, B. (2001). *Beyond mentoring: How to nurture, support, and retain new teachers.* Newton, MA: Teachers21.

Harry K. Wong (harrykrose@aol.com) is a former high school science teacher. He and his wife, Rosemary, are the authors of The First Days of School *and a monthly column, "The Effective Teacher," on Teachers.net. He is the coauthor of a new book,* New Teacher Induction: How to Train, Support, and Retain New Teachers.

RESOURCES

Louisiana FIRST www.doe.state.la.us/DOE/OQE/certification/LaFirst.asp

Louisiana Principal Internship Program www.teachlouisiana.net/pages.asp?PageName=prinInternship

New Haven Unified School District www.nhusd.k12.ca.us

New Leaders for New Schools www.nlns.org

NewTeacher.com

Teachers.net

The Effective Teacher video www.effectiveteaching.com

About the Authors

ANNETTE L. BREAUX is a curriculum coordinator for the Lafourche Parish Public Schools in Thibodaux, Louisiana, and a former elementary and middle school teacher. As a sixth- and seventh-grade teacher, she developed the TEAMS (Teamwork Enhances Achievement, Motivation, and Self-Esteem) program for successful classroom management. She is the author and coordinator of the FIRST (Framework for Inducting, Retaining, and Supporting Teachers) program, an induction program for new teachers that has been hailed as one of the top induction programs in the United States. Her FIRST program has been chosen by Louisiana as the model for all of the state's induction programs. She has given several hundred presentations to educators at professional conferences and to school districts across the country. She also provides training for school districts in implementing induction programs. Her audiences always agree that they come away from her presentations with user-friendly information, heartfelt inspiration, and a much-needed reminder that they truly have chosen the most noble of all professions—teaching.

Annette Breaux's professional affiliation and personal contact are as listed:

Lafourche Parish Schools
110 Bowie Road
Thibodaux, LA 70301
alb24@email.com

HARRY K. WONG, a former high school science teacher, is the most highly sought-after speaker in education today. Along with his wife, Rosemary, he is coauthor of the best-seller *The First Days of School*, which has become one of the most popular and widely read education books of all time. He has spoken to over a million people at every major education convention and in thousands of schools and school districts around the world.

Through his speaking and writing, he was introduced to the concept of new teacher induction in the early 1980s, when a number of districts were training their new teachers with many of the methods he espoused. As more and more school districts began to implement induction training, Harry became a "de facto clearinghouse" for ideas that districts were sharing with one another. In *New Teacher Induction* he shares the ideas, resources, and experience he has accumulated over the course of 20 years.

If you would like to share what you are doing to help train, support, and retain new teachers, please send your information to him as follows:

Dr. Harry K. Wong
943 North Shoreline Boulevard
Mountain View, CA 94043
harrykrose@aol.com

Index